A Demographic Analysis of East Afri~~ca~~
A Sociological Interpretation

KU-536-097

A Demographic Analysis of East Africa

A Sociological Interpretation

Mette Monsted and Parveen Walji

NOTTINGHAM UNIVERSITY LIBRARY

The Scandinavian Institute of African Studies, Uppsala 1978

© Mette Monsted and Parveen Walji 1978
ISBN 91-7106-126-6
Printed in Sweden by
Bohusläningens AB, Uddevalla 1978

Contents

Acknowledgements

This publication was initiated in 1974, when the authors were lecturer in demography and tutorial fellow respectively within the same field, as a response to the lack of relevant teaching material analyzing the population in East Africa. The earlier drafts in 1974—75 have been used by demography students and we appreciate the many comments and discussions of the drafts from this phase of the work.

The work on the textbook has received encouraging support from the Department of Sociology. We have greatly benefitted from comments and critiques received from members of staff in the Department. Especially Drs. Diane Kayongo-Male and Tarsis Kabwegyere have contributed with essential comments in the discussion of the chapters. We are very grateful to the chairman of Department of Sociology, Professor Phillip M. Mbithi, who followed this project in all the phases and whose support and detailed comments have been a great encouragement, and who made the writing of this book possible.

We also want to express our gratitude to the Danish Council for Development Research, whose contribution of a grant made publication of the book possible, and finally, thanks are due to the Scandinavian Institute of African Studies for the technical work involved in its publication.

The book is the result of a joint effort by both authors. The outline and all the chapters have been thoroughly commented on and discussed by both, and Parveen Walji has been responsible for the editorial revision of all the chapters. The book could be divided in two sections, the one being more general, containing the Introduction, the Demographic Theories and the Sources and Evaluation of Data (chapters 1, 3, 5, 6). This section is the result of a joint effort of the authors. The other section on the demographic variables and empirical contributions, is divided between the authors, and these chapters are predominantly the responsibility of one of the authors. Parveen Walji has been the main author for the chapters on Nuptuality, The Labour Force and Growth of Population (Chapters 9, 12, 13), whereas Mette Monsted has the main responsibility for the remaining chapters.

Chapter I

Introduction

This book has grown out of the frustrations of teaching demography in East Africa on the basis of the very technical and Western approach to the discipline, which has limited value for the African data and perspectives.

The point of departure has been the question of the relevance of demography for social and economic development planning in the East African context. The analysis of population dynamics appears basic for macro-economic planning. However, the question could be raised about the extent to which this statistical analysis of population has contributed to the understanding of the development processes. The authors perceive this as a relevant question, as the narrow statistical approach to demography has been developed in countries with abundant statistical data on population, and focuses on the same basic variables, independent of the specific social and historical context. This basis for the development of the discipline may lead to weaknesses in relation to the analysis of development problems in the African context. One of the problems appears to be the bias in the analysis due to the choice of variables. Why are mortality, fertility, population size, growth, distribution and structure, important variables for planning? How do we relate these to the problems of poor health, poor living conditions, employment problems, problems of famines and drought and limitations in the infrastructure? The demographic variables tend to give a constraining bias in the understanding and explanation of development phenomena. Thus population, which is the target of development efforts, may in many cases appear to be the major constraint in development, whereas other structural phenomena are not given as much explanatory value as they deserve, since they are much more complex and cannot be limited to simplistic quantitative indices or equations, such as the rough population data.

On the other hand, the limitations of the narrow demographic approach are also shown in the data collection methods. The large scale quantitative research surveys, which appear to be the major tool in demographic research, may not reveal the underlying social and economic problems, and may therefore represent a serious weakness in methodology compared with most sociological analyses.

The concern of the authors has been to try to analyse the available African demographic data and data collection methods from a sociological point of view, thus trying to reveal the weaknesses of the narrow statistical approach for the understanding of development processes in East Africa.

Theories within sociology and economics concerned with the population factor are very weak in their explanatory value. This weakness in the theory thus limits the possibilities of explaining the phenomena and the relationship between them, and leads to an even greater emphasis on the empirical approach and on the need for more data.

One of the purposes of this book is to tie the analysis of demographic data to a sociological framework. The authors do not pretend to introduce new or innovative factors or components in the study of population. That could be the outcome at a later stage. The authors attempt to change the focus or approach relating to the basic or conventional variables towards a more analytical sociological interpretation. Thus we have aimed at making the analysis of demography more relevant within the development and planning processes of the East African countries. This could be perceived as the first step towards a more analytical developmental discipline.

The other main purpose of the book is to produce a textbook in demography which analyses East African demographic data within a sociological framework. As most of the students of sociology are trained for administration and planning work, it is perceived as most important to train sociology students in the field of demography such that they are familiar with the conventional techniques applied in planning and administration, and also to give them a critical understanding of population dynamics as well as of the validity and relevance of the data.

Even for those sociologists and economists, who are not dealing specifically with demography, statistics on the distribution and structure of the population are often used for comparisons and for sampling frameworks. A thorough training within the field would provide the basis for evaluating these statistics in their proper context.

Chapter II

Historical Trends in the World Population

Data on the development of the world population are a basis for many comparisons, and are now used to a large extent in the discussions by ecologists focussing on the relation between the global resources and the global population.

The trends in the global population however can only give an indication of the "sum of trends" in the populations of different regions and continents, whereas even within the regions the historical conditions and specific development trends may be of a very different nature. The description of these trends does give a general picture though, and an introduction to the differential patterns and trends of single demographic variables in the regions.

The important issue however is, how does the population develop in different regions and what factors are important for the explanation of the trends of population? The most important factor in the historical development of population seems to be the mode of production. Thus a hunting-gathering society is less capable of exploiting the production capacity and can therefore maintain a smaller population in a given area, than a community using higher levels of technology in their production i.e. agricultural cultivation of the land. Also in relation to pastoralists, agricultural cultivation seems to provide a more productive economy, though this may not be valid in marginal dry land area without access to any irrigation. The main issue raised here is the higher efficiency of the agricultural production relative to the other modes mentioned, and therefore the better capacity of absorbing more people on the land. In relation to this the development from only agricultural production towards an industrial production and an urbanization, also changes the society's capacity to absorb more people. But even in this case the basis is the capacity of agriculture to support more people, namely also the urban dwellers.

Other main factors of importance for changing trends of population are related to wars, epidemic diseases, and to the regulation of the number of births. The importance of these other factors has played a very different role in the world's major regions, and therefore the regions will be covered separately.

The information on the early history of the world population is extremely inadequate and is based on estimations by groups of archaeologists, anthropologists, geographers, economists, historians etc. A kind of average figure covering the estimation of growth for long periods of time should not be accepted without a lot of reservation (see table 1).

The only aspect of which we can have a certainty, is that the increase in population has not been at a constant rate. The population increase has fluctuated between high growth, due to an improvement in the conditions for agricultural growth, and periods of decline during famine and epidemics.

The essential point in table 1 is that the population has been very small and has been increasing very slowly until approximately 1000 years ago. The first jump in the growth rate came with the transition in the most populated parts of Asia from hunting-gathering to agricultural production and the domestication of animals around 6000 B.C. This was the first step towards a surplus agricultural production, an economic differentiation and agglomeration. This implied that the total community was less exposed to natural calamities and had higher agricultural production. The early centuries A.D. were characterized by a considerable population increase in the old centres of the agricultural-urban civilization (the Mediterranean and Asia), but with fluctuations and some occasional heavy losses due to famine, wars and epidemic diseases. The vast movement of the nomadic population had a powerful impact on the Eurasian demographic history. In the fifth century A.D. the Roman Empire collapsed and was overrun by the German tribes. Also the Huns flowed from the Russian Plateau towards the west into France and eastward towards Asia. The Arabs expanded in Asia, Africa and up in Europe. In the Far East the Mongols expanded and conquered China and the Russian areas. In this period and later, there is a great discrepancy between the economic basis of the different continents and therefore the description of the regions will be treated separately. However, since they are still very much interrelated through the flows of population, trade, colonization etc. a summary of the general trends will provide a useful basis for further analysis. Before turning to the description of the different regions, it is important to consider: (1) the development in the relative proportion of the world population in the continents, and (2) the resulting densities now.

Table 1. *Growth rate of the world population.*

Year	World population in millions	Annual growth in percent
1 Mill. B.C.	0.1	0.0003
300,000 B.C.	1	0.0004
23,000 B.C.	3	0.003
6,000 B.C.	5	0.1
3,000 B.C.	100	0.04
A.D.		
1	300	0.04
1650	550	0.3
1750	730	0.4
1850	1,170	0.6
1900	1,610	0.9
1950	2,500	1.9
1965	3,300	2.1
1970	3,632	
2000 (projection)	6,920	

Source: Calculations by Revelle, Harvard University Centre for Population Studies. Quoted by G. Tschannerl, An Analysis of population dynamics in a political perspective. In: *Maji Maji.* Dec. 1972. Dar es Salaam.

Table 2 shows that the Caucasian race has been increasing very strongly compared to others during the last century. The Asian population has actually decreased relatively from having 60 % of the world population in 1650 to 56 % in 1965. Still more crucial is the situation for the African population, having an estimated 18 % of the total population in 1650, and only 7 % in 1900. This is mainly explained by the severe decrease in the actual population caused by the transportation of slaves from Africa to the Americas. The Europeans, however, have increased their number and share, and have spread to other continents also, mainly to the North America. They have never had as large a share of the world population (one-third) as in this century.It was largest in the 1930s just before the populations in the developing world began increasing their growth rate. With this distribution in mind, it is evident that the history of world population cannot be analyzed on the basis of the history of the European population, which only forms a minor share of the global population. However, it is important to relate the steady increase in the European population to the development of the populations in other continents, because the growth, or mostly decline, of Third World continents is largely related to the economic development in Europe and North America, and to the kind of relationship existing between Third World and First World countries. Most important is the transfer of Africans as slaves to North and Latin America, where they worked to increase production and wealth for the European population. The migration of Europeans to the American continent and their import of slaves from Africa not only dislocated the development in Africa for a very long period, but also destroyed the fundament for economic activities for the indigenous population in America (the Indians). The third point is the European colonization, which affected populations in Africa, Asia and in Latin America.

Table 2. *Distribution of world population in the different continents from 1650 to projected 2000, (pop. in millions).*

	1650[a]	1750[b]	1800[c]	1850[b]	1900[b]	1930[c]	1950[c]	1971[c]	2000
World, total	543	791	978	1260	1630	2069	2513	3706	6920
Africa	100	106	107	111	133	164	222	354	865
Asia excl. USSR	327	498	630	801	925	1120	1381	2104	4050
Latin America	12	16	24	38	74	107	162	296	670
Europe & USSR	103	167	208	284	430	534	572	711	965
North America	1	2	7	26	82	134	166	228	340
Areas of European settlement	118	187	241	350	592	786	914	—	1904
Percent of world population:									
Africa	18	13	11	9	8	8	9	10	12
Asia excl. USSR	60	63	64	63	56	56	55	57	59
Latin America	2	2	3	3	4	5	6	8	10
Areas of European settlement	20	22	23	25	32	33	30	—	17

Figures for Oceania are not included.
Source: a Carr-Saunders, *World Population.* b Durand, The Modern Expansion of World Population. In Nam (ed): *Population and Society.* c United Nations.

15

The development in the proportion of the world population in the different continents is shown in table 3. This is based on the annual population growth rates in the different areas since 1750, and summarizes some of the trends in the growth fluctuations, as well as the difference between the earlier high population growth in Europe and very low growth or stagnation in Africa, compared with the later high growth for all the Third World countries. For a thorough comparison of the continents, however, other aspects of the population, such as mortality, fertility, age-sex structure, employment etc. are also necessary, but these will be covered by chapters specially devoted to these concepts.

Table 3. *Estimated average annual growth rates of population 1750—1965 in major regions of the world (percentages).*

Regions	1750—1800	1800—1850	1850—1900	1900—1950	1950—1960
World, total	0.4	0.5	0.5	0.8	1.9
Africa	0.0	0.1	0.4	1.0	2.2
North Africa	0.2	0.5	1.2	1.4	2.5
Remainder	0.0	0.0	0.2	0.9	2.1
Asia	0.5	0.5	0.3	0.8	2.0
China	1.0	0.6	0.0	0.5	1.8
India-Pakistan	0.1	0.3	0.4	0.8	2.2
Japan	0.0	0.1	0.7	1.3	1.1
Remainder excl. USSR	0.1	0.6	0.8	1.2	2.4
America	1.0	1.5	1.8	1.5	2.2
Latin America	0.8	0.9	1.3	1.6	2.8
Northern America	—	2.7	2.3	1.4	1.7
Europe excl. USSR	0.4	0.6	0.7	0.6	0.8
USSR	0.6	0.6	1.1	0.6	1.6
Oceania	—	—	—	1.6	2.2

Source: UN. *Determinants and Consequences of Population Trends*, p. 32.

Table 4 on population density provides some basic averages, and may be used as a rough comparison of the levels of population density in the different parts of the world, as well as between different parts of Africa. However, it also shows how little evidence there is for defining the Third World countries as absolutely "overpopulated", as they show some of the highest, but also some of the lowest densities. Also within the industrial nations there are high and low densities. The world average is not high, showing only 27 persons per square kilometer, the variations in the major regions being from 2 in Australia to 280 in Japan. However the figures are only rough indications of the relation between area and population since the proportion of arable land or industrialization, both of which affect the carrying capacity of the area, are not considered. The last of these is important for a comparison of population densities between industrialized countries and Third World agricultural countries, and the first is important considering the large desert and semi-desert areas of Africa and Asia. One example showing the nonsense of using the crude population density as a measure of "overpopulation" can be drawn from Egypt, where there are 33 persons per square kilometer, but where most of the

16

population is concentrated along the Nile Valley, resulting in a densi valley of more than 500 per square km. There are practically no people i remaining land as almost all of it is desert.

Table 4. *Population, area and density for the world and major regions 1970.*

Areas	Estimated mid-year population (millions)	Area (km²) (thousands)	Density (population per square km)
World, total	3,632	135,781	27
Developing regions	2,542	74,468	34
More-developed regions	1,090	61,312	18
Africa	344	30,319	11
Western Africa	101	6,142	16
Eastern Africa	98	6,338	15
Middle Africa	36	6,613	5
Northern Africa	87	8,525	10
Southern Africa	23	2,701	8
Asia excl. USSR	2,056	27,532	75
East Asia	930	11,757	79
Mainland region	765	11,129	69
Japan	103	370	280
Other East Asia	61	258	237
South Asia	1,126	15,775	71
Middle South Asia	762	6,771	113
South-East Asia	287	4,498	64
South-West Asia	77	4,506	17
Europe excl. USSR	462	4,936	94
Western Europe	149	995	149
Southern Europe	128	1,315	98
Eastern Europe	104	990	105
Northern Europe	81	1,636	49
Latin America	283	20,566	14
Tropical South America	151	13,700	11
Middle America (mainland)	67	2,496	27
Temperate South America	39	4,134	10
Caribbean	26	236	109
North America	228	21,515	11
Oceania	19.4	8,511	2
Australia—New Zealand	15.4	7,955	2
Melanesia	2.8	525	5
Polynesia and Micronesia	1.2	30	41
USSR	243	22,402	11

Note: Because of rounding, the totals are not in all cases the exact sum of the parts. Population totals for the world, developing and the more-developed regions have been adjusted to take into account discrepancies between regional assumptions of immigration and emigration.
Source: UN. *Determinants and Consequences of Population Trends*, p. 161.

Differences in densities as well as in other demographic variables as mortality and fertility are often used to characterize or define differences between First World and Third World countries. The weaknesses in the density measure should be revealed, but the differences in mortality and fertility are more

he different life conditions in rich and poor nations. Mortality
Third World countries, the difference is in the range of an
ife at birth of 50 years in Third World countries, and around
rial nations. Within the Third World major differences are
erent history and general life and health conditions in the
d supply, nutrition and spread of epidemic diseases.

With respect to fertility, the differences are greater. The average number of children born to a woman in the industrial countries—the total fertility rate—is around 2.5, i.e. between 2 and 3 children born to every woman who lives throughout her fertile period. In Third World countries this figure is around 5—6 showing some variations, in different social and cultural systems. The much higher number of children born per woman in the Third World countries, and the mortality being only a little higher, implies a much higher rate of growth for these countries. The natural growth rate is defined as the difference between the number of births and number of deaths related to the total population. The growth rate is thus, on average, 2.5 percent per annum in Third World countries, while it is only 1 percent in industrial nations.

Africa

There is no written evidence on the history of population development in Africa. The sources of material are few, especially before the colonial period. We have indications only from late 18th and the 19th centuries based on members of European expeditions, and later only from the colonial administration. These indications and guesses tend to show a much higher population density in West and Central Africa, than in East Africa.

The most important factors for population development within Africa, before the colonial period and also to an extent during the colonial period, were related to the development of agricultural production, to the settling of pastoralists and the change of gatherer-hunters to semi-agriculturalists and agriculture gave way to a higher potential for population growth. Land was relatively abundant in the late 18th and early 19th centuries and the main restriction was limited to the methods of agricultural production.

Specifically for West and parts of Central and East Africa, the transportation of the African population as slaves to the Americas during the trade period from 1442 to the late 19th century had an extremely high impact on the population size, structure, and the living conditions and production of the remaining population. The prosperous Kingdoms of West and Central Africa were demolished and the remaining populations mainly of old people and isolated small groups, could not keep up a sufficient production, but were left to poverty and famine. It is estimated that 20 million Africans were captured, many more affected, and only around one-third survived to start working in the plantations in America and the West Indies.

Estimates from the Congolese Kingdoms showed that the prosperous rich societies with approximately 2 million people in the 16th century had declined to approximately one-third at the time of the colonization after 3 centuries of slave trade. The societies were poverty-stricken and did not reach their original level of population until the late 1960s.[1]

The East African population was much smaller and more scattered. The population seems to have been slowly increasing until around 1890 due to a slow expansion in agricultural production. The slave trade carried out by the Arabs with Zanzibar as the main station was by no means as large as in West and Central Africa. But it increased especially after the 1850s when new markets opened at the plantations of Mauritius, Reunion and Zanzibar. However, the impact on the small population was severe. The depopulation of certain areas led to problems of producing enough among the isolated groups, and the trade became restricted by size of market and isolation.

In most periods, occasional famine had affected the population in local areas, but in 1889 in East Africa the combination of a major famine followed by rinderpest, which decimated the cattle population and gave basis for a spread of many epidemic diseases, killed people in large numbers.

The caravans and many expeditions spread many other epidemic diseases to which the African population had no immunity, such as chickenpox, measles, poliomyelitis, plague, influenza, whooping-cough, jiggers infection and sleeping sickness. All came either from Europe or were spread by the expeditions from West and Central Africa to East Africa, where they had not been known before.[2]

In East Africa the population was also limited by the First World War 1914—18, where an estimated 350,000 people were recruited as porters, many died in the war or later by the diseases spread by the porters.

Colonization affected the population in many ways, also through induced migration of Arabs to West Africa as a trading and artisan class, and to East Africa of Asians for building the railway and later as a trading-artisan class.

Since 1800 the population of North Africa grew very fast due to a highly developed irrigated agriculture, and a profitable trade. The natural growth in this area remained high, and the Arabs expanded trade and migrated to the shores of West and Eastern Africa.

The total number of people in Africa has been estimated in several different ways; to show the discrepancy in the estimates the three of them are given in Table 5. The basis for these estimations are guesses of population size by leaders of expeditions, and later by the administrators. Some of the estimates later than 1900 also include data from surveys of a small area, but all those up to 1900 are of a very questionable origin, which explains the great unreliability and variations. Only one aspect they tend to agree on, this is the decline or stagnation in the population from 1750 to 1850.

[1] S. Axelson: *Culture Confrontation in the Lower Congo*, Uppsala 1970, p. 91. Quoted by S. Amin: Underpopulated Africa.

[2] R. M. A. Zwanenberg with Anne King: *An Economic History of Kenya and Uganda 1800—1970*, Nbi. 1975 p. 9—10.

Table 5. *Estimates of population in Africa, 1750—1960 (population in millions).*

	1750	1800	1850	1900	1950	1960
AFRICA					217	303
Estimates by:						
Carr-Saunders	95	90	95	120		
Wilcox	100	100	100	141		
Durand-variants						
Low level	60	69	81	115		
Medium	106	107	111	133		
High level	153	142	145	154		

Source: Revelle's calculations, Princeton, Quoted from G. Tschannerl, An analysis of population dynamics in a political perspective. *Maji Maji*, Dec. 1972. Dar es Salaam.

Europe

In Europe the population increased substantially from the beginning of the first century. But even though the general trend was an increase, the population growth fluctuated, and occasionally local famines and epidemics increased the mortality and resulted in local declines of the population.

In the 14th and 15th centuries the majority of the European countries were affected by the "Black Death", which eliminated up to half the population in some areas. In Central Europe, wars, and especially the epidemics following the wars, restricted the growth of the population.

After 1000 A.D. the major growth of population in Europe shifted from the Mediterranean to the Central, Northern and Eastern areas. The increase in the European population averaged 6 per thousand in the 1850s, when the mortality began to decline, and the growth rate went up to nearly 1 percent. The increase in the population continued in spite of the streams of overseas emigration.

The increase of population in the 15th and 16th centuries can be seen in the light of the land consolidation of the common grazing land in the communities. This increased the intensification of the agricultural production and opened the way for a surplus agricultural production.

The increased growth in population during late 1800s around the time of the industrial revolution can be related to the expansion of the medical research and of the medical facilities as well as the slowly improving sanitation in the cities. The latter facor was important for the improvement of the health conditions for the urban population. Up to the 18th century the population in the cities could not maintain itself by its natural growth, because of extremely high mortality in the cities. The increase in size of the cities had to be supplied from the inmigration of rural population.

Mortality began declining during the late 18th century, beginning in England and Scandinavia, and approximately 100 years later the fertility began declining. This development can be illustrated by a graph which shows these trends in Scandinavia, where they were very clear. The development of mortality and fertility has been the basis for the "demographic transition theory", where the fertility decline is expected to follow the decline in mortality also in other areas, i.e. in developing countries.

There are however clear exceptions to this model also in Europe. Both France and Ireland experienced a fertility decline before the main drop in mortality. Especially in Ireland the fertility declined and outmigration took place following years of famine and very high mortality (1846—47).

In England and Scandinavia and later in Eastern and Southern Europe the high population growth beginning just before 1900 together with the problems of agricultural production in the marginal agricultural areas, caused large-scale emigration to North and South America, and later to Oceania. The first big flow of population from marginal agricultural areas—marginal because of the land tenure system or the quality of the soil—was from Ireland and from Sweden.

Graph: 1: *Development in crude birth rate and crude death rate in Denmark 1735—1965. "The demographic transition model."*

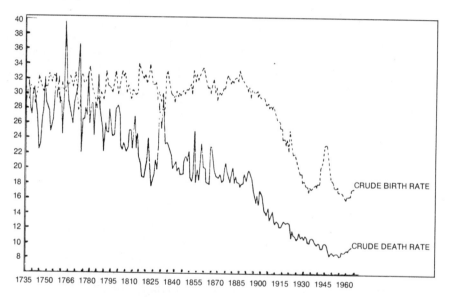

Source: P. C. Matthiessen: *Some Aspects of the Demographic Transition in Denmark.* Copenhagen 1970, p. 21.

Asia

Registration of tax-payers, soldiers and households has taken place in some parts of Asia for a long time; e.g. in different parts of China and India. In China this registration was a part of the Emperor's administration system, and it took place long before our time schedule. However, an estimate of the total population is very difficult due to a lot of changes in the boundaries of the empire, and to the many internal wars, epidemics and famines. In the 17th century the decline of the Emperor's dynasty and internal wars led to declining population. Later the growth fluctuated very much, but after 1949, when the war was over and the living conditions for the population improved, the growth increased.

India too had very long periods of stagnating population up to 1600 A.D. The Indian-Pakistan region however increased its population after 1700 and the growth accelerated, especially after 1950.

In Japan the population has increased more steadily except for the decreases during the 18th century. After this period the population increased in spite of a high emigration to other Asian regions. Many of the migrants, however, came back to Japan in 1945 after the war.

The rest of Asia has been influenced by the many dominating populations in their expansion periods; first the Mongols, later the Chinese and the Japanese migrated to and conquered other areas. The European colonization also influenced the growth of these populations. However, in all areas except China, the growth seems to have accelerated, on average, since 1800.

America

North America: This continent was only sparsely populated by the Indians who were semi-agriculturalists and mainly hunters. The indigenous population was practically eradicated in the 19th century, when the Europeans settled and not only took over the land for agricultural production, thus reducing necessary hunting land, but also fought the Indians in endless wars. Wars were followed by spread of diseases from Europe, and the Indian population rapidly became decimated. However, the total population living in North America did increase due to a heavy immigration of Europeans and to the very high fertility among the settler population. In the USA the population increased approximately 35 % in each decade from 1790 to 1860.

Latin America: In Latin America as well as in North America the indigenous population of Indians has been decimated, and in vast areas it has completely disappeared after the Spanish Conquest. Both the war and the imported diseases eradicated the population, and the estimated 7—12 million (note the margin in the estimation) in 1650 can very well be only a fraction of a population that was previously much larger.

The European settlement and the import of Africans as slaves in the plantations were insufficient to compensate for the decline in the indigenous po . tion.

The growth in the population has been resuming slowly, and after the 1950s the growth has been among the highest in the world (3.5 % per annum in 1960), because of a very high fertiliy and a rapidly declining mortality.

Oceania

Oceania, especially Australia and New Zealand, was very sparsely populated at the time of European settlement. The indigenous population was small. Even with the immigration of the European population, the population is still small in relation to the enormous land areas. As the population is mainly a result of an immigration over a short period, the population structure has fluctuated— showing late in the 19th century a population dominated by males of working age. After an "import" of European females, the high fertility level among the settlers has contributed to a high increase.

Conclusion

It is important to note in this chapter that firstly, the development in the population increase is mainly related to the forms of production in the society and the level of productivity Secondly, Europe, the Near East and the Arab world, i.e. some of the first areas to have high population density and an increase in agricultural productivity, have all exploited labour and land of other people in other continents for their own further development.

Therefore the population development in Third World countries is not only related to the internal form of production and local famines, but also to the contact with the colonizers and other exploiters, who through war, capture or spread of diseases increased the level of mortality in the first contacts.

Supplementary reading

1. Carlo Cipolla: *Economic History of World Population*. London 1965. Chapt. 1, pp. 17—32 and chapt. 4, pp. 77—94.
2. R. M. A. Zwanenberg with Anne King: *An Economic History of Kenya and Uganda 1800—1970*. Nairobi 1975, pp. 3—12.
3. UN. *Determinants and Consequences of Population Trends*, N. Y. 1974. Chapt. II, pp. 10—32 and Chapt. VI. A, pp. 160—173.
4. G. Tschannerl: An Analysis of Population Dynamics in a Political Perspective. *Maji Maji*, Dec. 1972, Dar es Salaam, 20,.
5. Samir Amin: Underdevelopment and Dependence in Black Africa—Origins and Contemporary Forms. *The Journal of Modern African Studies*. Vol. 10, no. 4, pp. 503—524.

phic Theories

Demographic theories are usually theories within sociology or economics, where population is seen as an important independent or dependent variable. All demographic theories thus concentrate on the relationship between social or economic variables (mainly at macro-level), and the development of demographic variables. As can be seen in this chapter, most of the "theories" are not scientific theories, but mainly empirical models with no explanatory or predictive value.

Historically, different social systems and different periods have emphasized different theories of population. The evaluation of the theories must be related to the specific context within which they were propounded. Because of the narrow relationship between a theory and the specific historical context, the theories developed in Europe in the 18th and 19th centuries will probably not be valid for the description or explanation of the patterns and changes in population in present-day Africa.

The European approach is related to the theoretical development and with the development of world population history. For example, in the Medieval Roman Empire, the lack of soldiers and the need for Roman inhabitants in the newly occupied areas, led to an emphasis on the necessity of high population growth for prosperous economic development. This chapter covers firstly a few of the major theories from Europe, some of which have had an impact on the discussion of the development of population in the Third World. Secondly, some of the newer theories which have a special relevance for the situation in African and other Third World countries are discussed. In evaluating the relevance of these theories for Africa, the specific social and economic conditions within the continent as well as the possible development of population are considered. The population theories are therefore highly dependent on the history of population in the different parts of the world.

Malthus and neo-Malthusianism

The reason for discussing Malthus' theory is not that it is more outstanding or a better description of population dynamics than the other theories, but because the theory has had long-term implications for population studies and thought.

Malthus was a British clergyman and economist in the late 18th century. The political background for his writings was (1) the outbreak of the French Revolution, which scared the upper classes ·in other European countries, and

(2) the British discussion on the improvement of social security and welfare laws for the poor. Against this background Malthus wrote "An Essay on the Principle of Population" (1798). In this political pamphlet he emphasized the need to curb the increase of the poor in the population. His basic argument was that food production increased by arithmetric progression 1, 2, 3, 4, 5, 6, ... whereas the population increased by geometric progression 1, 2, 4, 8, 16, 32, ... This of course endangered the food supply and made it necessary to curb the population growth. The other basic assumption was that the population, i.e. the poor, "bred like animals", and his moral solution was that they should restrain their sexual life by late marriages and abstinence. If fertility could not be controlled in this way, the only inevitable check would be "misery and vice" leading to high mortality, and thus curbing the population increase.

If this check was to be controlled, it was not advisable to improve social security for the poor as this would only lead to increased fertility. The conclusion therefore was, that the poor should control their numbers, permanently renounce and not be allowed to improve their social conditions as this would only encourage them to have more children. On the other hand Malthus argued: The demand for goods was an important incentive for the economy. The upper classes should therefore expand their consumption in order to create this incentive.

Similar ideas, specifically in relation to labourers and salaries, were launched in Ricardo's "The Iron Law of Wages" in 1821. He stated that high fertility among the labourers led to a high supply of workers, which in turn caused low salaries and high unemployment; this then pressed the workers to marry late and therefore resulted in lower fertility. The next generation would then provide a low supply of workers creating a high demand for labour and high wages, leading to high fertility, etc. The conclusion according to Ricardo was that there was a need to find a low level balance for salaries in order to avoid these heavy fluctuations.

Population theory was thus legitimizing the low salaries for the workers. The importance of this theory, however, is not so much linked to this phenomenon as to the revival of the considerations on the restriction of the number of poor people in the Third World by the neo-Malthusianists.

Neo-Malthusianism expanded in the 20th century, when the actual decline in fertility (and thus in population growth) had taken place in Europe, and Malthus' doomsday perspective thus had proven not to be valid in Europe, after it had been proven that the population *could be* restricted. The neo-Malthusianists now focused not so much on the poor in the industrial countries, but on the very high growth of the poor populations in the Third World, after the mortality began declining there.

The main arguments for restricting the population growth are of a macroeconomic nature:

1. Even with high economic growth, the growth per capita is stagnating due to a very high growth of the population. Or, phrased in a popular form "The population growth is eating up the economic growth".

2. The number of people of working age relative to those of dependent age is very small, when fertility is high. This reduces the economic capacity of the population since there are too many consumers in relation to producers, and therefore too much has to be spent on social overheads.

3. Population pressure on land is already high, and the high population increase results in a surplus population which has to migrate from the land to other forms of employment. This creates very heavy pressure on employment and high population growth in the cities.

4. High population increase means heavy pressure on employment, and when capital for creating new production is lacking, the result will be increasing unemployment and increasing urban social problems.

The essential characteristic of Malthusian thought is the focus on population as the crucial obstacle to economic development, thus explaining poverty and stagnation by increasing population, and not treating population as one of the variables to be combined with other economic structural variables.

The recent ecological theories are largely an extention of neo-Malthusian theory, but on a global scale. The main points raised are related to the limits of natural resources on earth, and the 1.9 % increase in world population. The implications of these perspectives are similar to the neo-Malthusian ones, i.e. the need to curb population growth in order to secure energy and more than "standing space" only for the coming generations, as well as to control the hazards of pollution.

A setback to these theories is the lack of recognition of the global distribution of resources. A child born in an industrial nation consumes approximately 10 times as much energy as a child born in a developing country, and the global point of view should thus lead to an emphasis on restricting the expensive children in the industrial nations, rather than the children of the Third World. The global standards also imply a theoretical redistribution of population, but why should Africa as a continent with a low population density limit its growth according to some global standards, as there is no wish in Africa to be the expansion area for other more densely populated areas?

Demographic Transition Theory

The transition theory is a description of the actual demographic transition from high fertility-high mortality via high fertility-declining mortality, via declining fertility-low mortality to a stage of low fertility-low mortality, which took place in Europe and North America. The smoothest pattern of this model was found in the Scandinavian counties, whereas deviations were found in other places. For example, France initially had a relatively low level of fertility and very low growth rates throughout the transition period, whereas in Ireland fertility declined before mortality and thus created a negative growth or decline of the population.

Later, when the USSR, Eastern Europe and even Japan experienced a more rapid decline of mortality followed also by a decline in fertility, this "model of transition" was seen as a theory which predicted how populations changed from high levels of fertility and mortality to low levels of these variables.

When Third World countries after 1945 experienced a rapid decline in mortality and thus an increasing population growth, the supporters of this theory interpreted this as the first stage fulfilled in the transition, and expected the fertility to decline as well. However in Europe, and in the other nations where the transition has taken place, the conditions for reducing family size were changing very fast in the expanding urban sector during the industrialization process. The changes in relation to the previously dominant rural life were towards fixed salaries, increasing costs of children and lack of benefit from their labour, limited housing, work away from home making it difficult for women simultaneously to work outside the home as well as to take care of their children. A comparable change in living conditions has not occurred for the Third World countries, where the majority of the population remains rural and with no immediate increase in the costs of raising children.

The model of transition as a demographic theory may thus be seen merely as an empirical description of how demographic variables changed in the industrial countries, but not as a "theory" specifying the conditions for the changes, or with any predictive value for countries under totally different conditions for the population.

European marxist view on population

Karl Marx did not see population increase and population pressure as isolated independent variables, but clearly as part of the economic structure and the working relations. He strongly opposed the view that population pressure limited economic growth. He used Ireland in 1846—70 as an example, where the population decreased throughout the period due to famine after the failure of the potato harvest (1846) and later due to the heavy outmigration of the population to America. Throughout this period of decreasing population, economic development and employment should have increased according to the Malthusian view, but on the contrary, the economy stagnated and unemployment increased. This trend was a result of changes in the production and the increased mechanization leading to declining need for manual labourers.

Marx' argument was that each economic system had its own laws of population. He emphasized that the capitalist mode of production had its own specific laws of population. He specified how, within such an economic system, a population could be changed to a surplus population or an industrial reserve army.

He operated with three forms of surplus population: (1) floating population consisting of people displaced by machinery and structural changes within industry. (2) Latent population consisting of that part of the agricultural population on the verge of migrating to the cities, mainly as a consequence of the commercialization and capital input into agriculture. (3) The stagnant population comprising workers with highly irregular employment and the lowest levels of living.

Over-population is thus perceived not as a general population law creating obstacles for economic growth, but in relation to this specific economic system and the development of the productive forces therein. The implication being that a surplus population in one economic system may well be an economically active population in another economic system.

Another aspect covered in Marx's arguments was the relationship between the productive and the dependent age groups. He rejected the static perception of the population structure, arguing that each individual is dynamic and that although he starts as a consumer, he becomes mainly a producer during the working ages and again later becomes a dependent and primarily a consumer again. Therefore the expenditure in education should be seen not as social costs, but as investments in the training of the future labour force.

This emphasis on the specificity of the population laws laid the foundation for the laws of population in the socialist states, where the increasing population numbers are not perceived as a burden to the economy, but as primary producers and thus an asset. The limitations in Marx' theory are obviously related to his description of the actual economic development and capital accumulation in Europe in the early part of the Industrial revolution, and therefore his analysis may not be used as the basis for a general theory which could be applied to systems in the developing countries with different economic conditions.[1]

Theories related to the Third World

The appearance of overpopulation in Europe between 1700 and 1900 was that of a poor urban working and unemployed group of people, increasing rapidly during the Industrial revolution period due to the high migration to the urban areas.

In different parts of the Third World, different relationships between population and land resources or employment seem to be emphasized in the different theories.

In Asia and especially in India and Java, the focus is on 1) the crowded cities 2) the lack of access to land and pressure on land, and 3) the high unemployment. This leads to the application of the neo-Malthusian approach and the theories emphasize population as the obstacle to economic growth. The relationship between overpopulation and the economic system is however clarified in China, where until 1949 there was a large surplus population, but where the appearance of over-population disappeared when the population became engaged in productive work for the collectivity after the revolution. In Africa

[1] Karl Marx: *The Capital.* Vol. I, chapt. 23.

different theorists have emphasized different aspects of population *vs.* resource relationship.

Ester Boserup, in her historical studies of the development of agriculture and the increase in productivity in agriculture, has emphasized how population growth and density influence technological development. She argues that in the historical development of agriculture, a high population density and growth rate seem to create the conditions for increasing the technological level. The evidence is found in the historical development of African agriculture, where the high population density has covariated with higher development of agricultural technology, whereas practically no technological development in agriculture has taken place in sparsely populated areas, even though resources have been abundant. The point is that population pressure not only makes change necessary, but also that increased productivity usually requires a higher input of labour. The theory thus emphasizes the trend from hunting-gathering through simple shifting cultivation toward more developed permanent agriculture. However it does not reveal how changes occur later on, or how agriculture will tend to develop under the present conditions, nor is it a deterministic or causal theory, stating that high population pressure automatically leads to higher productivity in agriculture, but only that this is one of the responses, and that high population density seem to be one of the conditions for this development.

Samir Amin, focussing on the availability of arable land which is not yet cultivated, presents the theory of underpopulated Africa.[2] In this he argues that Africa could have much higher productivity in agriculture and better infrastructure if there was a higher population which could work on the land and share the costs of an infrastructure. This is partly based on the evidence collected by Ester Boserup, but also on his own economic analysis, where it appears that the costs of a rapidly increasing population are outweighed by the benefits of a large adult population later on. For example in many thinly populated areas, a higher population could support the development of transport and water and thus improve the infrastructure necessary for the development of the area. Samir Amin's perception of the many acres of arable land which are not cultivated focuses on a central issue for the development of the agricultural potential, but in countries like Kenya, where there may still be uncultivated arable land, there is also very little which is not already privately owned. Thus Amin does not discuss the effects of land adjudication and distribution of land in this overall perception of population per arable land unit. This point seems to be essential when the open land frontier is an argument for the need of a much higher population. However, the perception that unemployment and under-development are a result of the economic

---

[2] Samir Amin: Underpopulated Africa. In: *Manpower and Unemployment Research in Africa*, no. 2, 1972, Quebec.

structure and not of population growth is very clear in his writings and is comparable with Marx' theory of the European population.

Arthur W. Lewis emphasizes other aspects of overpopulation when he discusses the surplus population in agriculture which, because of its large numbers, decreases the marginal productivity of agriculture. His proposal is that this surplus population should be diverted into industrial production. But he sees a problem in absorbing this population in the very slowly developing modern sector of the economy that exists in most developing countries. He suggests that the "bazar economy" (equivalent to the "informal sector") could absorb it. His main point is to get this surplus population away from agriculture, into this temporary sector, where it apparently neither dies nor lives, but survives, because here it does not present a severe drain on the productive resources, for example in agriculture.[3]

Many of the theorists working with development problems, however, seem to have difficulty in finding out the impact of the population factor, and some include it as only one of the factors. The population factor has many dimensions in relation to the economy, and what seems to be essential is the development of the system, such that it makes full use of the people in working ages and does not let them become a passive burden to the economy. One of the theorists, Gunnar Myrdal in his "Asian Drama", emphasizes the structure of the economy, for example, the structure of agricultural employment, where there is a lack of labour in certain peak seasons, but where most of this labour force cannot find employment outside the season, resulting in a pattern of seasonal employment and thus an under-employment problem, which is costly for the society. However, he also underlines other constraints in utilizing the labour force efficiently. The health status and the educational structure of the labour force seem to be important factors. Extinction of parasites like hookworm and mosquitoes would increase the capability of the working population. In relation to education and training, a more diversified and technical education of the labour force would lead to the possibility of increasing the employment.[4]

Theories at micro-level. Decisions on limiting family size

The previous theories are all concerned with macro-level economic discussions, mainly emphasizing the impact of population increase on the development process, whereas individual families do not necessarily follow the recommended macro-level birth-rate. Changes at the micro-level are based on decisions taken within the family as regards the planning of families. In Europe the decisions were related to 1) the initial improvement in economic conditions for young

[3] A. W. Lewis: *The Theory of Economic Growth.* 1963, p. 327.
[4] G. Myrdal: *Asian Drama.* Part 3 1968, p. 959—1532.

urban employees, followed by a declining age at marriage and 2) later economic constraints resulting in increased economic strains on the urban families, coupled with a decline in the economic value of children as labourers (urban setting and labour laws) and the increase in the costs of raising them. The urban families thus started practising family planning, limiting family size from around 5—6 children to 2—3 children.[5]

Other important variables affecting these decisions seem to be: Women's employment outside the home and the farmstead, improved education and general level of knowledge. However, the large scale change only affected the urban areas, whereas agricultural rural families did not change their behaviour until recently. The large impact on the total birth rate has been a result of the rapidly increasing proportion of the urban population with no relation to agriculture. A lot of the theoretical and empirical work in the analysis of the decisions on family size, from a micro-perspective is based on economic explanations, mostly using income as a determining variable. A more recent approach is the use of utility models or explanations based on consumer behaviour. However, the problem with these is to treat a highly complex behaviour as purely economic behavior based on conceptual frameworks derived from Western experiences, where most of the population is engaged in the urban wage economy.

In relation to Africa the pattern is different. The majority of the population is in agriculture. With increasing school enrollment, as is the case in Kenya, the costs of raising children are increasing, and this tends to affect the value of children. Yet the children are still contributing valuable labour for the family production, even if they are attending school, and they are still responsible for the old age security. These different tendencies in the costs and benefits of children do not press families uniformly towards having smaller or to maintain large families, since the pressures are working in different directions. In the East African case the conditions for having large families tend to change among rural poor peasant families in some areas, especially areas of high population pressure, while in other areas with low population density or among better-off families there is apparently no tendency to change the family size, or the attitude to having many children.[6]

In relation to the social and economic benefits and costs of large families, new attempts to develop sociological theory are arising. J. C. Caldwell calls his approach a 'restatement of the demographic transition theory' and argues, that "whether high or low fertility is economically rational is determined by social conditions: primarily by the direction of the inter-generational wealth flow". This flow has been from the younger generations to the older generations in all traditional societies, and it is apparently impossible for a reverse flow—at the great divide—to occur before the family is largely nucleated both emotionally

[5] J. M. Beshers: *Population Processes in Social Systems.* N. Y. 1967, pp. 33—130.
[6] Mette Mønsted: Conditions for a Changing Family Size in Selected Rural Areas of Kenya. Working paper. Centre for Development Research. Copenhagen 1977.

and economically.[7] This restatement is supported by other research findings in East Africa. For example, Tarsis Kabwegyere found definite social benefits arising from having many children in the study of some Akamba families in rural areas of Kenya. Reasons for having large families appear to be largely social, but once the children grow up, the benefits also tend to be of economic nature.[8]

The micro-level aspects of changing family size, have mostly been covered within the models of communication, i.e. how can poor illiterate people be persuaded and taught to limit their family size? In this respect the theory is not very clear and it may be added that the determining factors seem to be the living conditions and the social and economic basis for the large families, rather than communications on family planning.

Conclusion:

The above chapter reveals the weaknesses of the existing demographic theories and the need for an evaluation of theory in relation to the specific historical conditions described. For example, in many African areas land is abundant and is not a severe restriction on the population. This is a case which never existed in Europe, and it is now changing in many parts of Africa. But this will affect the population development and increase the pressure for changing agricultural technology.

Within the African continent, the relationships between population and land resources are so diverse that a uniform population theory or policy cannot be adequate as a framework for analysing them.

The research priority should be to examine and analyse family size and structure in relation to different social and economic conditions in the different regions. The studies at the micro-level could concentrate on:

1. Different types of production systems, and the extent of technological use in small-scale agricultural production, thereby trying to assess the role of children as labour contributors.

2. Income earning and expenditure patterns within the industrial families, to show whether children press on resources, and if they do to what extent.

3. Detailed anthropological studies to determine the social and cultural values about reproduction and their relationship to the overall economic context.

This raises serious methodological issues. Most demographic investigations have relied purely on large scale sample surveys for data collection. However, for the type of micro-level studies required for establishing adequate theoretical frameworks, one must argue for the need to utilize multiple methodological

[7] J. C. Caldwell: Toward a Restatement of Demographic Transition Theory. *Population and Development Review* vol. 2 no. 3–4 1976, p. 355.
[8] Tarsis Kabwegyere: Determinants of Fertility: A Discussion of Change in the Family among the Akamba of Kenya. Staff seminar no. 19. Dept. of Sociology. Univ. of Nbi. 1976.

techniques. Thus sample surveys should be only one of the methods. In addition one could resort to participant observation for detailed information on the social and economic conditions and case studies to highlight certain relationships, time budgets, etc. These different approaches would yield more relevant information than the broad survey type only based on questionnaires, as for example the KAP (Knowledge, Attitude and Practice) survey which seems to be heavily relied upon for demographic statistical information.

Supplementary reading:

1. UN. *Determinants and Consequences of Population Trends*. N. Y. 1974. Chapt. 3, pp. 33—63 and chapt. 12, pp. 398—465.
2. National Academy of Sciences: *Rapid Population Growth. Consequences and Policy Implications* (Vol. 2) Baltimore 1971.
    a. T. P. Schultz: An Economic Perspective on Population Growth, pp. 148—174.
    b. Theodore W. Schultz: The Food Supply—Population Growth Quandary, pp. 245—272.
    c. Gavin W. Jones: Effects of Population Change on Attainment of Educational Goals in Developing Countries, pp. 315—367.
3. Roushdi A. Henin: The Applicability of the Theory of Demographic Transition to African Countries. In: OECD. *The Demographic Transition in Tropical Africa*. Paris 1971, pp. 15—28.
4. Ester Boserup: *The Conditions of Agricultural Growth*. London 1965.
5. Samir Amin: Underpopulated Africa. In: *Manpower and Unemployment Research in Africa*. No. 2, 1972. Quebec, Canada.

[9] KAP: refers to the Knowledge, Attitude and Practice of contraception among women and men. These surveys have been carried out on a large scale in different countries, based on communication models, with the purpose of assessing the ignorance among people in the developing countries regarding family planning.

Chapter IV

Introduction to Demographic Variables

Demography is defined as the discipline studying human populations with respect to size, distribution, structure, and the dynamics of these variables. It is concerned with the general quantitative characteristics, and the analysis of changes in them. This implies a study of the geographical distribution of the population, the urbanization, the age-sex structure and also household and marriage structure.

Perceived in the most narrow sense, demography can be seen as population statistics. This is only static and measures the existing population structures. But in order to make demography a relevant social discipline, the dynamics and changes of population become the essential part of the analysis, together with the relevant parts of sociology and economics for the explanation of the demographic phenomena.

In the registration of movements and changes in the population, the demographic variables, i.e. variables influencing the size and structure of the population, are in focus. These are births, deaths, migrations, marriages, divorces.

The relationship between size of population and the variables may be illustrated by the following flow diagramme:

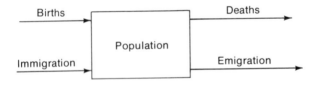

With respect to a special population such as the population of married women in a country, the variables affecting the size of the population are the following:

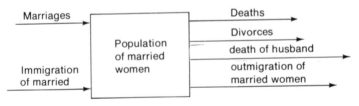

Thus all the variables affecting the changes, all inputs and all outflows in the population are essential for the measurement of changes in the population, and sometimes as part of the basis for the estimation of the total size of the population.

Demographic methods and demographic variables may also be used outside the narrow population study, as processes of change in special populations such as school or university populations and the drop-out rates, or the size and supply of the labour force, involve the same considerations and the same methods can be applied. In the case of school enrollment in Kenya, the important input variables would be: enrollment of the 7-year-old in Standard 1 plus all other later enrollments after an interruption of their schooling, as well as immigrating school-children. The outflows will consist of: graduations at exams, drop-outs and deaths as well as outmigration of school-children. These variables are important for determining the size of the school-population if the size is known at some point in time, and the size at a later point in time has to be estimated on the basis of the changes in the population.

In the analysis of all the demographic variables, the chapters will cover:

1. Sources and evaluation of data: the kind of data available, and the evaluation of official statistics, censuses, and sample surveys.

2. Measures and methods for the calculation and estimation of demographic variables.

3. Description of demographic variables in East Africa, related to an analysis of the variations and changes in the variables.

4. Analysis of the explanations, causes and consequences of these differential patterns of the variables and structures of population.

This book emphasizes the analysis of the data available for East Africa, and focuses the demographic processes, i.e. how the accumulation of the variety of social, psychological and economic factors affect the decisions relevant for the demographic variables, and how these change.

Demography deals with the incidences of births and migrations and marriages, all of which seem to be related to individual patterns of causes and personal decisions. The family level of decisions therefore should be considered in the analysis. But concerning the statistics of large figures of population, there seems to be a kind of pattern and regularity because the basic economic conditions and other social factors are similar for large groups of the population. This often leads to what is called the "law of large figures"—where aggregates of individual decisions show certain common patterns.

Chapter V

The Source and Nature of Demographic Data in East Africa

The major sources of demographic information are population censuses, vital registration systems and sample surveys. If a country has complete and accurate censuses and vital registration, one can get a good picture of its population characteristics. Most western countries have these, and this has led to the development of techniques of population analyses, on the assumption of the availability of complete and accurate data. However, the situation for most developing countries, and especially for Africa, is quite different. Not all countries have population censuses, and in those that have, the accuracy and reliability is questionable. Moreover, in most African countries registration is non-existent or incomplete. Therefore, many of the techniques developed in demography, especially those using vital registration, have limited use because of the nature of the data available to us. In the East African countries a heavy reliance is placed on estimates based on censuses, and sample surveys also contribute a lot to demographic knowledge.

Population censuses

A census is a complete count or enumeration of the population usually carried out during a specific time period, and at regular intervals of about five or ten years (the Kenyan one however has had an interval of seven years between the last two censuses because the second census was delayed). The census provides information on basic demographic characteristics like size, distribution, age-sex structure, marital status, education, occupation, etc. In addition, one can also derive estimates of fertility and mortality on the basis of certain questions included in the census, as has been done in the East African countries.

Prior to 1948, the East African population was estimated on the basis of mere guesses of the tax-paying population, thus making the validity of these counts highly questionable. As early as 1878, the population of Uganda was estimated by Stanley to be 780,000, while the population of the East African Protectorate was estimated to be 2.5 million in 1897 (almost comparable to Kenya except for the Western Province). In 1902, the estimate for Uganda was 3.5 million and for Kenya 4.0 million. Between these early guesses and the first round of censuses, the estimates were made by the colonial administration based on tax-payers. The earliest estimate for the Tanganyikan African population in 1913 was 4.1 million, based on the number of adult male tax-payers and their dependants. In Kenya, the poll-tax, which was levied on every able-bodied male over 16 years old, was used as the basis for estimating the population. After a very uncertain age-estimation, the British administration decided that the adult female population made up 49 % of the total adult population, while children under 16 years made up 37 % of the total population. However this assumption was proved wrong by the results of the first census which showed a much higher proportion of children, around 48 %. Also, errors in the counting of the males made the final estimate too low, by as much as 25 %. Around 1931, some attempts were made to count the population in Uganda and Tanganyika, but the first proper census in all the three East African countries was undertaken in 1948. However, even this one was not complete, as it left out the difficult forest and arid areas. The results of the censuses are given in table 6.

Table 6. *African population in East Africa, 1948 (in thousands)*.

Country	Last estimates		1948 Census
Kenya	4,055	(1946)	5,251
Tanganyika	5,838	(1947)	7,408
Uganda	3,988	(1947)	4,918

Source: S. H. Ominde: *The Population of Kenya, Tanzania and Uganda*. Nairobi 1975, p. 3.

The first round of the census is not considered accurate, but is supposed to have provided a fair estimate relevant for the evaluation of the labour force and the tax-payers. The results of the non-African population were reported in detail, whereas the published results of the African censuses were more limited.

The 1948 census was followed by another census, also before Independence, in Tanganyika in 1957, in Uganda in 1959 and in Kenya in 1962. This census followed basically the same procedures as the 1948 census. The Kenyan one was slightly modified, abandoning the different stages of enumeration, and resorting to a single enumeration using two forms; a simple one for the rural areas and a more detailed one for the urban areas. Kenya has also published a very detailed and thorough analysis of the 1962 census, and Volume III on the African Population is of special interest. However, the data is old and the fact that the census took place just before Independence, limits the general validity of the data in many of the areas where fights had been taking place. Also, data on the major inmigration areas like the Rift Valley and the major towns, are too old to contribute any useful information on the current situation.

All the East African censuses over the years have differentiated between the African and non-African population. Table 7 provides the numbers and distribution of the African and non-African population in East Africa for the 1948 census as well as the later censuses.

Table 7. *African and non-African population ii the East African countries in the 3 censuses (population in thousands).*

Country	1948	Second Census		Third Census	
Kenya: African	5,253	8,366	(1962)	10,753	(1969)
Non-African	155	270		189	
Tanganyika: African	7,410	8,623	(1957)	11,482	(1967)*
Non-African	70	123		122	
Uganda: African	4,918	6,451	(1969)	9,456	(1969)
Non-African	41	87		92	

* Mainland only. For the whole of Tanzania including Zanzibar 12,313,469 in total.

For each of the three East African countries, only three censuses are available, and only one of these was undertaken after Independence. Thus the last census for Kenya was in August 1969, for Tanzania in 1967 and for Uganda also in 1969. This reflects the absence of recent or current data on the East African societies, and the need for, and dependence on, estimations and projections on the basis of the last round of censuses. However, of the three countries, only Tanzania has prepared a thorough analysis of its 1967 census. As this is the only detailed analysis of the last censuses, a lot of reliance has been placed on it to describe East African data in many of the chapters of this book. For Kenya, the raw data collected in the 1969 census, have been published but no analysis or evaluation of the data or the methodology has been published as yet. The information collected in the Kenyan population census of 1969 is published in the following volumes:

1. Kenya Population Census 1969. Vol. 1. Statistics Division, Ministry of Finance and Planning, 1970. (Information on geographical distribution of population in Provinces, Districts, Divisions, locations, sub-locations. Density, adults/children and the sex distribution of the total populations, as well as the age and sex distributions for districts and provinces).

2. Kenya Population Census 1969. Vol. II. Data on Urban Population (Population by size of urban centres, Population in Urban Centres, area density, tribe, population by sex, age, education in urban centres, number of centres of different sizes, population by sex, relationship to head of household and urban centre).

3. Kenya Population Census 1969. Vol. III. Data on education, relationship to head of household, sex, tribe, age, birthplace and sex, age and marital status.

This census is a *de facto* enumeration of the population. *De facto* refers to the counting of the people actually present at the registration time i.e. a question on "Who stayed in the house last night?" This differs from the other principle for censuses referred to as *de jure* or counting persons usually belonging to an area but not necessarily residing in the place at that particular moment. Thus the question would ask "Who usually belongs to this household and has permanent residence here?" The census consisted of a total census, as complete as possible even in the remote areas, as well as a more detailed survey of a sample of the population. The more detailed survey provided information on place of birth, number of children born alive per woman etc.

As regards the validity of the data in the censuses of all the three countries, the last one seems to be the most complete. In Kenya the 1969 census is the first to try to cover the North Eastern Province. However even this census is questionable in relation to a few specific areas. For example, the figure for Eldoret town in the census was 18,196 people. However, Eldoret Municipality has estimated the population in 1969 to be no less than 27,500, based on the water consumption and average earnings. These differences are most likely related to the definition of the town and only to some extent may affect the total number of people in the area. However town boundaries are difficult to define and other similar errors may easily be found. Thus census data have to be used with a lot of caution, and various evaluation and correction procedures have to be used to correct the data. Some of these are covered in the next chapter.

Sample surveys

Because of the limitations of censuses and vital registration, sample surveys are increasingly being used to provide demographic information as they can be used to get both registration and census type of data. Information from the census can be supplemented by intercensus or post-enumeration surveys, which, because they are more definite in scope, may get better and more detailed information. However, the major problem with surveys is that of representativeness and sampling errors which may cause large biases in the results. Still, surveys are widely used in the East African countries, where most of the data on fertility and mortality trends have been derived from these surveys (e.g. Kenya 1969 census). In Kenya, sample surveys are regularly carried out on specific issues by the Central Bureau of Statistics (Nairobi). Examples of importance are:

1. Demographic Baseline Survey Report, 1973—Central Bureau of Statistics, Nairobi, July 1975.

2. Internal Migration Patterns in a selected area in Kenya Deomographic Working Paper No. 1—Central Bureau of Statistics, Nairobi, October 1975.

In addition, for Kenya, all Statistical Abstracts, Economic Surveys and Development Plans provide essential materials and estimates of the population, in between and after the censuses.

Also, special surveys with other than demographic purposes can provide data on the population. An example is the "Report on the Demographic Studies of the Joint Machakos Project" by P. G. Blok, Medical Research Centre, Nairobi, in 1975. This provides information on the population in the Machakos area which supplements the previous census data.

In Tanzania and Uganda similar surveys have been conducted; of special importance is the Rungwe Survey of Tanzania, a post-enumeration survey following shortly after the 1967 Tanzanian census. The purpose was to check on the reliability of the census results by using a much more comprehensive survey.

Vital registration

The third source of data refers to a record of vital events like births, deaths, marriages and divorces, occurring in an area, usually in a given year. However, although registration of births and deaths is legally compulsory in all the East African countries, it is very incomplete and inadequate for demographic analysis.

In Kenya registration has to take place within a month of a birth or death. However, this cannot be fulfilled in most of the rural areas. Only in Nairobi and Mombasa is vital registration estimated to be around 90 % complete. In the rural areas, the quality of registration varies; it is estimated to be the best in the densely populated areas of Central Province and parts of Western and Nyanza Provinces, but even in these areas it is not very reliable. It has been estimated that in Kenya only one-fifth of all the births and a quarter of all the deaths are registered. Nairobi seems to have almost complete coverage of registered births (perhaps because the majority of the births take place in hospitals); while registered deaths do not account for more than half of the deaths in the city.

Thus the current situation in the East African countries, as in other African countries, is that registration is either non-existent or very inadequate, which leads to a heavy reliance on censuses and sample surveys to obtain a comprehensive picture of the demographic situation in these countries.

The above description reflects some of the limitations of demographic data in East Africa. It is apparent that no reliance can be placed on registration data, and that the majority of the estimates of population trends are on the basis of censuses or survey data. However, these also have their limitations. Census data usually suffer from problems of completeness, coverage, misreporting, etc. and require rigorous analysis and evaluation. Sample surveys are the basic tools for getting information on the major components of population change, namely fertility and mortality estimates with the application of complex techniques for estimating from incomplete data. But too often, too much reliance is placed on these large-scale surveys and this can create serious methodological problems. The analysis of the relationship between the various population and socio-economic variables, and the trends in these may not be reliable or representative because of the problems of sampling in the rural areas. Very often the sampling techniques and strategies used are based on those adopted for the more literate urban societies of the West, or often only people who are available or willing to talk are interviewed, which can cause tremendous bias in the information. Therefore, too much reliance on such data can distort the actual picture and affect policy implications. Cases in point are the large-scale KAP surveys. (Cross-cultural surveys on Knowledge, Attitude and Practice of

40

family planning in developing countries.) An additional problem is the operationalization of the concepts being used. So far in most surveys the types of questions asked are based on the socio-economic framework of Western societies; for example questions like "How many children do you have?" or "How many of your children have died?" may seem perfectly straightforward questions to a Western woman, but could be highly sensitive and suspicion-laden questions for the rural African woman.

The argument being made here is the need for more relevant types of survey techniques and sampling procedures. In addition, a clear background knowledge of the social, economic and cultural aspects of a population is required before the formulation of any questions, so that one is getting information on what one asks and not on the respondents evaluation of what one is asking, since sample surveys are still very important as tools for demographic data collection together with population censuses.

Supplementary reading

1. S. H. Ominde: *The Population of Kenya, Tanzania and Uganda*, Nairobi 1975, p. 3—9.
2. *Kenya Population Census 1962*. Vol. III, African Population, pp. 1—18.
3. B. Egero & R. Henin (eds): *The Population of Tanzania*. An Analysis of the 1967 Population Census. Census vol. 6, Dar es Salaam 1973, pp. 14—37 and pp. 231—246.
4. *Kenya Population Census 1969*. Introduction in Vol. 1, Vol. 2 and Vol. 3.
5. R. M. A. Zwanenberg with Anne King: *An Economic History of Kenya and Uganda 1800—1970*. Nairobi 1975, pp. 7—20.

Chapter VI

Evaluation of East African Population Data and Simple Techniques for Correction.

As pointed out in the preceding chapter, population data collected in East Africa are distorted and unreliable and need to be thoroughly evaluated and corrected before they can be put to any useful purpose. Errors in population statistics can result both from inaccuracies in the basic population data as well as from inaccuracies in the assumptions used to derive population estimates. Once it has been revealed that the data are inaccurate, it is possible to adjust them through the use of simple correction techniques. Therefore one needs to investigate the basic population data, and this will be very much related to the evaluation of the data collection procedures. This will indicate the representativity, completeness, reliability and validity of the statistics. In addition, apart from the technical evaluation, it is also very important to get the basic economic and sociologicial evaluation in terms of validity and reliability, so that one can judge how consistent the data are with the other social and economic information in the area being studied.

Factors affecting completeness

Omissions (in censuses and surveys).

A major problem in both population censuses and sample surveys is that of omissions of certain groups or individuals in the population. These omissions are not distributed equally, instead some groups tend to be systematically left out while others are included. For example, it is usually difficult to have a complete enumeration of people in remote and inaccessible areas like mountains, forests, deserts, etc. Also, all the nomads, semi-nomads and other migrant groups of the population have a much higher probability of being omitted from the count than the permanently settled population. Certain age groups have a higher risk of being left out than others. Thus in the analysis of the Rungwe District after the 1967 Tanzanian census, it was revealed that young men from approximately 20 to 35 years were covered very incompletely in the census due to their high rate of mobility.[1] Omissions of very young children are also very frequent . All these omissions lead to the undercounting or under-representation of certain groups of people, thus resulting in unreliable data. In a

[1] Klaas de Jonge and J. Sterkenberg: The Rungwe Survey. In: B. Egero & R. Henin eds: *The Population of Tanzania*. An Analysis of the 1967 Population Census. Census vol. 6. Dar es Salaam 1973, p. 237.

census there is usually a problem of locating all the people for enumeration. Besides, there is a lack of qualified interviewers who might try to trace everybody. Problems of under-enumeration can also arise depending on the type of census count being used. In Nigeria it has been found that "a *de facto* enumeration tends to underestimate the population,... on the other hand a *de jure* enumeration tends to overestimate the population...".[2] However, the degree and type of bias in carrying out a population estimate will vary from country to country and one cannot say for certain that a *de facto* count will always lead to under-enumeration.

Sample surveys should be easy to administer as they demand a more limited number of interviewers. However, sample surveys are often very unreliable as the sample framework or the population from which the sample is drawn is often not precisely known, leading to major difficulties in generalizing for the whole population. This also implies that it is not very clear what the size of the sample should be, i.e. whether it should be 8 % or 10 % of the population.

The length of time for the census

In carrying out a census, which involves enumerating a large population one of the major problems is to find enough qualified interviewers to quickly finish the enumeration (within one week). If a census takes too long, it is more prone to omissions and double counting due to movements of the people. An example from the USA shows that in the 1930s when the census enumerators were following a group of agricultural labourers in their migration with the harvest season towards the North, there was an over-enumeration of the population by as much as 30 %!

Time period

Another problem is the time of year that the census is taken. Different seasons will show different patterns of population distribution and structure in some areas. One example is that of a coffee plantation area, where the population density will be higher, with more people in working ages during the harvests than during other seasons; or in the Rift Valley region, where there will be far more working males during maize planting, weeding and harvesting than during the other seasons.

Interviewer instructions

It is important to have consistent and complete instructions about the interpretation of concepts and definitions to be used in the census, especially regarding the definition of a household. Also, the interviewer should be clearly instructed whether the enumeration should cover a *de facto* or a *de jure* popula-

[2] O. O. Arowolo, *Problem of Population Movement and Enumeration in Nigeria: The example of Ife Division in the Western State*, Population Studies Centre, University of Pennsylvania 1970.

tion. In the 1967 Tanzanian census some of these problems were quite consider-able, as the definition of "a household" was not clear in relation to polyga-mous households. Some interviewers defined the household of the husband and those of all his wives as one household while others interpreted each wife's house as a separate household.

Lack of knowledge

In the rural areas of East Africa people do not always know their exact age or that of members of their household. Old people especially, may know approxi-mately what major historical events occurred around the time of their birth and the age-set they belong to, but not their exact age. This leads to a difficult process of estimation and is a major source of error in the data. However, younger people in most areas are now increasingly able to give their exact ages. Additional problems also arise because most people do not fully comprehend the significance of the census and tend to be very suspicious, thus withholding or giving false information.

Because of the difficulties in carrying out population counts, and the result-ing errors, one needs to know and evaluate the limitations of population data and the degree of unreliability before one can meaningfully utilize the statistics. Such an evaluation is usually closely related to other aspects of the population.

Evaluation of the reliability of the absolute population number

The absolute population in most African censuses is often systematically un-der-enumerated; omissions are more frequent than double-counting and they are systematically skewed. Some indicators used to reveal under-enumeration are:

a. Too high a growth rate between two censuses: This usually indicates that the earlier census has been more under-enumerated than the latter. For example, the annual growth rate in Kenya between 1962 and 1969 was calcu-lated to be 3.4 % per year (the population figure for Kenya in 1969 was 10.94 million and in 1962 it was 8.64 million). On the basis of the analysis of the other variables, this growth rate appears far too high, and it is likely that the 1962 census may have under-enumerated the population by as much as 5 %. This method is a check on the internal consistency of the demographic data by use of the "balancing equation".

b. The age-sex distribution: This will usually reflect under-enumeration. It may be revealed if there are gaps in the age-structure especially for young men 20—34 years old and young children under 5 years. The age pattern however, is not only an indication of under-enumeration but also of incorrect statement of age of the enumerated population, which may show some of the same traits. If the sex ratio (i.e. number of males per 100 females in the population) is unrealistically high, one may suspect an under-enumeration of females, especially in some age groups where the surplus of males cannot be explained by migration.

c. The size of nomadic groups: These are often under-enumerated and other surveys or estimations on the consistency of the data have to be applied for the evaluation.

Evaluation of errors in the age-sex distribution

In the rural areas of East Africa the registration of birth dates is very limited, and has been non-existent for most adult groups of the population. People do not know their exact age, although they do know their relevant "social age" or age-set. These age groups are reflected in the development of social roles in societies, such as infants, young (uncircumcised) children, young circumcised men (e.g. morans), adults, elders. Usually old people also know approximately what historical, local or national events occurred around the time of their birth. Therefore, for an estimation of age in an area a list of historical events (major droughts, famines, good harvests, wars, etc.) should be prepared to assist the interviewers. The instructions to the interviewers in the Tanzanian 1967 census were as follows: "If actual age is not known, an estimate is to be given. To get a better age estimation, various generally known facts are to be used. For example, children who cannot walk are usually under 1 year of age, children begin to lose milk teeth at the age of 6. Age of puberty is usually between the age of 13 and 16 years for males and 12 and 15 for females, etc. Some generally known historic events might be very helpful in the estimation of ages."[3] Ten such events were listed covering the years 1890—1964 (ages 3—77 years). These events help locate time of birth, although they also provide a basis for heaping of people in certain age-groups (just around these events).

On the basis of such instructions one can expect many errors to arise in the reporting of age data, as a lot of dependence is placed on the judgement and discretion of the interviewers.

There are two different kinds of errors in the age-sex information, both having a different impact on the population data:

1. Digital preferences: This refers to a tendency to state the age in certain preferred age-groups. Mostly this is in age groups ending with digits 0 and 5, and to a lesser extent with digits 6 and 8. This affects the age distribution so that there are often more people recorded in the preferred age groups than in the other groups.

2. Age-misreporting i.e. systematic over- or under-estimation of certain age groups. Thus respondents place themselves in the wrong age groups not because of rounding but because they choose to, or believe themselves to be

[3] Egero and Henin: op. cit. p. 202.

younger or older than they really are.

An evaluation of digital preference or age-heaping is only possible when information is collected for one year intervals of age. One index (Whipple's Index), shows the degree of heaping in age-groups ending with 0 and 5. The index is simple to compute and its values range from 100—500. If there is no heaping at 0 and 5, Whipple's Index = 100, but if there is maximum heaping at these digits, the Index = 500 showing that the data is completely distorted.

However, Whipple's Index gives no indication or evaluation of heaping at the other ages. Therefore, in East Africa, much more information on the different types of age-errors can be derived directly from the age-sex pyramid based on one-year intervals (see graph 2).

Correction of age errors due to rounding

The age-heaping as shown in the graph may be smoothened by grouping the data into 5-year intervals. However, if these are the normal intervals, i.e. 0—4, 5—9, 10—14 etc. there will be considerable systematic errors. Whereas if the intervals are such that the ages with the heaping are in the middle of the interval, i.e. 3—7, 8—12, 13—17 etc. then there will be fewer systematic errors.

Example of men in Kenya, 1962

In graph 3 an example is shown where heaping has occurred at ages 25, 30, 35. Somewhat less heaping is also revealed at ages 28, 32, and 38. The heaping, for example at age 30, results from men 29 years old, being classified as 30 years

Graph 2. *Age-sex pyramid for the African population of Kenya (excluding Northern Province) Recorded figures by single years of age with smoothed curve, 1962.*

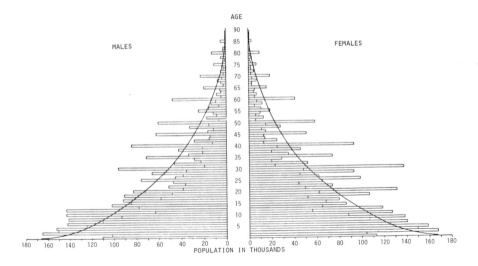

Graph 3. *Number of men in single years of age from 20—61 years in Kenya, 1962.*

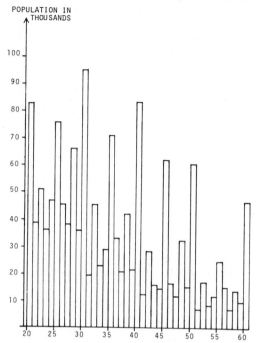

POPULATION IN THOUSANDS

Source for Graphs 2 and 3: Kenya Population Census 1962. Vol. 3, p. 28.

old. The age group 29 is therefore much smaller in relation to the actual population, whereas 30 is too large. In addition, the heaping at age 30 is also a result of men aged 31, 32 and maybe even 33 years being classified as 30 years old.

a.   If the normal 5 year age-groups are formed, then 30—34 would be: 121,000 + 35,000 + 61,500 + 37,500 = 255,000. However this age group contains a surplus of people who should actually belong to the 25—29 year age-group, and also lacks some men 34 years old who may have been wrongly classified as 35 years old and thus are included in the 35—39 age groups.

b.   If other intervals are used, placing the ages with the major heapings in the middle of the interval, then the misplacement of the people will be much less, since heaping mostly involves misplacement from neighbouring age-groups e.g. from 29 to 30, or from 31 to 30.

If the age intervals instead are 23—27, 28—32, 33—37, then the misplacement would occur and remain within the correct 5-year age-group. For example, 23—27: 69,000 + 79,000 + 13,500 + 82,500 + 65,000 = 309,000. In this case heaping does not create any major misplacement, except for minor problems around age 28. All other heaping will take place inside the 5-year age-group, towards age 25.

Another method of smoothening or graduation of the age distribution is related to a comparison with population models, which are built up as averages of different population distributions and smoothened for these kinds of errors.

The major problems of age-errors is however related to a systematic over- and under-statement of certain age groups. This is a problem in Africa, Asia and Latin America, but the pattern of misreporting is very different due to different ages of marriage and the differential evaluation of social age in these countries.

The African pattern of age-misreporting is described in the Kenya Population Census 1962 as follows:

1. An under-enumeration of children of both sexes under 5 years.

2. A general understatement of the ages of older boys and young men, resulting in an inflation of the 5—9 and 10—14 year age-group, and deficits in the late teens and twenties.

3. A general overstatement of ages of older girls and young women, this overstatement resulting from displacement from 10—14 to 15—19 age group, from 15—19 to 20—24 age-group, and from 20—24 to 25—29 age group. However, also a certain downward trend from the 10—14 years age group, and an underestimation of girls under puberty, resulting in an inflation of the 5—9 year age group.

4. A general overstatement of ages among old people, which is more pronounced among males than among females.[4]

The age-misreporting may sometimes be revealed in the actual age distribution, but it is usually difficult to detect. However, it is reflected in the sex-ratios for the different age-groups, as the pattern of misreporting is different for males and females.

If there is not considerable migration, the pattern of higher mortality for males throughout life should lead to gradually declining sex-ratios toward the higher age-groups. The very high sex-ratios at old ages can be explained by misreporting of age, mainly the overstatement of the ages of old men. The incorrect statement is not only a result of the respondent's false reporting, but just as much a result of the interviewer's evaluation of the respondent's ages, which may be based on totally wrong criteria.

Graduation of the age-sex data is often carried out. However, all graduations smoothen out the actual as well as the erroneous deviations from a smooth age-sex pyramid, which confuses rather than adjusts the age-sex distribution. Therefore the data must first be evaluated in relation to their consistency with other information on the area. For example, if migration has taken place or is taking place, then the age-sex structure will be affected, especially since migration tends to be selective by age and sex, and these bulks or gaps in the distribution should not be smoothened out. Also, if mortality among certain age-groups has been high in some years, this will be revealed in the actual distribution, or if fertility has been fluctuating the pyramid will reflect this. All

---

[4] *Kenya Population Census 1962.* Vol. 3, p. 26.

Table 8. *Sex-ratio in 5 year age groups for Kenya 1962 and 1969 and Tanzania mainla, and Zanzibar 1967**

Age	Kenya 1962	Kenya 1969	Tanzania mainland 1967	Zanzibar 1967
0— 4	99	101.1	98	98
5— 9	102	102.6	101	97
10—14	118	107.7	111	123
15—19	103	102.8	90	94
20—24	71	95.1	70	67
25—29	76	85.0	80	89
30—34	82	93.9	89	91
35—39	96	95.2	101	126
40—44	101	96.0	94	98
45—49	119	105.3	108	145
50—54	114	95.2	97	103
55—59	132	112.1	105	165
60—64	118	108.4	93	119
65—69	124	117.8	103	185
70—74	} 141	} 108.1	94	116
75—79			124	163
80—84			114	105
85—89			134	102
90—94			132	104
95+			127	81

* Number of males per 100 females

Source: Calculations on Kenya Population Census 1962 and 1969. And Egero and Henin: op. cit., p. 203.

these factors may create deviations from the model of a smooth pyramid, which results from a stable level of fertility, mortality and no migration. Thus the use of these models will also level out all the actual deviations, giving a distorted picture. Therefore a smoothening on the basis of stable population models can only properly be done if there are no other indicators of changes in mortality (for a few ages), and fertility or if there is no major migration. This implies that the age-sex structure for sub-populations in towns, provinces and districts in East Africa cannot be smoothened.

Graduation of an age-sex structure is done on the basis of selecting the population model which best fits the actual age-sex structure. Population models are age-sex distributions of the population, stabilized in a projection using specific levels and patterns of mortality, fertility and natural growth rate. These models are mostly found in:

1. Coale and Demeny: Regional Model Life Tables and Stable Populations, Princeton 1966.

2. UN. Manual IV, Methods of Estimating Basic Demographic Measures from Incomplete Data, N. Y. 1967.

In order to use these models, a certain knowledge about the mortality and fertility picture of the country is needed. In Kenya in 1962, models were selected on the basis of the estimated mortality level and the growth rate. The

49

percentages of the population in the age groups 25—34, 35—44 in the models were then compared and the one that best fitted the data was applied as the correct smoothened age-sex structure.

This kind of technical smoothening levels out some of the major errors caused by age misreporting but must be utilized with caution. It may sometimes be better to have the actual age-sex structure showing both real and 'false' bulks and deficits, if some of the real can be explained, as this tells us much more about the structure and the changes in the structure.

Supplementary reading:

1. *Kenya Population Census 1962.* Vol. III, pp. 25—33 and p. 89.

2. B. Egero and R. Henin (eds): *The Population of Tanzania.* An Analysis of the 1967 Population Census. Census vol. 6. Dar es Salaam 1973, pp. 202—211.

3. L. Bondestam: *Some Notes on African Statistics—collection, reliability and interpretation.* Scandinavian Institute of African Studies. Research report 18, Uppsala 1973, p. 50.

4. UN. *Manual II, Methods of Appraisal of Quality of Basic Data for Population Estimations,* N. Y. 1955, p. 4—23.

5. *Demographic Baseline Survey Report 1973.* Central Bureau of Statistics. Republic of Kenya, Nairobi 1975, pp. 1—22.

Chapter VII

Structure and Distribution of the Population

Age-sex composition of the population in East Africa

In all societies the age and sex structure of the community are important factors for the reproduction as well as for the production.

In traditional pastoral and/or agricultural communities, age and sex are the main variables determining the division of labour, and the prescription of roles in social as well as economic functions were based on the division of the population in sex and age groups. The important groups were related to the functions in the society, e.g. at the age after circumcision boys were expected to engage in warfare, a certain age was prescribed for marriage, and the role of old men as elders.

All of these functions were based on the division of the ages into age-sets, which cannot exactly be translated into five or ten year age groups, as they do not fit them, and vary in the different tribal groups, and closely related to the expected role of the age-sets in these groups at different times.

A balance between the two sexes has usually been important for the mating and reproduction in a community, though it may not necessarily be important for the organization of the production as the work of the two sexes may not be equally important for survival. However, in all societies a balance between adult producers and children has been important to secure sufficient production for the whole group of producers and consumers (consumers = young children and old people beyond working age).

In the traditional agricultural societies there was no need for more detailed information on the age-sex distribution than the division into age-sets, and more detailed information was thus not available or registered.

However, age information of a more detailed character is necessary for planning and projections of schools, health services and employment in the more complex society of today. The methodology developed within demography is highly dependent on correct and uniform age-sex data for the whole society, as it is developed in countries with a registration of births and thus access to accurate age-registration. Later, methods have been developed to correct and smoothen the age-data of a poorer quality, which are often a result of the transition from the traditional agricultural society to a modern complex society in most Third World countries.

In this transition period the data on age are often very inadequate, especially for certain age groups (see chapter VI). The analysis of age-sex structure is, however, extremely important both for the estimation of other demographic variables, and for the evaluation of human resources, demand for education, health and employment in a region. Therefore the data have to be calculated, evaluated and maybe corrected for a proper use of the age data.

The sex-ratio: The sex ratio is defined as the number of males per 100 females, and this is varying in the different ages. At birth the sex-ratio is usually about 105—107 male births per 100 female births, i.e. a few more boys than girls are born. Estimations from Kenya give a sex-ratio of 102 in 1962 and 104 in 1969. Factors which influence the sex-ratio at birth are mainly related to mortality as this is higher for males, both prenatal and just after birth. The higher the level of mortality the lower the sex-ratio. The sex-ratio at birth is however also related to the time of registration. The later the ratio is registered after birth, the lower the sex-ratio due to higher male mortality. The sex differential mortality continues at all ages, as a result not only of biological differences, but also of social factors, e.g. the higher occupational risk of accidents or disease among men of working ages. Only in areas with very high fertility are the mortality risks for females affected, and may be higher during the reproductive ages. There is always a certain risk when giving birth, and the risk of dying is higher the more children a woman gives birth to.

The described pattern of mortality ought to provide a gradually declining sex-ratio throughout the ages, only with a relatively constant level in the women's reproductive ages. The expected patterns according to models of societies, thus without age-misreporting or migration, are shown in graph 4.

However, the pattern does not come out like this in the actual figures from the censuses. The examples from Kenya in 1962 and 1969 (in graph 5) show how the age-misreporting affects the sex-ratio, where especially the systematic overestimation of men's age contributes to a gap in the early adult years and increasing sex-ratios in the older ages.

The main patterns of reported sex-ratios for certain major age groups are provided for Kenya, Tanzania and major regions of Africa as well as overall characteristics for developing and developed countries for a comparison (in table 9). The table also reveals the difference between the smoothened and the

Graph 4. *Sex-ratios in different ages derived from a stable population with mortality and fertility levels equivalent to Kenya, 1969.*

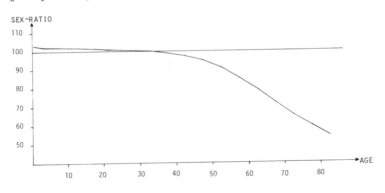

Graph 5. *Sex-ratios reported in the Kenyan Census 1962 and 1969.*

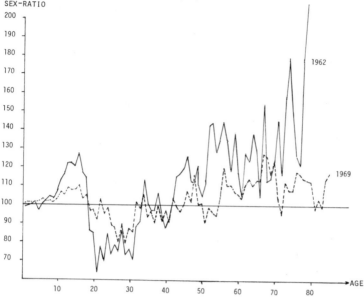

Source: Kenya Population Census 1962, vol. 3 and 1969, vol. I.

actual enumerated data, reflecting the distortions especially over-evaluating the middle age and old men's age (see chapter VI).

The sex-ratios of most importance for planning are those for working ages. These are important both for employment and for housing development. The extremes among the Kenyan regions in 1969 are Nairobi with 184 males 15—59 years (205 if only 20—49 years) per 100 females in the same ages, and Nyanza with 88 males 15—59 years per 100 females (82 if ages 20—49). These two deviations can be explained by the migration pattern.

Table 9. *Sex-ratios for major age-groups in Africa*

Area	under 15	15—64 yrs.	65 and over	Total
Developing regions	103.2	102.3	87.8	102.2
More-developed regions	104.3	92.8	65.6	93.0
Africa	100.3	99.6	82.6	99.4
West Africa	99.5	102.9	84.8	100.9
East Africa	99.3	96.9	79.1	97.4
Middle Africa	97.8	93.6	77.7	94.8
North Africa	103.6	100.8	88.1	101.6
Kenya 1969 enumeration	103.3	97.9	111.4	100.4
Kenya 1969 model graduation	101.1	100.8	81.0	100.4
Tanzania 1967 enumeration	101.9	88.5	113.3	95.5
Tanzania 1967 model graduation	95.8	95.0	82.0	95.5

Source: UN. *Determinants and Consequences of Population Trends.* 1974, p. 263, and calculations on Tanzanian and Kenyan Censuses.

Age distribution

The age distribution shows very large discrepancies between different areas, especially in a comparison between low fertility areas (developed countries) and high fertility areas (developing countries). The proportion in major age-groups for different regions is given in table 10. These age-groups are chosen as they approximately represent important economic groups: pre-school + school age (0—14), working ages (15—64), old age (65+). In relation to this kind of division in age-groups the working ages are perceived as the labour force and the younger and older age-groups as dependents or consumers draining the surplus generated by the working population. The dependency burden defined as dependents (population 0—14 yrs. + population 65 and over) per 100 in working ages, should thus give an indication of the burden of non-working (consumers) on the working population (producers). This will be discussed further in the chapter on Labour Force.

Table 10. *Age distribution in major age groups for regions (%).*

Area	under 15	15—64	65 and over	Dependency burden
Developing regions	41.6	55.1	3.3	81.3
More-developed regions	28.1	63.0	8.9	58.8
Africa	43.5	33.7	2.8	86.2
West Africa	44.3	53.3	2.4	87.5
East Africa	43.6	53.6	2.8	86.4
Kenya 1969 enumerated	48.4	48.3	3.6	107.5
Kenya 1969 graduated	47.2	50.4	2.4	98.3
Tanzania 1967 enumerated	43.9	50.5	5.6	98.1
Tanzania 1967 graduated	43.9	53.3	3.0	83.0

Source: UN. *Determinants and Consequences of Population Trends.* 1974, p. 265; *Kenya Population Census 1969; Tanzania Population Census 1967.*

Population structure as a result of fertility, mortality and migration

The population structure is a result of the number of people flowing into the population, i.e. births and immigrations, and the number flowing out of the population due to deaths and emigration, as these flows are related to specific age-groups.

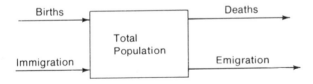

The influence on the age structure can be attributed to which ages are inflated or drained, i.e. births only contribute to the number of infants, while deaths are distributed over all age-groups, though mainly to older people, and migrations are especially related to the age-group 20—40.

As to outline the impact of fertility and mortality and migrations on the age-sex structure, we try to take up one factor at a time, and keep the others constant until we try to combine them in the actual pyramids. Thus what kind of impact on the age structure do the factors have, and what is their relative power?

Suppose we have a population with no deaths before the maximum age of 100, i.e. all people lived until their 100th birthday and then died, and there was the same number of births every year and no migrations, then the age structure could be illustrated as a box, with the same number of people in each age-group (graph 6 a).

Suppose, however, we introduced the effect of mortality in the different ages that is a realistic pattern of mortality, but maintained the same number of births every year and no migrations, then the effect of mortality could be seen (in graph 6 b).

If, instead, we tried to introduce a variation in the number of births, that is, using the assumption of no deaths before 100 years of age, no migrations, but a high fertility, i.e. an increasing number of births every year, then this would also result in a pyramid (graph 6 c). The main question, after these unrealistic assumptions, is how strongly each of the above factors influences the age pyramid, when they are affecting the pyramid, at the same time.

The assumptions of no migrations, which is not so unrealistic for nations and for very isolated and traditional groups, is maintained for the moment until we

Graph 6. *Age-sex pyramids with different mortality and fertility assumptions.*

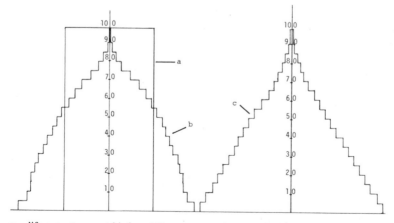

a. life expectancy at birth = 100 years, growth zero. b. life expectancy at birth = 40 years, growth zero. c. life expectancy at birth = 100 years, increasing number of births—high growth.

know what the impact of the combined fertility and mortality on the age-structure is.

In order to make these comparisons we compare the age structures with that of Kenya 1969. The first comparison is with the age structure where mortality fell drastically but no change occurred in the fertility (graph 7 a shows conditions after these trends have stabilized). This should show the effect on the age structure of a drastically declining mortality (graph 7 a). The drastic change in the mortality is from a Crude Death Rate of 17 per thousand to less than 10 per thousand, or from an expected life at birth of an average of 47 years to an average expected age of 70 years. The decline does not have very high impact on the structure. With declining mortality nearly all age-groups benefit from higher rate of survival. The small changes at the bottom of the pyramid can be ascribed to the fact that the infants and children benefit slightly more from the better chances of survival than other age-groups.

If on the other hand we compare the Kenya 1969 age structure with an age structure as it would be after a drastic decline in the fertility, and measured after the population has stabilized the change, then we can see that the age structure changes considerably. The change is equal to a change from an average number of 6 births per woman to an average of 2, while the mortality does not change (graph 7 b and table 11).

Graph 7. *Age structure in Kenya 1969, compared with results of drastic change in mortality or fertility.*

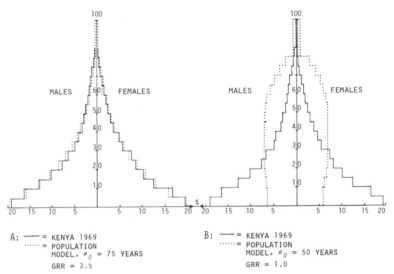

A: —— = KENYA 1969
    ······ = POPULATION
    MODEL, e_0 = 75 YEARS
    GRR = 3.5

B: —— = KENYA 1969
    ······ = POPULATION
    MODEL, e_0 = 50 YEARS
    GRR = 1.0

Source: Calculations on Kenya Population Census 1969 vol. 1 and UN. Manual IV. Methods of Estimating Basic Demographic Measures from Incomplete.
Data. N.Y. 1967 p. 101 + 106 + 113 + 118.

Table 11. *Age structure under different levels of mortality and fertility.*

Proportion in broad age groups with:

	Under 15	15—59	60+
High mortality—high fertility	48.4	46.2	5.4
Low mortality—high fertility	47.3	48.4	4.3
High mortality—low fertility	17.8	60.5	21.5
Low mortality—low fertility	19.5	58.6	21.9

High mortality: e_0 = 20 years, low mortality: e_0 70 years, High fertility: GRR = 4, low fertility: GRR = 1

Source: UN Pop. Studies no. 26: The Aging of Population and its Economic and Social Implications, 1956.

This table should also reveal some of the single effects of the isolated change in one of the variables, and the combined effect of changes in the mortality and fertility.

The reason for the very high impact of the fertility on the age structure is that very high fertility means a large increase in the number of births every year; if this number is limited, then the base of the pyramid is limited, and the total basis for the percentage calculation is smaller, therefore the whole structure changes and the percentages of population also in the non-reduced age-groups will be affected; this is illustrated with some constructed figures in table 12.

Table 12. *Age structure for a population with a high fertility, and for the same 15 years later, when the fertility has been reduced to half of the original level.* *

Age	High fertility abs.no.	%	Low fertility abs.no.	%
0— 1 years old (under 1)	100	5	50	3
1— 4 years old	380	19	190	13
5— 9 years old	420	21	210	14
10—14 years old	380	19	330	22
15—59 years old	600	30	600	40
over 60	120	6	120	8
Total	2000	100	1500	100

* Constructed figures.

This example should show that a reduction in some age-groups affects the percentages in all the age-groups, as the total number which is the basis for the percentages is also changed.

The conclusion of this is that the fertility level has a very high impact on the age structure, and a much higher impact than the mortality.

If we do not only treat large areas, with many people, but also small areas with a high level of migrations, then all the deviations from the smooth pyramid will often be ascribed to the migration, especially if it also affects the symmetry of the pyramid, with the "male side" deviating a lot from the "female side" of the pyramid.

For example, the shape of the pyramid in Nairobi (graph 8) does not show that particularly many boys were born between 15 and 40 years ago in Nairobi, but that many in these age-groups have migrated from other areas to Nairobi as adults.

However, graph 8 also reflects that the method of constructing the age-sex pyramid provides different structures, which may lead to quite misleading results if the interpretation is not correct. The usual way of constructing the pyramid is by taking each sex separately, so that each sex totals 100%. This is used because it is easy to make comparisons with other countries with different sizes of population. However, if there appear to be very heavy migrations among one of the groups, i.e. heavy immigration of males in a certain age, then the pyramid gets "skewed" and appears to have fewer male births and male children than female (see graph 8a). This does not explain the shape of the pyramid, but that because the adult age groups of the men become much larger due to the migration, the male children become—not absolutely but relatively—a smaller group among the males. While among the females, where there is no heavy migration of adult females, the girls will make up a relatively larger part of the female population.

The graphs for the relative numbers of the total male and female population show this difference. Here the statistical basis of the pyramid does not contain this kind of pitfall, but is nearly symmetric at the bottom.

In smaller housing areas, where age structures are also used to provide the basis for planning of needs of schools and employment possibilities, the pattern may be much more skewed, and totally dominated by the migration. This will be the case in the bungalow areas of Nairobi West and in the planned Dandora

Graph 8. *Age structure of the population of Nairobi in 1969. The age structure is constructed both as relative numbers for each sex separately and relative of the total population.*

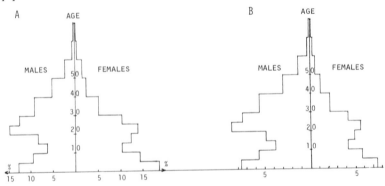

A = Total of males is 100%. Total of females is 100%.
B = Total of males + females is 100%. Total of males is 60%. Total of females is 40%.

Source: Calculations on Kenya Population Census 1969. Vol. 1.

Graph 9. *Hypothetical age-sex structure for new bungalow middle-class area in Nairobi.*

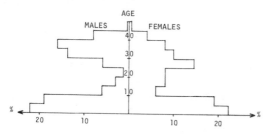

Scheme. Unfortunately we do not have the figures, but the expected structure (constructed figures) is provided as an illustration of what such a graph may look like (graph 9). The settlement pattern in such a newly-built middle-class area may provide many children for young school classes and especially for nursery schools, but hardly any for older classes or secondary schools. The over-population of certain classes in the schools may follow all the way up through the school. Also it may be expected that the husbands are between 25 and 45 and the wives a little younger, and that there will be some young girls working in the area as housegirls (middle class area assumed).

Regional and rural-urban distribution of the population in East Africa

Information on the geographical distribution and density of population provides an important input to the evaluation of the distribution of economic and human resources in an area.

The density of population per square kilometre is in many cases used as an important characteristic of the area, whether it is over-, under-, or optimally populated. However, the problem with this measure is that it gives the same weight to high potential land as to low potential land, and thus does not reveal the population in relation to agricultural resources.

The overall population densities for Kenya in 1969, Tanzania in 1967 and Uganda in 1969 were 19, 14, and 40 per square kilometre respectively. That is a very much higher population density for Uganda, and approximately the same for Tanzania and Kenya.

However, it is important to be able to use these figures in some kind of evaluation or planning of economic potential to compare this with the proportion of high potential land in the area. The population density and percentage of estimated high potential land in the districts of Kenya are shown (table 13).

Table 13. *Estimated population density and land potential in Kenyan districts, 1973.*

Area	Total land in hectares	% high potential land	Pop. density	Area	Total land in hectares	% high potential land	Pop. density
Central				*Rift Valley*			
Kiambu	244	48	194	Baringo	1,067	16	19
Kirinyaga	143	68	181	Elgeyo-Marakwet	273	38	77
Nyandarua	353	75	50	Kajiado	2,096	1	5
Nyeri	329	49	110	Kericho	489	78	142
Murang'a	187	84	180	Laikipia	972	13	9
				Nakuru	702	41	61
Western				Nandi	274	85	105
Kakamega	352	92	222	Narok	1,852	49	9
Bungoma	308	82	112	Samburu	2,081	7	4
Busia	163	100	123	Trans Nzoia	247	84	73
				Uasin Gishu	6,082	87	73
Nyanza				West Pokot	378	20	22
Kisumu	208	94	193	Turkana	507	1	3
Siaya	253	—	151				
Kisii	220	100	307	*North Eastern*			
South Nyanza	571	99	116	Garissa	4,393	0	1
				Mandera	2,647	0	2
Eastern				Wajir	5,650	0	4
Embu	271	24	66				
Isiolo	2,560	0	1	*Coast*			
Kitui	2,939	2	12	Kilifi	1,241	8	32
Machakos	1,419	9	50	Kwale	825	15	33
Marsabit	7,273	0.05	1	Lamu	651	1	4
Meru	993	24	10	Taita	1,696	2	9
				Tana River	3,878	2	2

Source: P. Mbithi & C. Barnes: *Spontaneous Settlement Problem in Kenya.* Nairobi 1975, p. 84—85.

The potential of the land is determined by soil fertility, rainfall, altitude and topography. The basic needs of land for subsistence agriculture will therefore be different in different areas. If a family should have subsistence and an annual income of K.£100 (family of 6) the average acreage needed for this would be in Kisumu + Siaya District = 4.5 acres; South Nyanza District = 7 acres; Kisii District = 2.5 acres; Western Province = 3.5 acres.

In areas with a wider range of land quality as in Machakos, the need for the family defined above would be 4 acres in terms of high potential land, 7 acres of medium potential land, or 25 acres of low potential land.[1]

Even if the quality of the land is evaluated, there will be differences in population density due, for example, to ecological factors such as vegetation and tsetse flies and especially historical, economic as well as political factors. The last point will explain the differences between the previous "reserves" and the previous "White Highlands". Still, the "White Highlands" are characterized by good soil and low population density and are to some extent capable of absorbing a larger population. However, an analysis of Rift Valley Province

---

[1] Mbithi and Barnes: *Spontaneous Settlement Problem in Kenya.* Nairobi 1975, p. 88—90.

revealed that some of the areas with very low population densities—Samburu, Turkana and Kajiado—also have an over-population, as the land was poor even for grazing and overgrazing took place in the area.[2]

The distribution of the population in East Africa on rural-urban areas mainly meets the difficulties of comparison due to definitions of what is rural *vs.* urban, and the lack of a standard definition of towns in East African censuses. This problem of comparison by the same standards becomes even more difficult in East Africa, where the dominant pattern of settlement is dispersed homesteads, i.e. villages with high population concentration are not found, and only urban areas of a certain size will show the clear pattern of the concentrated population with clear boundaries to the surrounding rural areas.

In the Tanzanian Census, two principles for classifying urban areas were applied, namely, size and the administrative role. The definition thus contained towns and former townships (classified as such in the administration) and their sizes, all of which had to be more than 1000 inhabitants.

In Kenya all agglomerations with more than 2000 inhabitants were classified as urban areas. For comparison with other countries the size criterion is often used, classifying the urban areas as agglomerations with more than 2,000, 5,000 or 20,000 inhabitants.

Table 14 shows the development in the number of cities in the different groups, and also the development of the level of urbanization, defined as percentage of total population living in towns in the three East African countries.

Table 14. *Development of cities in East Africa from 1948 to 1969. Number of towns classified according to size.*

Size of urban centre	Kenya			Tanzania*			Uganda	
	1948	1962	1969	1948	1957	1967	1959	1969
2,000— 4,999	10	16	25	9	8	8	19	13
5,000— 9,999	3	11	11	6	4	7	3	9
10,000—19,999	2	3	7	2	9	3	3	7
20,000—49,999	—	2	2	1	1	9	1	3
50,000—99,999	1	—	—	1	—	1	—	1
100,000 and over	1	2	2	—	1	1	1	1
Urbanization = % of pop. in towns over 2000	5.3%	7.8%	9.8%	2.4%	4.0%	5.7%	4.3%	7.0%

* Mainland only

Source: S. H. Ominde: *The Population of Kenya, Tanzania and Uganda.* Nbi. 1975, p. 91 and 94; *The Population of Tanzania,* op. cit. p. 81 and calculations on these.

[2] op.cit. p. 88—90.

The characteristic pattern of urbanization in the three countries, as with most countries in the Third World, is the prevalence of one or perhaps two very large cities, which contain most of the urban population, and very few cities in the medium size category, as is found in the early urbanized countries in Europe, Asia and even in North America. This is illustrated by table 15 showing the size of the major cities and their proportion of the total urban population.

Table 15. Proportion of population in primary East African cities of the total urban population, 1969 (Tanzania 1967).

City	Population	% of urban pop.
Nairobi	509,286	47 %
Mombasa	247,073	22 %
Dar es Salaam	272,821	40 %
Kampala	330,700	48 %

Source: Calculations from Censuses.

Even if comparisons between different regions are difficult because the patterns of settlement and definition of cities and boundaries of towns are not alike, comparisons between urbanization in different regions of the world are provided. The definition is restricted to population in cities over 20,000 as errors in this group of towns are less than at a lower level. The comparison is provided to show the relatively low urbanization in East Africa. The growth of the cities is just as high as in other developing regions, but the proportion of the population residing in cities is much lower than in most other places.

Table 16. Urban population as proportion of total population in major regions of the world, 1960.

	% urban*
Developing regions	15 %
More-developed regions	46 %
Africa	13 %
East Asia	19 %
South Asia	14 %
Europe	44 %
Latin America	33 %
North America	58 %
Oceania	53 %
USSR	36 %

* Defined as agglomerations of more than 20.000 people.

Source: UN. Determinants and Consequences of Population Trends. 1974, p. 188.

Supplementary reading:

1. UN. *Determinants and Consequences of Population Trends.* N.Y. 1974, chapter VIII, pp. 262—292.

2. Simeon Ominde: *The Population of Kenya, Tanzania and Uganda.* Nairobi, 1975. Chapter 4—6, pp. 59—96.

3. B. Egero & R. Henin (eds): *The Population of Tanzania.* An analysis of the 1967 Census. Census Vol. 6, Dar es Salaam 1973. Chapter 3, pp. 38—55, chapter 5, pp. 76—97.

Chapter VIII

Mortality

Factors affecting mortality

The causes of mortality are usually very difficult to isolate in areas of high mortality as in Africa, especially 40—50 years ago. In such areas a combination of factors is often the real cause of mortality. To illustrate this point, an analysis of the major "killer—diseases" in different areas and times is useful. Some of the previous large scale killer diseases are the same as those existing now, such as the epidemic diseases of cholera and influenza. The important differences between areas where these diseases are killing on a large scale and those where they are not, may usually be explained by differences in "general health conditions", especially nutritional status and resistance to these kind of diseases. For example, in 1918 there was a famine in some parts of Kenya, and in 1919 the influenza epidemic broke out. The death toll from influenza was much higher in the famine striken areas than in other areas.[1]

On a world basis and in areas within Africa, famine and food-shortage are still major factors having serious impact on mortality. This is not because very many die directly from hunger, but mainly because of the decline in the general health and in the lower resistance toward diseases, which makes even a weak attack of the disease fatal.

The mortality due to famine in areas of Africa is not precisely known. Areas affected by famine are often remote areas, where transport and health facilities, and thus also information, are poor. The major droughts in north-west Africa and in Ethiopia cost very many lives, but the majority of the people died from diseases due to low resistance because of *poor and unsatisfactory* nutrition.[2]

This implies that the actual effect of droughts and famines on mortality follows much later after the famine has occurred, because people have become weak, and it takes a long time to restore their health. Droughts and famines have been relatively regular phenomena in local areas within Africa. In some areas of Kenya like Machakos, there have been drought conditions every second or third year, and famine-relief has been a regular feature of these areas since the 1930s.[3] Machakos District is an area with high rain-uncertainty, but it is not a remote area, and transport of food for the people has been possible. We know much less about famines and their effects in Northern Kenya and other

[1] Vogel et al.: *Health and Disease in Kenya.* Nairobi 1974, p. 94.
[2] J. C. Caldwell: The Sahelian Drought and its Demographic Implications. OLC no. 8. Canberra, Dec. 75, pp. 23—31.
[3] Mary Matingu: Rural to Rural Migration and Employment. A Case Study in a Selected Area of Kenya. M. A. Thesis. 1974. Dept. of Sociology, Nairobi.

remote dry areas of East Africa.

What is even more important for the mortality level and for the resistance against diseases is the composition of the nutrition. The major group of people in an area may be affected by other variables such as: 1) Rinderpest, which kills off the cattle in an area, and thus removes the main access to protein. This has happened several times in Western Kenya and Uganda. 2) Droughts affecting both crops and the survival of cattle. 3) Introduction of cash-crops: coffee, tea, sugar, sisal, which in some areas decrease the production of vegetables and food crops grown, especially if the area is a monocultural production area. 4) Urbanization and employment of the groups in the low income bracket, may also affect the nutritional status, because of low salaries for many of the employed and the high prices of protein-rich food.

In East Africa in the 1890s there are clear indications of a declining population. Relating to the above factors, Zwanenberg describes it as follows:

Around 1890 there were (a) widespread wars in Uganda and (b) widespread famines and epidemic diseases which followed the famines, throughout East Africa. Famine began in 1889 and in some areas continued sporadically until the end of the century. Rinderpest decimated cattle; drought and locust invasions upset crops; smallpox and dysentery killed people.[4]

A major spread of epidemic diseases also reached East Africa in this period. Diseases like smallpox, chickenpox, measles, poliomyelitis, plague, influenza, and whooping-cough all seem to have reached East Africa through contact with the Europeans, who brought them either from Europe or from other African areas through which the expeditions passed. These expeditions also spread jiggers to East Africa, resulting in jiggers infection. Sleeping sickness was by far the most serious of the new diseases.

By 1898 sleeping sickness reached epidemic proportions in Busoga and the next few years (until about 1905) it was a rife around Lake Victoria, and then continued to occur sporadically up to early 1920s. Between 1900 and 1905 sleeping sickness alone is estimated to have killed at least 200,000 people on the western side of the lake, about two-thirds of the estimated population at that time.[5]

Epidemic diseases have been especially severe during and after periods of famine or war since no resistance against diseases existed. For instance during wars, the losses due to epidemic diseases have been much higher than the deaths in active battle, e.g. in the First World War, of the 4,300 Kenyans that died, only 30 % were killed in battle.[6]

Generally better health conditions due to better social and economic development are the best means of reducing mortality, and at present in some areas they appear to be a necessary condition for reducing mortality.

[4] R. M. A. Zwanenberg with A. King: *An Economic History of Kenya and Uganda 1800—1970*. Nbi. 1975, p. 9.
[5] Ibid. p.10.
[6] Vogel, et al. eds.: *Health and Disease in Kenya*. Nbi. 1974, p. 94.

5 – A demographic...

The main factors leading to high mortality, will vary in the different areas, and very often they are related both to the natural surroundings and to social and economic conditions of the people in the area. A type of classification of the areas is therefore one way of illustrating these differences and the impact on the morbidity pattern:[7]

Urban and periurban areas

In urban areas, epidemic diseases are likely to spread quickly due to the high concentration of population. However, sanitation is the crucial factor, i.e. water supply and sewage system. Improvements in these would be important preventive measures against the diffusion of epidemics. Urban areas however, also have much better health services than rural areas, and with a concentrated population it is also possible to provide the services at a much lower cost. In urban areas, the cost of protein-rich food in relation to the salaries is also of importance for the general nutritional status and resistance against diseases. Therefore there is a major social difference between the different status groups according to these factors, and the difference in mortality will reflect class differences much more clearly in urban than in rural areas.

Low land humid areas

In African low-land areas, the basic health problems are related to epidemic diseases. In Kenya, the Coast and the lower parts of Nyanza and Western Provinces show a very high frequency of stomach diseases, and many kinds of children's diseases. Malaria seems to be endemic in these areas and in some areas it even seems to be increasing; an increase in rates of malaria and schistosomiasis has been reported after the introduction of the Ahero irrigation scheme (the same is found for the Mwea-Tebere scheme).[8]

The Highlands

In the highlands, the main problem seems to arise from the very cold nights and the extreme temperature changes which implies a high frequency of all respiratory diseases. Pneumonia and bronchitis are the most frequently reported to the health personnel.

The evidence of the reported pattern and the level of mortality from different diseases has to be based mainly on hospital statistics and reports from health personnel. The problem with this is that hospital deaths have been estimated to account for only 10 % of all deaths.[9] Even though this proportion is increasing due to increasing hospital attendance, it is still a small fraction of the deaths,

[7] Ibid. p. 82.
[8] Ibid. p. 65.
[9] Ibid. p. 76.

and is not representative, as the urban and upper-classes of the population are expected to be overrepresented.

It is reported that of all deaths occurring in hospitals in Kenya, respiratory diseases are responsible for 30%, infective and parasitic diseases for 26%, and diseases of the digestive system (especially for children) for 14%. Children account for one-eighth of the total number of deaths in hospitals.[10]

Public health in the form of improved access to health clinics in rural areas is an important factor in eliminating the existing diseases. However preventive measures, like establishing access to clean water may be the most important and efficient for controlling the spread of diseases and removing the conditions for epidemics. In addition, insecticides against malaria mosquitoes as well as against tsetse flies can be used as preventive health measures in large areas.

Description of mortality trends in East Africa compared with other parts of the world

The level of mortality in East Africa has been declining since the early fifties from around 30—40 per thousand (equivalent to an expected life at birth of approx. 30—40 years), to around 13 per thousand in 1973 (equivalent to an expected life at birth of approx. 52 years). The decline has not been equally distributed all over East Africa. There are still areas with high mortality while in other areas mortality has declined to a lower level than 13 per thousand.

In comparison with the African continent, Kenya has relatively low mortality. The northern and southern parts of Africa have the lowest mortality at around 13—16 per thousand, whereas tropical Africa has an average level of mortality of 17—21 per thousand. Variations within tropical Africa are very large, and even within East Africa the crude mortality rate varies in subregions between 13 and 31 (based on the censuses in the late 1960s). The 1967 census of Tanzania indicates variations ranging from a low mortality of 13.6 per thousand in the rich regions of Kilimanjaro and Arusha, to around 16 per thousand in Dar es Salaam, rising up to a general level of around 25 in the poorer regions of Dodoma and Mtwara.[11]

Africa as a whole is a continent with the highest level of mortality, and where the mortality decline has started later. Generally the causes of the initial mortality decline in Africa can be attributed to improved medical services and insecticides which contributed to the limitation of malaria mosquitoes, tsetse flies, ticks and other insects affecting people, cattle and also crops. But the improved transport of crops and improved food prodoction can be seen as important for the mortality decline in the last 10 years.

In Europe the mortality fluctuated around 30 per thousand (equivalent to a

[10] Ibid, p. 79 and 82.

[11] B. Egero & R. Henin: *The Population of Tanzania*. An Analysis of the 1967 Population Census. Census Vol. 6. Dar es Salaam 1973, p. 179.

life expectancy at birth of 30—40 years) before 1780. Just before 1800, around the time of the "industrial revolution", the mortality began to decline more systematically due to: 1) increased productivity in agriculture, 2) better sanitation and water conservation, 3) medical improvements and 4) improved transport facilities. This was important in order to facilitate the transport of food to local famine areas, as local famines have been a regular phenomenon all over the world, resulting in high regional fluctuations in the mortality level. The mortality in Europe declined until around 1940 to a level of 10 per thousand (equivalent to a life expectancy of 70 years). After that time only little change has occurred, and in fact at present the life expectancy appears to be declining for men due to the increased pressure on labourers in industry and to increased pollution (in northern Europe).

In Asia the mortality has declined, but here the decline is very unequally distributed. In Japan, the mortality has declined to around 9 per thousand, and in China it is also less than 10 per thousand, but in the rest of Asia the variations are great and parts of India, Pakistan, Bangla-Desh and Indonesia seem to have a high mortality ranging from 16—25 per thousand. In these areas the level of mortality fluctuates a lot during droughts, floods, famines, epidemics etc.

Explanations of the mortality decline in East Africa, and differentials of mortality

The decline in mortality in Europe was caused mainly by structural changes due to the increased productivity in agriculture and changes in the living conditions in the cities where an increasing proportion of the population was living. Improvements in the sanitation and sewage systems had a major impact in controlling the spread of infectious diseases. Transport of crops was important for the reallocation of crops from surplus areas to deficit areas. The advances in medical science only had a minor effect on the decline in the early period, but were of course important for the declining mortality especially for infants and children. In most parts of Europe the decline in mortality took a very long time, between 120—150 years in most parts. In Africa and Latin America the decline lasted only 30—40 years whereas in Asia it took around 80 years.

The differences in the time period reflect the different causes of the mortality decline. In countries where mortality decline has been experienced after 1945, the major reason for the initial decline can be attributed to medical and veterinary programmes. Vaccination campaigns and access to health clinics in rural areas have improved the chances of survival, especially for children. The control of rinderpest and tick fever has also improved the chances of survival for many other groups of the population. The improved transport facilities have made it possible to bring food to drought-striken areas, thus preventing the worst famines.

However, the most important cause for bringing down the mortality seems to have been the provision of better living conditions for the people, and access to better nutrition. Children in particular are very vulnerable to disease when they are not well nourished. Malnutrition provides the background for high mortality due to diseases like measles, pneumonia, digestive and parasitic diseases. These are fatal if the nutrition and general health are not good. The extent of malnutrition has varied in time according to the living conditions of the people. Around 1925 the food available for employees on Kenyan farms was generally much poorer than that obtained in the "Reserves",[12] resulting in poor health and malnutrition among the labourers. The large numbers of parasites, together with malnutrition because of insufficient wages, caused high mortality among the labourers, i.e. around 22 per 1000 employed (1922).[13] At present the extent of malnutrition varies according to areas because of variations in living conditions. Surveys in some cashcrop areas within Machakos district have revealed that the highest protein calorie malnutrition rates were in these kinds of areas, going up to as high as 50 % in some cases. This is because the protein-rich vegetables which were previously provided in the subsistence agriculture are no longer cultivated.[14]

The regional variations in the morbidity and mortality patterns are estimated on the basis of the life expectancy at birth and the infant mortality. These are provided for Kenya on the basis of the 1969 census (Table 17). In this table the much lower mortality in Nairobi in relation to other areas is revealed. The table also shows interesting discrepancies in the life expectancy and the infant mortality rates. Apparently, infant mortality is relatively high in the Coast and Nyanza Provinces in relation to mortality in other age groups.

Table 17. *Estimated life expectancy and infant mortality for the provinces of Kenya in 1969.*

Province	Life expectancy[1]		Infant mortality[2]	
	Males	Females	Males	Females
Nairobi E.P.D.	59.9	63.8	79	62
Central	53.0	56.3	81	66
Coast	54.0	57.5	152	136
Eastern	47.3	50.0	115	100
North Eastern	43.9	46.2	121	107
Nyanza	49.6	52.5	183	168
Rift Valley	45.1	47.5	*	*
Western	47.3	50.0	150	131
Kenya	47.0	51.0	126	112

[1] Life expectancy at birth e_0. [2] infant deaths before 1 year birthday per 1000 births in same year.
* Sampling errors have led to severe underestimation of this measure showing only 94 for males and 77 for females. The measure is expected to be much higher.

Source: S. H. Ominde: *The Population of Kenya, Tanzania and Uganda.* Nbi. 1975, p. 37 and S. H. Ominde: Demography and Ethnic Groups. In: Vogel et al., p. 42.

[12] R. M. A. Zwanenberg: *Colonial Capitalism and Labour in Kenya 1919—1939.* Nbi. 1975, pp. 38—39.
[13] Ibid. p. 62.
[14] Vogel et al. op. cit., p. 66.

In a demographic survey of Kenya carried out by the Central Bureau of Statistics in Nairobi, infant mortality was estimated at around 94 for females and 113 for males, thus indicating a mortality decline since 1969. In relation to expectation of life at birth, the average has increased from 47.0 and 51.0 for males and females respectively in 1969 to 51.9 and 59.2 in 1973.[15]

Graph 10. *Age-specific mortality rates in 5 year age-groups for males and females with 2 different levels of mortality.*

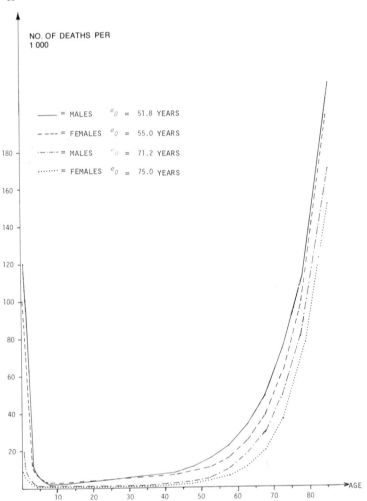

Source: Manual IV. Methods of Estimating Basic Demographic Measures from Incomplete Data. N.Y. 1967, pp. 88 and 92.

[15] *Demographic Baseline Survey Report 1973.* Central Bureau of Statistics. Nbi. 1975. pp. 47—48.

Mortality differentials have already been mentioned in relation to the problems of age structure and the reliability of data. A comparison of the two sexes shows that in all countries and at nearly all ages, males have higher mortality than females (see graph 10).

The differentials are also prevalent for the different age-groups: mortality is higher for the very young under 5 years of age and for the old, as can be seen from the age-specific mortality shown in graph 10. One set of curves shows the pattern of mortality under conditions of relatively high mortality, similar to the pattern in Kenya, and the other set shows typical curves for males and females under low mortality conditions. The problem in Africa, however, is often that the specific rates at certain ages deviate from the models and from the early European age-pattern of mortality, e.g. child mortality for age-groups that change diet from mother's milk to other food is especially high. Clear evidence of this has only been revealed in some intensive surveys, as shown in graph 11.

The demographic baseline survey in Kenya 1973, does not go into details

Graph 11. *Child mortality in ages 0—4 years in two African countries compared with Europe before 1900.*

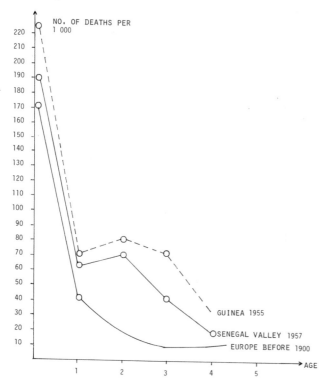

Source: T. N'Doye: Infant Mortality and Nutritional Problems. In: OECD. *The Demographic Transition in Tropical Africa.* Paris 1971, p. 251.

71

about the increase in child mortality around the age of 2, but it has detailed information on the proportion of children surviving at the age of two. For both sexes together, the proportion living at the age of 2 out of 1000 infants born was 874 compared with 857 in the census 1969. In 1973 867 males and 882 females were still alive at 2 years of age. The pattern varied also by rural and urban areas. In the urban areas, 906 males and 919 females reached 2 years, and in the rural areas 858 males and 876 females reached this age.[16]

Apart from age-sex differentials, mortality differentials also exist between regions, i.e. drought-striken areas, monocultural crop areas, rich and poor regions etc. Differences in the urban-rural mortality have existed in all countries. In Europe there was earlier a much higher mortality in the cities than in the rural areas. Now the pattern is the same all over the world, namely that cities have a much lower level of mortality than the rural areas.

This is primarily because they have better access to medical care, but the average socio-economic status and therefore the average living conditions of the people in the cities also tend to be higher, on average, than the rural areas. The difference thus not only reflects the differential access to medical care but also the socio-economic differences.

Variations in the socio-economic conditions provide a basis for the very different access to good nutrition and care for the children; good housing, clean water and medical treatment, all of which are important for better health and lower mortality. We do not have information on these aspects in the Kenyan census, but in Tanzania these mortality differentials have been estimated by socio-economic status (see table 18).

Table 18. *Mortality estimates for socio-economic groups in the mainland of Tanzania, 1967.*

Socie-economic group	Infant mortality per 1000	Survival to age 5 per 1000
Urban top-level white collar	62	904
Urban middle-level white collar	82	868
Rural top-level white collar and urban blue collar workers	104	829
Rural middle-level white collar and rural blue collar workers	115	808
Agricultural labourers and persons without occupation	140	762
Farmers	155	739

The socio-economic grouping of the women is based on residence and occupation of the head of household.

Source: B. Egero & R. Henin: op. cit., p. 183.

[16] *Demographic Baseline Survey Report 1973.* Central Bureau of Statistics. Nbi. 1975, p. 45.

This table reveals that despite the shortcomings in the socio-economic groupings, the infant mortality shows substantial variations. Among the urban top-level white-collar people, infant mortality is in the region of 62 deaths per 1000 births, while among the farmers it is 155 per thousand births. The proportion surviving until 5 years of age varies between 90% and 74% (or 900 per thousand and 740 per thousand respectively). The result is a very heavy loss of children born to rural farm families, where one-fourth of the children born die before they reach 5 years of age.

The estimates in the Tanzanian census on differential mortality for different educational levels largely reflect the same differences, as there is a very high correlation between socio-economic status and education. The groups of people with no school education had an infant mortality of 155 per thousand, and those with 5 or more school years had a rate of 82 per thousand. Although mortality in Tanzania is higher than in Kenya, the pattern of differential mortality is expected to be the same in the two countries.

Even within the same status groups, there may often be differences in mortality for those in different occupations, according to the amount of risks involved in the job. Usually miners, drivers and some kinds of industrial workers appear to have a higher risk of accidents or disease than those in white collar jobs. These differences however, have not been studied in Africa, and only to a very limited extent in other continents.

Implications of a decline in mortality on the age structure of the population

The shape of a population pyramid is influenced by mortality, fertility and migration. If the number of births were the same each year for a country and there was no major migration, the changes in the shape of the pyramid could be attributed to the mortality changes in the different age-groups of the population.

However, if the number of births were increasing then the base of the pyramid would increase every year, and this would also affect the shape of the pyramid. Actually, we know from the work on population models, that changes in fertility have a very high impact on the population structure, while changes in mortality only have little impact on the structure, because deaths are usually distributed over the different ages. Even during a very steep decline in mortality, all the groups of the population will be affected, and the structure therefore will only be altered to the extent that a few age-groups may be affected more than others, i.e. the infant mortality might be declining much more than mortality in other age-groups. If infant mortality is declining most rapidly, the change in relation to the pyramid will be similar to the effect of increasing the number of births, i.e. an increase in the number of infants. To illustrate this, a population pyramid with two very different levels of mortality

Graph 12. *Age pyramids for different levels of mortality.*

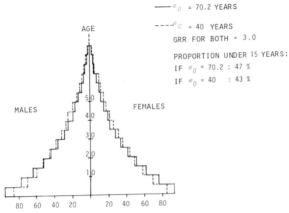

— e_0 = 70.2 YEARS

---- e_0 = 40 YEARS

GRR FOR BOTH = 3.0

PROPORTION UNDER 15 YEARS:

IF e_0 = 70.2 : 47 %

IF e_0 = 40   : 43 %

AGE

MALES   FEMALES

80 60 40 20   20 40 60 80

Source: UN. *The Concept of a Stable Population.* Application to the Study of Populations of Countries with Incomplete Statistics. N.Y. 1968, p. 172.

is presented. This shows that there is very little difference in the structure, even when the decline in mortality is very drastic, and the life expectancy at birth is increased from 40 years to 70 years.

Measures of mortality with a discussion of the cohort versus the calendar approach

The measurement and the estimation of the factors which influence the age-sex population structure first covers mortality then fertility and finally migration. The reason for this has nothing to do with the relative importance of the factors, but reflects the development of the methodology and techniques. The measures of mortality are necessary for developing the more complex fertility and migration measures.

An event or incidence, e.g. death, may be measured in many ways. However, for any mortality measurement we want to be precise about:

a. *the time period* referred to

b. *the group of people* referred to. Either the generation or, in other cases, the *population at risk.*

Crude Death Rate

The first measure, "the Crude Death Rate" or CDR, is a very crude measure, evaluating the number of deaths in a population in relation to the total population at risk in a given year.

$CDR = D/P \cdot 1000$

In other words the CDR is equal to the number of deaths in all the age-groups occurring in a population at a given time interval times 1000, and divided by the number of people in the population who are exposed to the risk of dying during the same time interval as the deaths are registered.

The specification of the persons in the denominator exposed to the risk of dying is important. If we study mortality over a one-year period in Kenya, for example from 1.1.74 to 31.12.74, then it is important to note that a person who died in September was not exposed to the risk of dying for the whole year, and neither was the child born in July. People who migrate to the country in November are only exposed to the risk of dying in Kenya during November and December. The population at risk is therefore equal to the "person-years lived", i.e. the number of people multiplied by the time period. This method is very cumbersome and would be possible only in very small communities, even if this were the correct measure. Instead, we assume that the number of births, deaths and migrations are equally distributed throughout the year. If this is the case (and it is a fairly good assumption) then the *mid-year population* provides a good approximation of the numbers of person-years lived for the whole population.

To calculate the mid-year population, we find the population at the beginning of the year, and the population at the end of year. We add these up and divide by two (this gives the average). The method is best if it is used for only very short periods, like one year, as the assumption about the equal distribution of demographic events is most reasonable for shorter periods. But usually there is a period of 5 to 10 years between the censuses, and even in such cases this method is used. If in Kenya there had been a census in September 1974, then this would have been exactly 5 years after the 1969 census. Then if the total number of deaths in this period is found, the person-years lived between the two censuses could be found by adding the population in September 1969 to the population in September 1974 and dividing by two. This would give the average population per year, but since we are referring to a 5-year period, we should multiply by 5. If the total number of deaths in this period is known, we can calculate the CDR. Thus:

$$CDR^{69-74} = \frac{D^{69-74}}{(P^{69} + P^{74}) \cdot 5/2} \cdot 1000$$

This is equal to the total number of deaths in the population in the period 1969 to 1974 times 1000, divided by the average population per year multiplied by the 5-year period (population at risk).

If the time period is longer then we would have to account for it, e.g. if the census in Kenya was in 1978, then the period would be 9 years and the population at risk would be the sum of the two populations at the end of the interval, multiplied by 9/2 instead of 5/2. However, in some areas, where the statistics are incomplete, we often have to use the nearest count of the population as the estimation of population at risk. How good an approximation this is

Table 19. *Estimated crude death rate and expectation of life at birth for major areas and regions of the world, 1965—1970.*

Major area and region	CDR per 1000	e_0	Major area and region	CDR per 1000	e_0
WORLD TOTAL	14	53	MORE DEVELOPED REGIONS	9	70
DEVELOPING REGIONS	16	50	*Europe*	10	71
Africa	21	43	Western Europe	11	71
West Africa	24	39	Southern Eur.	9	70
Eastern Afr.	22	42	Eastern Eur.	9	71
Middle Afr.	24	39	Northern Eur.	11	72
Northern Afr.	17	50	*Latin America*	10	60
Southern Afr.	17	48	Tropical Am.	10	60
Asia			Middle Am.	10	60
East Asia	14	52	Temperate S. Am.	9	65
Mainland region	15	50	Caribbean	11	58
Japan	7	71	NORTHERN AMERICA	9	70
Other E. Asia	10	60	OCEANIA	10	65
South Asia	17	49	USSR	8	70
Middle S. Asia	17	48			
South-East Asia	16	50			
South-West Asia	16	51			

Source: UN. *Determinants and Consequences of Population Trends.* N.Y. 1974, p. 110.

Table 20. *Crude deaths rates in selected countries in Eastern Africa[1] (per thousand).*

Country	Year	CDR per thousand
Kenya	1962	20
Kenya	1969	17
Kenya	1970—75	15.7[2]
Tanzania Mainland	1957	24—25
Tanzania Mainland	1967	21—23
Zanzibar	1957	20—21
Zanzibar	1967	20—21
Tanzania	1970—75	21.1
Zambia	1970—75	18.8
Burundi	1970—75	23
Rwanda	1970—75	21.1
Ethiopia	1970—75	22.9
Madagascar	1970—75	21
Mauritius	1970—75	7.2
Reunion	1970—75	8.5
Uganda	1970—75	15.9

[1] 1970—75 figures are estimated on the basis of trends and the last census data.
[2] At the Demographic Baseline Survey 1973, the CDR is estimated to be 13 per thousand.

Source: Demographic Handbook for Africa, 1971 and 1975. Addis Ababa 1971 and 1975, table 21.

depends on the time span of deviation from the person-years lived as estimated above. Another problem in Africa is that the numbers of deaths per year are not completely or adequately registered and therefore the measure has to be estimated in many cases, and not calculated directly on the basis of the number of deaths.

Crude deaths rates and life expectancy for different regions of the different continents can be seen in table 19. For comparison, variations in crude death rates are provided for selected countries in Eastern Africa (table 20).

Age-specific death rates

The crude death rate is indeed a very crude measure, as all members of the population are not exposed to the same risk of dying. We know from an earlier section on mortality, that old people are more likely to die than young people, and infants are more likely to die than children over 3 years (see graph 10). The age-specific mortality or death rate can be used for measuring mortality for subgroups of the population, i.e. in different age-groups and for each sex seperately. We usually use the following notation for the age-specific mortality rate:

$$_n m_x$$

where the suffix x is the beginning of the age interval, and the prefix n is the length of the interval.

The mortality rates for females between 10 and 15 years old would be:

$$_5 m_{10}^f = \frac{_5 D_{10}^f}{_5 P_{10}^f}$$

Number of deaths among females between 10 and 15 years of age divided by the mid-year population of females between 10 and 15 years in the same population and same calendar year.

The main problem with this measure as with the CDR is that the exact number of deaths is not registered, and has to be estimated in the African countries. However it may be estimated from census data on the basis of reported deaths and the age of the deceased in the 12-month period before the survey or census as has been done in some countries, e.g. in Tanzania 1967.

Standardization

As indicated above, the mortality is much higher in the older ages of the population than among the younger age groups. Therefore, if we use the crude death rate as a measure of the mortality, it not only reflects the mortality level, but also the number of people in the ages with a high mortality risk. This implies that in a population with very many young people and few old people, there will be relatively few deaths in relation to the size of the population.

77

Whereas if there are many old people in the population, there will be a higher number of deaths per 1000 in the population, even if the level of mortality is the same. This is because a population with many old people has a higher risk of many deaths than a population with many young people—other things being equal.

The implication of this is that the CDR not only provides a measure of the mortality level, but is also to a large extent determined by the age structure. In order to eliminate the effect of the age structure on the mortality measure, a standardization of the CDR may be worked out.

The idea behind standardization is that in a comparison of the CDR of two countries, the difference reflects both differences in the age structure as well as differences in mortality levels, but when we standardize by using one of the age structures as the standard population, we are keeping the age structure constant. Thus in the comparisons any variation in the figures can only be caused by differences in the mortality level. An example is given below to illustrate this:

Table 21. *Examples of standardization. CDR for USA and Taiwan and standardized CDR for USA using Taiwan as standard population and for Taiwan using USA as standard population (per thousand).*

Mortality level	Age structure as in the	
	USA population	Taiwan population
USA mortality	9.2	(5.0)
Taiwan mortality	(12.7)	8.2

The CDR for the USA is 9.2 per 1000 and that for Taiwan 8.2 per 1000. A comparison of the two rates reflects both differences in mortality and in the age structure. The comparison is distorted because the age structure is mainly the result of the fertility level, thus other factors are involved in the comparison of mortality. Standardization shows that while the CDR of the USA is higher than that of Taiwan, this can be attributed to differences in the age structure, with more young people in Taiwan than in the USA, whereas in actual fact the Taiwan mortality is higher regardless whether the USA or the Taiwan population is used as the standard population. Thus, the standardized rate of 12.7 for Taiwan is higher than the CDR for the USA (9.2) and the CDR of 8.2 for Taiwan is higher than the standardized CDR for the USA (5.0).

In standardization we calculate the "hypothetical number of deaths" or the number of deaths that would occur in Taiwan if it had the same age structure as the USA.

$_5\hat{D}_x = {_5}m_x^{Taiwan} \cdot {_5}P_x^{USA}$ (^= this is hypothetical)

As the CDR is the total number of deaths divided by the total population (in this case the total USA population), then we may just as well divide by the total population in each age-group and thus use the *relative* age structure.

An example is shown in table 22 comparing the CDR of the USA with that of Mauritius by means of standardization. For this one needs the age-specific mortality for Mauritius, and the relative age structure for the USA. The age structure for Mauritius is only provided to show the calculation of the "CDR proper" for Mauritius.

Table 22. *Comparison of the crude death rates for Mauritius 1968 and USA 1971 by means of a standardization, using USA as the standard population.*

(1) age	(2) Maur. 1968 age distr per thous.	(3) Maur. 1968 mort. per thous.	(4) USA 1971 age distr per thous.	(5) =(2) · (3) 1000 Maur. mort. Maur. age	(6)=(3) · (4) 1000 Maur. mort. USA age distr
Less than 1	29	73,6	18	2.134	1.325
1— 4	123	7,6	66	0.935	0.502
5— 9	145	1,6	93	0.232	0.149
10—14	130	1,2	101	0.156	0.121
15—19	120	1,6	95	0.156	0.152
20—24	85	2,0	87	0.170	0.174
25—29	57	3,1	68	0.200	0.211
30—34	56	3,0	57	0.168	0.171
35—39	47	4,2	54	0.197	0.227
40—44	52	4,7	57	0.244	0.268
45—49	39	7,3	59	0.285	0.431
50—54	34	12,7	54	0.432	0.686
55—59	26	20,5	49	0.533	1.005
60—64	21	30,0	43	0.630	1.290
65—69	16	43,5	34	0.696	1.479
70+	20	80,0	66	1.600	5.280
Total	1000		1000	8.768	13.481

Source: calculations on data from *Demographic Yearbook 1972.*

CDR for Mauritius 1968: 8.8 per thousand; CDR for USA 1971: 9.4 per thousand; Standardized death rate for Mauritius 1968, if it has the USA age structure 1971: 13.5 per thousand.

The CDR proper for Mauritius is found by multiplying the numbers in each row of column 2 by the same row in column 3. This is done in column 5 and the sum is the CDR. Using the USA as the standard population, we multiply the figures in each row of column 3 by the same row in column 4. The result is shown in column 6, and the sum of this provides the standardized death rate for Mauritius, if the USA population is used as the standard population. The comparison thus reveals that even though the original CDR for Mauritius is lower than the CDR for USA, the mortality level in Mauritius is higher, and the difference between the two rates can be ascribed to the difference in the age structure, i.e. Mauritius has a much younger population than the USA.

The purpose of standardization is to enable a comparison of mortality levels for two countries without the distorting influence of the age structure, as this implies that not only mortality, but also levels of fertility are being compared. In this work the purpose is also to show how important the age structure is for the measure "Crude Death Rate", as this is a measure most often used in superficial comparisons between different countries.

Age-specific mortality for selected age-groups

We have already covered the age-specific mortality for certain age groups under the section on differential mortality. However one of the best indicators of the mortality and health level in a population is the infant mortality rate. In addition the comparison between the registered infant mortality and the infant mortality rate estimated on different bases provides a good basis for the evaluation of the quality of the data.

The infant mortality $(_1q_0)$ is defined as the number of deaths among infants under 1 year of age in a given year divided by the number of births in the same year. For example, the infant death rate for 1975 would be:

$$_1q_0 = \frac{_1D_0^{75}}{B^{75}}$$ ($_1D_0$ = Deaths among children under 1 year old in 1975)
(B^{75} = Births in 1975)

The infant mortality rate is thus different from the mortality rate of other age-groups, because the numbers of deaths are not related to the population at risk, i.e. the number in the age-interval, but to the number of births in the same year. Some of the infants dying thus do not belong to the group born the same year. The reason for the approximation related to births in the same year is that mortality is highest among infants immediately after birth and then it rapidly declines throughout the first year. To show the difference, the age-specific death rate for another age-group of the population, that of children between 1 and 5 is calculated below:—

$$_4m_1 = \frac{_4D_1^{75}}{(_4P_1^{1.1.75} + _4P_1^{1.1.76}) \cdot {}^1/_2}$$

Thus age-specific mortality is defined as the number of deaths in a given age-group in a year, divided by the mid-year population of this age-group (population at risk or person-years lived). While the infant mortality is related not to population at risk during the interval, but to the population at the beginning of the age-interval, i.e. the number of births.

In order to evaluate the level of infant mortality some estimates are provided. The infant mortality has been estimated per thousand as follows: Kenya 1969: 112 for females and 126 for males; Kenya 1973: 94 for females and 113 for males; Tanzania 1967: 160 for both sexes together.

80

In the rural survey in Ethiopia 1964—67: the recorded infant mortality was 84, whereas the estimated rate was 200.

Exact data on mortality for the different age-groups are usually difficult or impossible to find, just as it is impossible to find data on differential mortality for certain status or income groups. However, mortality for the different age-groups is estimated on the basis of census data through the means of a life-table which is covered later in this chapter.

Calendar versus cohort principles

The idea of differentiating between *calendars* and *cohorts* (or generations), is reflected not only in everyday thought, but also in most sociological research. Often, Africans think of their own generation, meaning those born in the same year, or in some cases those circumcized at the same ceremony. Many will tend to compare their own generation at specific ages with that of other, especially younger, generations. For example "when I was your age, I always obeyed my mother..." etc. This could be a comparison of 14—16 year-old girls in 1976 with girls of the same age in 1936, that is the same age, but from different cohorts and at different time periods.

It is important to clarify this principle as both time, age and cohort affect events and people.

a.   The time period or the year is significant, as the general economic and social conditions at a particular point in time will affect the people living at that exact time, for example the importance of primary education will depend on whether a person had this education in Kenya in 1950 or in 1976. The immediate usefulness of the education may be quite different.

b.   Age has always been an important variable in any social system with implications for the division of labour and other norms of behaviour.

c.   The cohort or the generation has implications regarding how new phenomena are perceived. A cohort will involve the sum of the specific experiences of the generation throughout the different ages, and the time period covered. Different generations will have different conditions, and may react differently to new ideas depending on the conditions under which they have been living, for example the services of extension officers may be perceived by older generations as a continuation of the colonial system, and they may respond differently to these compared to younger generations, who have not experienced the previous system.

We can use a table or graph to illustrate how time, age and cohort are interrelated, and how we can find, for example age, if we have information on generation and year. In a system of co-ordinates with time (years) as the horizontal axis and age as the vertical axis, the lines in the rows indicate the precise birthdays, and the lines in the columns the division between calendar years, i.e. between 31 December 1974 and 1 January 1975 (see graph 13). A generation born on the same day, e.g. on 1 January 1971, would in passing through the different ages, make a transversal line as shown in the graph.

81

Graph 13. *Lexi's diagramme.*

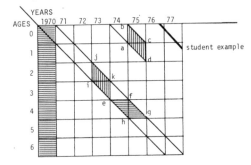

When an age-sex pyramid is constructed, we take the information during a year, and indicate the age distribution at that specific time, usually along a vertical line. If we want information on deaths in a population at a given year, we take the information in one column, e.g. in 1970, with an observation period of one year. This is the method most used for defining or organizing population data, since it represents different age-groups from different generations in one calendar year. The transversal band shows the generation group. This also represents different age-groups, but it follows the same generation, i.e. those who are born in the same year, up through all the age-groups, until all are dead. Data on such a generation is difficult to obtain, as persons have to be studied from birth until all are dead after 100 years. This gives a period of observation of 100 years. If this kind of information were available, it would show how a standardized generation of 100, 10,000 or 100,000 is reduced by deaths throughout all the ages. This cannot really be compared to the age-specific mortality as the latter refers to data on the generation at one point in time.

In time series studies to check for a phenomenon several points in time are comparable in principle. But these cover a much shorter time period than the study of a generation mortality would cover. But study of the total fertility behaviour of a generation, thus lasting until all have passed the age of 50 years, would be possible as a case of the generational approach to data collection.

The graph 13 also indicates some other problems of combining the three criteria for the identification of data by:
1. observation period—calendar (vertical lines)
2. age (horizontal lines)
3. generation or cohort (transversal lines)

These three do not fully correspond. To illustrate this we may start with another type of generation. If, instead of being concerned with mortality, we were concerned with the drop-out rate at the university distributed on the "study-age, or the time they have studied, then the study-age and the generation of the students would be the same for all students as all are enrolled at the same time of the year, e.g. in October. After 1 year, all the students are "1-year old" in the study, and after 1½ years they are all 1½-year olds in the study. In

1976 this could be illustrated by one of the transversal lines, but not the broad band (see graph 13).

Whereas in the case of university students, the generation and the age were exactly the same in the same year, this is not so in an actual population. The diagramme shows the problems arising from the situation, where the births or entrances to the population do not occur at one point in time, but are distributed during the whole year. The infants born throughout the year 1.1.1974 to 31.12.1974 will not all be 1-year old in 1975. Those born on 1.1.1974 would become 1-year old on January 1st 1975, and almost reach their 2-year birthday on 31.12.1975. Whereas the infants born on 31.12.1974 would not become 1-year old until 31.12.1976, and thus still be 0-year old or just under 1-year old. The generation born in 1974 will thus be distributed on 2 age-groups in 1975, namely the 0-year old and the 1-year old (see graph 13 abcd).

Usually however, we consider people's ages and a single observation year, instead of the generation, as shown in the graph column 1970. The infant mortality is also data of this kind, whereas there may be other problems of combining generation information with the other two variables:

i.   The generation born in 1970 will reach age-group 4 years (between 4th and 5th birthday) over two years; i.e. either in 1974 or in 1975 (see graph 13 efgh)

ii.   The generation born in 1970 will in 1973 be between their 2nd and 4th birthday (graph 13 ijke).

On the basis of this information it may be argued that generation data are not very imporant. But very often, especially in areas where statistical data are incomplete, we have to ask questions on data back in time, i.e. get retrospective information, and this kind of data is related to generations. In demographic surveys in Africa, there is always some retrospective data, e.g. for women in reproductive ages, questions are posed on the number of live children born and the number of them who are still alive.

In relation to historical information the relationship between generation and age is important, i.e. if there is information on the year a person is born, how old is she or he at the time of the interview? Or better, if a person can refer his time of birth to important events in the locality, then it is possible to calculate the other information. For example, a woman may not know her age but knows that her fertile period began in 1904—because it is related to a certain event. Her age and approximate year of birth may then be calculated and we can estimate her time of birth to be 1889—90, and thus in 1976 she will be around 86 years old.

The combination of age, time and cohort is important for the evaluation of age as a sociological variable, explaining differential behaviour. In relation to education, age is an important variable for explaining the level of education but this has not always been the case. The age differences in education are largely an effect of different conditions and access to education for the different cohorts. What matters is not whether a person is 20 or 50 years, but the conditions existing for the generation born 50 or 20 years ago concerning access to school education. One good indicator of this is that the age differences in education seem to be changing over time.

In relation to methodology, we always have problems with the causal relationships between events reported back in time, the registration of events are ex-post facto and that plays a major role for the memory and the perception of the event under the specific historical conditions. Rationalization of the perception is closely related to the age and time of the event, and also to the total accumulated experience of the cohort.

The life table

The life table shows how a standard generation is reduced by mortality through the ages, until all the persons have died at the maximum age, which is usually defined as 100 years.

Graph 14. *Examples of life table curves for high and low level of mortality (females).*

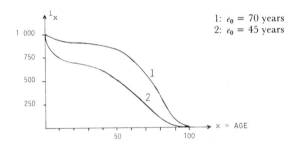

1: e_0 = 70 years
2: e_0 = 45 years

Source: UN. *Manual IV. Methods of Estimating Basic Demographic Measures from Incomplete Data.* N.Y. 1967, p. 86 and 91.

A life table ought to be based on generation data according to the definition. However such data are usually not available, and therefore the life table is based on a "false" generation. It tells us how a generation would die out in the different age-groups if it died according to the age-specific death rates in a given year. It is thus based on calendar data, but applied on a hypothetical generation.

The construction of a life table (see table 23) involves the following concepts, and the relationship between them:

l_x = the number of survivors of the generation at the exact age x (exact birthday).

l_0 = radix, this is an arbitrary number, which shows the standardization basis, or the original size of the generation. Usually it is 1,000, 10,000 or 100,000.

84

For constructing the life table the process is as follows:

1. $_nm_x = \dfrac{_nD_x}{_nP_x}$ The calculation of the age-specific mortality rates in the actual population. 'n' is the interval between the exact birthdays 'x' and 'x+n'.

2. $_nq_x = n \cdot {_nm_x}/(1 + n/2 \cdot {_nm_x})$ Calculation of the *probability* of dying between age 'x' (exact birthday) and the next age 'x+n' (birthday), on the basis of the calendar mortality rates. Here the calendar data are transformed to "generation" data. The formula is valid for all ages above 1 year of age.

3. $_nP_x = 1 - {_nq_x}$ Calculation of the probability of surviving between age 'x' and 'x+n' which is complementary to the probability of dying.

4. $l_{x+n} = l_x \cdot {_nP_x}$ Calculation of the number surviving in the life table. This is equal to the number of survivors at previous exact age multiplied by the probability of surviving to the next age. This is then the life table.

The above shows the calculations for ages above 1 year. Usually the age-interval n is 5 years long for all age-groups above the age of 5 years.

For those ages under 1 year of age, the bulk of the deaths occurs shortly after birth, and the $_1q_0$ is directly calculated as was indicated under the infant mortality rate, thus $_1q_0 = \dfrac{_1D_0}{\text{Births}}$ and thus leaving out the calculation of the $_1m_0$.[17]

Measures derived from the life table

In the life table we have information on the proportion in each age group who are expected to survive to the next age group, or in other words, the probability of dying before reaching the next age group; e.g. in Kenya for males in 1969 the probability of dying between 25 and 30 years of age is estimated to be 0.035, or of the number of males who reach their 25th birthday, 3.5% are likely to die before they reach their 30th birthday. The most important measure to be derived from the life table is the average life expectancy at age x, namely e_x.

We have earlier introduced the concept of the average life expectancy at birth

---

[17] If for some reason the numbers of deaths and births are not provided, but instead we have the mortality rate $_1m_0$, then $_1q_0$ can be calculated from this by another estimation, based on the skewed distribution of deaths, therefore the estimation formula is $_1q_0 = {_1m_0}/(1 + {}^3/_4 \cdot {_1m_0})$

Table 23. *Construction of a life table for Kenyan males, 1969.*

(1) Age	(2) $_nm_x$	(3) $_nq_x$	(4) $_nP_x$	(5) l_x
0	0.1385*	0.126	0.874	1000
1	0.0241	0.090	0.910	874
5	0.0085	0.042	0.958	795
10	0.0032	0.016	0.984	762
15	0.0054	0.027	0.973	750
20	0.0070	0.034	0.966	730
25	0.0072	0.035	0.965	705
30	0.0075	0.037	0.963	680
35	0.0084	0.041	0.959	655
40	0.0101	0.049	0.951	628
45	0.0128	0.062	0.938	597
50	0.0167	0.080	0.920	560
55	0.0226	0.107	0.893	515
60	0.0329	0.152	0.848	460
65	0.0464	0.208	0.792	390
70	0.0718	0.304	0.696	309
75	0.1074	0.423	0.577	215
80	0.1605	0.573	0.427	124
85	0.2494	1.000	0.000	53
100				0

* Calculated from $_1q_0$ by means of an approximation (see footnote 17).

Source: S. Ominde: *The Population of Kenya, Tanzania and Uganda.* Nbi. 1975, p. 37.

i.e. e_0, but this measure may be calculated at any given age, showing the average number of years remaining for those surviving to age x. The number of man-years lived by the population between age x and age x+n is important in this respect. This measure is $_nL_x$ and can be calculated as the area under the curve of the life table. The time survived for a generation in the life table between the ages x and x+n is estimated as the area under the life table curve:

Thus $\quad _nL_x = (l_x + l_{x+n}) \cdot n/2$

for intervals of 5 years, the calculation would be:

$$_5L_x = (l_x + l_{x+5}) \cdot 5/2$$

Graph 15. *Life table example with indication of the "area" survived between the ages x and x+n.*

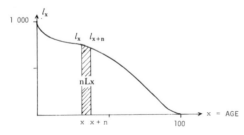

This measure $_nL_x$ is calculated for all intervals in the life table (see table 24). These are then added together from the last interval, i.e. 85—100 + 80—84 + 75—79 etc. in column T_x. Thus at each level the remaining area under the life table curve indicates the time survived for the generation in the life table from age x to age 100. By dividing this measure T_x at each level by l_x, we find the average number of years to be lived per individual in the group, i.e. e_x. In the equation, then $e_x = T_x/l_x$.

Table 24. *Life table and the calculation of e_x for males in Kenya 1969. e_x for females is provided for comparison.*

x Age	l_x Numbers surviving in the life table	$_nL_x$ Time survived by the generation between ages x and x+n	T_x Time survived by the generation between ages x and 100	e_x Average life expectancy from age x	e_x Average life expectancy from age x
(1)	(2) males	(3) males	(4) males	(5) males	(6) females
0	1000	911.8	46,921.7	46.9	51.2
1	874	3,277.4	46,009.9	52.6	56.6
5	795	3,892.5	42,732.5	53.8	57.1
10	762	3,780.0	38,840.0	51.0	54.1
15	750	3,700.0	35,060.0	46.7	49.7
20	730	3,587.5	31,360.0	43.0	45.7
25	705	3,462.5	27,772.5	39.4	41.9
30	680	3,337.5	24,310.0	35.7	38.1
35	655	3,207.5	20,972.5	32.0	34.2
40	628	3,062,5	17,765.0	28.3	30.3
45	597	2,892.5	14,702.5	24.6	26.5
50	560	2,687.5	11,810.0	21.1	22.7
55	515	2,437.5	9,122.5	17.7	19.1
60	460	2,125.0	6,685.0	14.5	15.7
65	390	1,747.5	4,560.0	11.7	12.6
70	309	1,310.0	2,812.5	9.1	9.8
75	215	847.5	1,502.5	7.0	7.8
80	124	442.5	655.0	5.3	5.7
85	53	212.5	212.5	4.0	4.4
100	0			0	0

(3) $_nL_x = n/2 (l_x + l_{x+n})$ (4) $T_x = \sum_{x=0}^{100} {}_nL_x$ (sum from bottom up)   (5) $e_x = T_x/l_x$

Source: Calculations on the Kenyan Census 1969.

The e_x shows the average number of years left to live for a person who has reached the age x if the level and structure of mortality remains the same as it was at the time the life table was constructed. In countries with a rapid decline in mortality, as in East Africa, the e_x thus provides a kind of minimum for the life expectancy at age x. The average age expected for each individual in the life table generation is not e_x, but is $x+e_x$, the obtained age plus the average expected number of years to live.

Usually we use the measure e_0 as the best indicator of mortality in a population. This summarizes the mortality experience in all ages, and is the most reliable measure for comparisons. Only in cases where we want to secure good information on specific age-groups such as infants and children 1—4 years old, do we need to supplement with e_1 and e_5. In countries like those of East Africa, with relatively high infant mortality, e_1 and even e_5 may often be higher than e_0, and the chances of surviving to older ages increase considerably when the first "dangerous" years are passed.

Information collected for the estimation of mortality

In Kenya in 1969 information was collected on the basis of 1) the number of surviving children for women, and 2) whether the parents of the household adults were still alive. This type of information implies that a lot of estimation operations are necessary, and the results in all the East African countries only provide information on the general level of mortality, as the results have a relatively low level of reliability.

The children and infant mortality estimates in Kenya 1969 are based on a question to all women over 12 years of age, on the total number of children they had given birth to before the census, and the number of children still alive. This is a typical retrospective data collection, where not only the people's reluctance to talk about the dead comes in, but also the mother's tendency to leave out those children born long before the census but who died just after birth. Thus the data from younger women, especially those 20—29 years old, provides the best and most reliable information for infant and child mortality. On the basis of this information an attempt is made to fit the data with a model or a standard life table in order to arrive at a reliable estimate. Life tables have been calculated and tabulated for different areas of the world, with different levels of mortality and different age-specific patterns of mortality. However, the estimation of mortality on the basis of model life tables is a complex process and is not to be covered here for the teaching of undergraduate students.

The information used for the estimation of adult mortality is data from the census on whether the parents of the adults in the household were still alive at the time of the census. This information, related to the age of the respondents, provides the basis for the estimation and fitts the data to the appropriate model life table.

In the Tanzanian 1967 census the information on family survival was supplemented by a question on the number of deceased in the household during the 12 months preceding the census. If there were any deceased, the sex and age of the deceased were registered. This calendar year approach seems to be very simple and may directly provide the age-specific death rate in the previous year, as well as infant mortality and crude death rate. However, many methodological problems of completeness and validity arise because of the following:

1. It is always difficult to get information on deaths. However, the problems increase when more detailed information on the deceased is demanded.

2. The definition and use of the exact registration or reference period is difficult. It may include deaths in a period of 10, 12 or 14 months before the census. This is a factor impossible to control fully and the result will be quite different depending on the reference period used.

On the basis of this kind of information in Tanzania, the estimated child mortality seemed to be overestimated, whereas the adult mortality seemed to be underestimated.

In order to give an evaluation of the exactness of the data and estimates on mortality in the East African countries, quotations from the *Kenya Population Census 1962*, vol. 3, and from *The Population of Tanzania*, edited by B. Egero and R. Henin are presented:

Kenya 1962:

The proportion of children surviving to census date indicated a level of child mortality which corresponds with those contained in various model mortality tables with expectations of life at birth of between 40 and 45 years. These models indicated that the Crude Death Rate among Africans (excluding the Northern Province) should be somewhere between 18 and 23 per thousand ... it appears unlikely that the Crude Death Rate in Kenya in the early 1960s was much in excess of 20 per thousand. (*Kenya Population Census 1962*, vol. 3, p. 75)

Tanganyika 1957:

A life expectancy at birth between 35 and 40 years and a crude death rate of some 24—25 per thousand may therefore be taken as the best estimates obtainable from the census data. (*African Census Report 1957*, Dar es Salaam 1963, p. 91)

Tanzania 1967:

The pattern of mortality by age is extremely difficult to establish. The Mainland infant mortality in 1967 appears to be as low as 160 per thousand or less, a considerable reduction compared to the only figure given in the 1957 census report, 190 per thousand. On the other hand, there is little doubt of a relatively high mortality in the ages between 1 and 5, possibly connected with weaning. The survival rates obtained were 800 or less per thousand to age 2, and 740 per thousand to age 5. Expressed in a different way, this means that 1 out of every 6 children born dies within his first year of life, 1 out of every 5 before his second birthday and 1 out of every 4 before reaching the age of 5 years. (Egero & Henin, op.cit., p. 84)

This could be supplemented by comments on the Kenyan 1969 census, where according to different methods of estimation, the infant mortality is "somewhere between 112 and 135 per thousand".[18] Variations in mortality measures can be found in different surveys. For example, in the demographic baseline survey in Kenya 1973, the figures from 2 control areas varied greatly, one sample showing a male infant mortality rate of 55 per thousand, while the other 115 per thousand. The highest figures from this survey are quoted for this text. Life-expectancy for males in the two samples was 51.9 and 58.7 years respectively.[19]

Examples from a health study in Machakos area reveal these difficulties; even with a regular check-up on deaths occurring in the households, the crude death rate was found to be 6 per thousand, which is evaluated to be severely under-registered.[20]

[18] *Demographic Baseline Survey Report 1973*. Central Bureau of Statistics. Nbi. 1975, p. 48.
[19] Ibid.
[20] P. G. Blok: *Report on the Demographic Studies of the Joint Project Machakos*. Medical Research Centre. Nbi. 1975, p. 49 and 64.

One may conclude this section by saying that in countries with incomplete registration of vital events, careful and complicated calculations must be carried out—based on recorded and retrospective data of events that have occurred during the past year. Also, the reliability of the data is very difficult to evaluate, and especially data on mortality where people show reluctance to talk on the subject or give any detailed information.

In relation to sociological analysis, the health and disease patterns are the most relevant variables. The methodology for the study of these events would differ from the large-scale surveys at one point in time. They would, instead, have to consist of time-series studies of local populations in order to contribute more essential information on the causes for the differential health pattern, and to reveal the major obstacles for further health improvement. Within the study of mortality, the demographic approach is very narrow and statistical, and does not focus the factors perceived to be relevant for the rural development or planning, whereas a combined sociological and medical approach—maybe with demographic contributions—would tend to focus other aspects of more relevance for the improvement of the life conditions for the people.

Supplementary reading

1. L. C. Vogel, A. S. Muller, R. S. Odingo, Z. Onyango, A. De Geus (eds): *Health and disease in Kenya*. Nairobi 1974.
  a) S. H. Ominde: Demography and Ethnic Groups, p. 27—48.
  b) J. N. Van Luijk: Social and Cultural Aspects of Health and Disease, p. 63—74.
  c) J. Bonte: Patterns of Mortality and Morbidity, p. 75—90.
2. *Demographic Baseline Survey Report 1973*. Central Bureau of Statistics. July 1975. Nbi., pp. 43—51.
3. B. Egero and R. Henin (eds): *The Population of Tanzania*. An Analysis of the 1967 Population Census. Census volume 6. Dar es Salaam. 1973. Chapter 11, pp. 176—185.
4. *Kenya Population Census 1962*. Vol. III, African Population. Central Bureau of Statistics. 1966, pp. 70—75.
5. U. N. *The Determinants and Consequences of Population Trends*. N. Y. 1974. Chapter V, pp. 107—158.
6. Julien Condé: Some Demographic Aspects of Human Resources in Africa. Conf. in Dakar 1973. OECD. Paris 1973, pp. 41—93.
7. Thianar N'Doye: Infant Mortality and Nutritional Problems. In: OECD. *The Demographic Transition in Tropical Africa*. Paris 1971, pp. 245—252.
8. R. M. A. Zwanenberg with Anne King: *An Economic History of Kenya and Uganda 1800—1970*. Nbi. 1975, pp. 3—22.
9. R. M. A. Zwanenberg: *Colonial Capitalism and Labour in Kenya 1919—1939*. Nbi. 1975, pp. 60—70.
10. J. C. Caldwell: *The Sahelian Drought and its Demographic Implications*. OLC Canberra. Dec. 1975, pp. 1—2 and pp. 23—31.

Chapter IX

Nuptuality

Nuptuality or the study of marriage, like the other demographic components, namely fertility, mortality and migration, is an important factor influencing population growth and composition. However, it is often not covered as a separate topic in demographic texts, perhaps because of the lack of good, adequate data on marital status, especially in the developing countries, or because it is often subsumed under the section on fertility due to the obvious relationship between marital status and reproductive behaviour in most societies. The importance of marital status data in demographic, sociological and economic analysis and planning renders it necessary to examine the definitional and methodological problems involved in the study of nuptuality, the type and sources of data available, and the use of such statistics for analytical purposes. This chapter attempts to point out some of the important issues related to the study of nuptuality within the African context from the demographic viewpoint.

Problems of definition

Although marriage has a definite meaning in African cultures and appears to be universal, a number of problems make it difficult to classify and define it in general terms.

a. The first problem is that of classification of marital status categories. The UN definitions do not cover all the wide range of marriage possibilities. As Van de Walle[1] has pointed out, marriage must be distinguished from free and consensual unions. He observes a gradient in marital status which moves thus:

Celibacy —	free — union (concubinage, unstable unions)	consensual — unions (socially recognised stable unions)	customary — marriage	religious/ civil marriage

The distinction between free and consensual unions becomes meaningful because of the implications for exposure to the risks of childbearing. In addition, within the customary forms of marriage, one can distinguish a variety of

[1] Etienne Van de Walle, "Marriage in African Censuses and Inquiries". In: Brass et al.: *The Demography of Tropical Africa*. Princeton University Press, 1968, p. 186.

practices like marriage by payment for service, marriage by exchange, ghost marriage, *iweto* (woman-woman marriage), levirate marriage etc. These different patterns would have varied implications for patterns of family formation, inheritance patterns and reproductive behaviour, but are rarely dealt with in demographic data collection. It is this multiplicity of marital categories which make the collection of data a dilemma for the census taker. He must clearly indicate the criteria he is using for drawing the line between a marital union and a non-union. In their study of North East Tanganyika, 1957—58, Roberts and Tanner observed:

The conjugal condition cannot be specified in categories more detailed than "currently married" and "currently not married" for it is impossible to distinguish their sub-divisions The latter include the divorced, widowed and not yet married. The married category includes those practicing any of the seven different types of marriage observable in the area, together with the participants in common law-unions.[2]

The general attitude towards marital status data collection seems to be best illustrated by the instructions given to enumerators in Ghana[3] and Ethiopia:

Ghana:
In general, your guide as to who is married or not married will simply be what the respondent tells you.

Ethiopia:
In general, if a person claims to be married, you should accept his word. If you express doubts, or enquire too much, you may embarass the informant and lose his cooperation.

This indicates the problem of classification that may exist in various parts of Africa. The definition in most cases is left to the respondent which may make international as well as regional comparisons very difficult. But also the perception of being married may be the most relevant distinction in relation to demographic analysis, especially in relation to fertility behaviour.

    b.   The prevalence of polygamous marriages in Africa also poses statistical problems and especially the vague definition of households. Should polygamous households with a number of wives and their respective children be counted as one household or several households? In the Rungwe survey in Tanzania,[4] some enumerators treated them as one household while others as several, thereby affecting the reliability of the data.

    — In the case of divorce of one of the polygamous husband's wives, the marital status of the husband would remain unchanged although that of his wife would change from "married to divorced". Similarly in the case of the husband's death, several widows would result.

    — The problem of restrictive legislation. In some countries the gap between

[2] D. F. Roberts and R. E. S. Tanner "A Demographic Study in an Area of Low Fertility in N.E. Tanganyika" in *Population Studies*, Vol. XIII, No. 1 July 1959, p. 64.
[3] Instructions to Enumerators for Post-enumeration Survey, Ghana 1960.
[4] B. Egero and R. Henin (eds): *The Population of Tanzania*. An Analysis of the 1967 Population Census. Census vol. 6. Dar es Salaam, 1973, p. 249.

custom and law may bring about an understatement of important social phenomenon like polygyny. Thus for example, polygyny was made illegal in the Congo after 1951, but polygamous unions were still formed and recognised by customary law. However, the second wives in plural marriages were recorded as living in consensual unions, thus distorting the actual picture.

c. Data on age at first marriage also causes difficulties because of ambiguities in the definition of marriage, as well as mis-statement of current age. Marriages at very young ages are common in Africa, though the spouses may wait to cohabit until the wife has reached puberty. Most African countries observe the international recommendation on minimum age for marital status which is 14 or 15 years. This can lead to the understatement of the number of married couples and an over-estimation of age at first marriage. Again, variations occur which affect comparisons between countries. Thus, Liberia used 10 years as the minium age in the 1962 census, Sudan used "over puberty" in the 1955—56 census, but 11 years in the Wadi Haifa census 1960, UAR used 16 years for females and 18 years for males, whereas Tanzania and Kenya included no information on age at first marriage in their last censuses.

The close connection between age at marriage and fertility levels which will be discussed later emphasizes the need for reliable data on age at first marriage.

d. The definition of categories like widowhood, divorce, and separation also creates difficulties.

— What type of unions are susceptible to termination by divorce? Free unions are most probably not included. Does one consider consensual unions?

— How does a union end in divorce? According to the UN definitions[5] a divorced person is one "whose marriage was dissolved by legal means and who has not remarried, including persons formerly living in stable *de facto* unions, but no longer regarded as forming part of such a union". However, with customary marriages, divorce can cover various situations, and also it is difficult to draw the line between divorce and separation. Most countries conveniently group the two together.

— False reporting can lead to distorted statistics. It was found that in small towns in the northern provinces of Ethiopia about one-third of the women aged 10 years and over were divorced.[6] This is an extremely high proportion and was probably due to the fact that these "divorced" women may really have been unmarried mothers who preferred to regard themselves divorced.

— The problem of widows in polygamous households has been mentioned. Also, the treatment of inherited widows (levirates) becomes ambivalent. Is levirate marriage a continued marriage, a separate marriage or should the woman be regarded a widow? However, information on this is lacking for the majority of the countries.

The preceding section has attempted to highlight some of the conceptual and methodological problems in the analysis of marital status statistics. Having

---

[5] UN. *Principles and Recommendations for National Population Censuses*. New York, 1958.

[6] *Population of Ethiopia*, Results from the National Sample Survey, 1st round 1964—67. Imperial Ethiopian Govt. Central Statistical Office, Statistical Bulletin No. 6, Addis, November 1971, p. 22.

pointed these out, one can now examine some of the existing data on marital status, and discuss factors affecting nuptuality and the relationship between nuptuality and fertility.

Factors affecting nuptuality

Marriage is regarded as a very important institution in African societies in that it serves certain basic functions; it is the primary institution for procreation, it serves as an alliance between different kinship groups, it is important for inheritance purposes and for the continuation of the ancestral lineage. There are thus various cultural, sociological, economic and religious factors affecting nuptuality in any society. A brief summary of the factors is given.

    a. Demographic factors: The age-sex composition as well as mortality and migration have an important bearing on marriage.

    — The age-sex composition determines the proportions in each age group and the sex ratio of the population.

    — Migration and mortality will also affect the number of men and women available for marriage.

    b. Social and cultural factors:

    — The value placed on marriage and procreation in society. Each society has culturally prescribed norms governing marriage, fertility, sterility, etc. This will influence the incidence of marriage as well as the type of marital patterns.

    — The type of inheritance patterns.

    — Education: marriage tends to be delayed especially if more young men and women are going through school for long periods.

    — Rural urban migration will affect the sex ratio in both the rural and urban areas. The absence of young men in rural areas could lead to more polygamous marriages.

    c. Economic factors:

    — The availability of bridewealth.

    — The availability of land and the related need for family labour.

    — The economic position can determine the type of marriage as well as the age at marriage.

    d. Religion: The influence of christianity could affect the incidence of polygyny because of the emphasis on monogamy. It could also undermine other traditional types of marriage customs, e.g. *iweto* (woman-woman marriage) and levirate (marriage of widows by husband's younger brother).

Nuptuality and fertility

The relationship between nuptuality and fertility will be discussed by looking at the following variables, which appear to have a significant effect on fertility levels.

94

1. Proportions married and age at marriage
2. Type of marital union, i.e. polygyny/monogamy
3. Marital instability

Proportion married, age at marriage and fertility

In their framework of the "intermediate variables" affecting fertility, some of the factors Davis and Blake (1956)[7] have included are "age of entry into sexual unions, permanent celibacy or proportion of women never entering into sexual unions, amount of time spent after or between unions". Given that in all societies, the majority of the births occur within a marital union, it is obvious that proportions married in a population and age at marriage are fundamental determinants of fertility, especially in those societies where fertility is not deliberately controlled through contraceptive use. It therefore follows that the higher the number of women remaining single, the lower the fertility rates[8] because of limited exposure to sexual unions. This has been the case in Ireland which seems to have the highest proportion of celibate women (as high as 30%). For tropical Africa, the available data indicate that marriage is almost universal. Between the ages of 20—45 about 70% of the men and 90% of the women were in some form of a conjugal union.[9] Marriage data exist for Kenya and Uganda in 1969. These show very high marriage rates for both men and women, though the rates are higher in Kenya than in Uganda. The variations according to age, show a high frequency of unmarried men before the age of 25 and of unmarried women below the age of 20. The declining percentage of married persons at higher ages is explained by the increasing number of unions terminated by the death of one of the spouses. The higher mortality for men as well as their higher age at marriage results in a rapidly declining percentage of married women and an increase in the number of widows from the age of around 50 years.

The proportion of unmarried in Kenya 1969 is 5.7% for both sexes from the age of 30 years, when most are married. The proportion of widowed women over 60 years is more than 50%, whereas the proportion of widowed men is less than 10%. The proportion of divorced is relatively stable for men and women, being around 2—3% from the age of 25 years.[10]

Various studies have been caried out to show the effect of age at marriage on fertility. Usually it is assumed that all other things being equal, earlier age at marriage for females would lead to a greater completed family size since earlier marriage implies more exposure to the childbearing period. However, although the theoretical relationship appears simple, various sociological and physio-

[7] K. Davis and J. Blake, "Social Structure and Fertility. An Analytical Framework". *Economic Development and Cultural Change*, 1956, p. 211—35.
[8] The conventional index for measuring marital fertility is the age-specific marital fertility rate which has been discussed in the fertility chapter.
[9] E. Van de Walle, op.cit. p. 196.
[10] *Kenya Population Census 1969*, vol. III. Calculations.

Table 25. *Percentage of married persons by age: Kenya & Uganda 1969 census.*

Age	Kenya		Uganda	
	Males	Females	Males	Females
10—14	0.4	1.4	0.4	1.9
15—19	3.4	33.4	1.6	46.2
20—24	26.0	75.6	6.0	80.3
25—29	64.4	86.6	63.0	85.6
30—34	81.9	87.6	71.5	83.8
35—39	86.0	86.2	75.1	81.7
40—44	} 87.8	} 80.1	75.2	75.1
45—49			76.0	80.5
50—54	} 88.1	66.4	73.7	59.1
55—59		76.1	53.3	
60—64	} 86.2	} 43.3	71.1	41.6
65—69			72.6	35.6
70—74	} 80.7	} 30.7	67.6	26.6
75+			65.2	19.8

Source: S. H. Ominde: *The Population of Kenya, Tanzania & Uganda*, Nairobi, 1975, p. 67 and 71.

logical factors may come into operation which may reduce the subsequent fertility of those marrying earlier, or raise it of those marrying later.

In his Lebanon study, Yaukey (1961)[11] shows that total fertility decreased systematically and markedly with increased age of the woman at marriage. An increase from 15.5 years to 25.1 years was associated with a decline in the total fertility rate from 7.74 to 4.46. Henin's study in the Sudan (1961–62)[12] also indicates that the highest mean number of births was recorded for women marrying at age 14 or under. However, Ryder (1959)[13] suggests that the reason for the low total fertility rates for women married at very young ages is that the high level of fertility at early ages represents an exposure to the greater risk of damaging the reproductive apparatus and may produce infertility at early ages. This is also suggested by the Mysore study in India (1961).[14] Here the effect of the rise in age at marriage is seen as two-fold: (1) that it tends to shorten the span during which women are subjected to the risk of pregnancy, (2) it could influence a woman's fertility during the period of marriage either positively in that postponement may raise fertility in so far as it improves the health of the mother during the reproductive period or negatively—in that if marriage was postponed beyond a certain age it would lower fertility. A similar conclusion has been drawn by Sinha (1951).[15]

[11] Yankey David, *Fertility Differentials in A Modernizing Country*: A Survey of Lebanese Couples, Princeton 1961, p. 48—9.

[12] R. A. Henin, "Patterns and Causes of Fertility Differentials in the Sudan", *Population Studies*, Vol. XXVIII, No. 2, July 1969, p. 181—83.

[13] Normal Ryder, "Fertility" in *The Study of Population* by Hauser and Duncan, The University of Chicago Press, 1959, p. 418.

[14] *The Mysore Population Study*, New York, 1961, p. 116.

[15] J. N. Sinha, "Fertility and Age at Marriage", *Bulletin of International Statistical Institute*, 33—34, 1951, p. 113—26.

Thus the relationship between age at marriage and fertility is not very simple. Moreover, the widespread use of contraception in certain communities could lead to a reversal of the relationship. However, it is an important variable and many countries in their efforts to lower fertility often raise the age of marriage as one of the policy measures (e.g. China, where age of marriage has been increased to 30 years). Data on age at marriage for the African countries is very poor because of biases in age-reporting associated with marital status, and sometimes data on age at marriage are not even available (Tanzania 1967) which makes it very difficult to evaluate the possible influence of that variable. The usual index used to indicate the mean age at marriage is estimated from census data on the proportions of single or unmarried by age groups. For Kenya, 1962, the mean age at marriage was estimated as 24.1 years for males and 18.4 for females,[16] for Tanzania 1967, it was 25.8 years for males and 16.8 years for females.[17] Thus women seem to be marrying at early ages in these countries.

Type of marital union and fertility

Data compiled for several African countries for 1955—64 seem to indicate that polygamous marriages are still widely practiced in Africa Usually two aspects of polygyny are measured: (1) the incidence of polygyny: the proportion of polygamists among married males, (2) its intensity: the average number of wives per polygynist. However, the actual incidence of polygyny is difficult to assess because most countries do not include questions on polygyny in their censuses. Table 26 shows the incidence of polygyny for selected African

Table 26. *Number of wives per husband for selected African countries.*

Country	Year	% of husbands with		
		1 wife	2 wives	3+ wives
Libya	1964	97.1	2.7	0.1
Sudan	1956	84.1	13.2	2.6
Egypt	1960	96.2	3.5	0.3
Ghana	1960	73.8	20.0	6.2
Guinea	1954—55	62.9	25.0	12.1
Togo	1958—60	68.1	21.6	9.3
Central African Republic	1959—60	75.6	19.5	4.9
Rep. of Congo	1960—61	67.2	24.2	7.7
Tanganyika	1957	78.9	17.2	4.0
Rungwe* (Tanzania)	1967	73.9	19.3	6.8
Nigeria* Urban	1972	92.8	5.4	1.8
Rural	1972	66.7	19.6	13.7

* Sample Surveys

Source: UN Demographic Handbook for Africa, April 1975; Egero and Henin: *The Population of Tanzania,* p. 248; Kwaku Adadevoh: *Sub-fertility and Infertility in Africa,* p. 58.

[16] *Kenya Population Census 1962,* Vol. III. African population. Statistics Division, Ministry of Economic Planning and Development, October 1966, p. 55.
[17] B. Egero and R. Henin, op.cit. p. 243.

countries in the 1950s and 1960s. There seems to be a high percentage of polygamists in West African countries and in the Congo and a low percentage for North Africa. However, comparisons with other areas are difficult because of limited data. Monogamy, however, was and is still the dominant union, even in areas with high levels of polygyny. Among polygynous unions, the union with 2 wives is by far the most frequent. Very few of the men have more than 2 wives.

The frequency of polygamous unions cannot be very high in larger areas unless a very exceptional age-sex structure exists. We know that in all areas the number of male and female births are nearly the same, sometimes with a small majority of male over female births. With a high frequency of marriage also for the men, there are many wives available per man at adult ages. However, men tend to have higher age specific mortality at all ages and at around age 20—30 years there will be a slight surplus of women to men. Also men tend to be older than their wives and where there is a high level of fertility men can thus select wives from younger generations. Therefore the practice of polygyny in many areas of Africa implies that all women, even where they were in surplus, could marry and that divorcees and widows could also enter into new marriage unions. But the level of polygyny is still clearly restricted by the age-sex structure of the population in the 15—45 age groups.

Variations in fertility occur according to the type of marital union (i.e. monogamous or polygamous). However, there is a lot of debate over the polygyny fertility hypothesis. This could perhaps be overcome with adequate research on the subject. Some studies indicate that polygyny tends to depress fertility. For example, the Rungwe survey in Tanzania (1967),[18] Henin's[19] study in the Sudan and studies by Dorjahn[20] (1959) show that in polygamous households there is a lower number of children born per wife than to those in monogamous households. Also, data compiled for a number of countries in Africa (Table 27) show that fertility rates consistently fall as the number of wives increases. Some of the probable reasons given are:

— There is a lower average frequency of coitus and therefore a lower chance of pregnancy for wives in polygamous marriages than in monogamous ones.

— That taboos on intercourse during certain periods are more respected in polygamous households.

— The age differences between husband and wife are greater in polygamous marriages and the youngest wives have a shorter duration of marriage.

— Women enter polygamous unions because they are already infertile to start with.

— Polygamous unions are more unstable than monogamous ones.

[18] B. Egero and R. Henin, op.cit. p. 243.
[19] R. A. Henin, "Patterns and Causes of Fertility Differentials", op.cit.
[20] V. R. Dorjahn: "The Factor of Polygyny in African Demography". In: *Continuity and Change in African Cultures*, eds. W. R. Bosom and M. J. Herskovitz. University of Chicago Press, 1959, pp. 109—112.

Table 27. *Fertility in monogamous and polygamous unions for some African regions*

Country or sub-region	Year	General fertility rate of women* when they are:			
		Sole wives	2 wives	3 wives	4+ wives
Guinea	1955	274	246	222	
Ivory Coast	1957—58	261	235	←——— 182 ———→	
Mali (Central)	1956—58	264	←————— 218 ————→		
Central African Rep.	1959—60	196	168	140	138
Republic of Congo	1960—61	188	163	114	78
Zaire	1955—57	211	←———— 141 ————→		
Gabon	1961—62	128	←—— 111 ——→		99

* Births per 1000 women aged 15—49.

Source: Demographic Handbook for Africa, U.N. 1975, p. 85, Table 19.

While some studies have shown lower age-specific fertility rates for women in polygamous households (Dorjahn, 1959)[21], others have failed to show any relationship between fertility and different marital types (Ekanem, Nigeria, 1972).[22] In the analysis of marital data from Rungwe district in Tanzania the differences between fertility among women in polygamous unions and in monogamous unions were very small.

Table 28. *Average number of children per woman in the Rungwe sample in Tanzania 1967.*

	1 wife	2 wives	3 or more wives
Average number of children	7.5	7.2	6.1

Source: Egero & Henin: op.cit., p. 251.

The difference is so small that it may well be explained by differences in duration of marriage for the youngest wives.

Thus there is little evidence and much dispute about whether polygyny increases or reduces fertility. Data on the extent of polygyny are not available for a large enough population in Africa to make possible a comprehensive study of the polygyny fertility hypothesis.

Marital instability and fertility

Marriage can be dissolved through divorce, separation or death of the spouse. A high rate of marital instability decreases the amount of reproductive period spent in unions, thereby leading to low marital fertility. In fact, it has often been argued that the Indian fertility rate would be much higher were it not for

[21] Ibid. pp. 109—112.
[22] Ekanem, I. I. "The Influence of Polygyny on Fertility in Eastern Nigeria." In: *Sub-fertility and Infertility in Africa*, ed. B. Kwaku Adadevoh, 1973, pp. 56—63.

the taboos on widows of remarriage. But again, studies show contrasting findings about the exact nature of the relationship. It is often argued that subfecund women are more likely to be divorced than fertile ones. It appears as if high marriage instability tends to increase the frequency of infertility but also infertility or low fertility can increase marriage instability. The factors are thus closely interrelated. In the Rungwe survey the average number of children was thus much lower for the women who had experienced more than one marriage. (See table 29).

Table 29. *Average number of children per married woman in Rungwe 1967, according to number of marriages.*

Married	1 time	2 times	3 or more times
Average no. of children	7.4	5.9	3.8

Source: eds. Egero & Henin: op.cit., p. 251.

In Tanzania (Rungwe District) the data thus seem to support West African data on a close negative relationship between the number of times married and fertility.

Sources of data

Registration of marriage has been enforced only in a few countries in Africa, and in previous years (between 1956—64) a number of countries (including Uganda and Tanzania) had omitted from their population censuses any inquiry into marital status.[23] This could be attributed either to the definitional and classificatory problems connected with various marriage customs found in most African countries or because they thought the data were of "insufficient value". There are, for example, in Kenya, five recognized forms of marriage, namely Christian, Civil, Hindu, Islamic and African customary marriage, but only three of these (which constitute a small proportion of all marriages) are registrable.

Wherever data on marital status are available, they are supplied mostly by censuses or sample surveys but only in very few cases by registration data since this is either very limited or non-existent in most African countries. Studies by social anthropologists can also provide very useful data on marriage for demographic inquiry, for example, the effect of marital customs on fertility, or the different types of marriage practices in different cultural areas. But these are rather limited because of the small size of the populations studied and may not always be adequate for statistical analysis. Thus, the reliance is mainly on census and survey data, and some of the types of data provided are (1)

[23] *Collection of Statistics of Marital Status in Africa.* ECA Working Group on Censuses of Population and Housing, Addis Ababa, June 21–29, 1965 p. 1.

proportions married, single, widowed, divorced, (2) age at first marriage (3) in a few cases, type of marriage (e.g. polygamous or monogamous).

The inclusion of this type of information is usually based on the UN recommendations on the compilation of marital status statistics which tend to be western oriented.

A study of country practices in population censuses and demographic surveys conducted between 1955—64 in Africa[24] showed that of the 39 countries covered, 12 collected no information on marital status, whereas of the remaining 27 that did collect such data, most of them followed the UN definitions. The Kenya 1969 and Tanzania 1967 censuses both give the usual type of information, i.e. the proportions single, married, widowed and divorced by age groups, but there is no information on age at first marriage nor questions on polygamy.

The marital status data that is available in most countries is however defective because of the types of errors involved in censuses and surveys, namely errors of coverage, age mis-statement, memory lapse about previous marriages, problems of classifying marital status categories, problems of defining households, etc. Some of these problems, especially of definition and measurement, should be examined to point out the constraints and limitations of data on nuptuality.

Supplementary reading:

1. B. Egero & R. Henin (eds): *The Population of Tanzania.* An Analysis of the 1967 Population Census. Census vol. 6. Dar es Salaam 1973, pp. 246—252.

2. *Kenya Population Census 1962.* Vol. 3, African Population, pp. 54—57.

3. Jane Chalmers: *Economic Change and Marital Stability: A Kenyan Study.* Radcliffe College, Massachusetts 1971, pp. 39—52, p. 60—79.

[24] Ibid., p. 17.

Chapter X

Fertility

Problems of definition

The definition of "fertility" and births creates more problems than the definition of mortality and deaths in the population. More concepts are involved, and many more factors of a sociological and biological nature are related to the definition. Therefore the following definitions, which are relevant for the analysis of fertility are provided.

a. Fertility is the actual performance of persons in terms of reproduction. This is measured by counting the number of live-births and should be distinguished from fecundity.

b. Fecundity is the biological capacity of persons to reproduce themselves. Fertility is always lower than fecundity, as all societies have some kinds of restrictions on reproductive performance. Fecundity is thus a theoretical concept, which cannot be measured. It is only sometimes estimated on the basis of "natural fertility" i.e. fertility in groups with practically no restrictions on fertility, and with norms advocating very high fertility.

c. Infertility is the incapacity of a woman to carry a pregnancy to a live-birth. It is not necessarily the incapacity to conceive (infecundity or sterility). Infertility is measured through the absence of a live-birth. It may occur before any live-births to a woman (total infertility) or after some children have been born.

d. Subfertility is a low level of fertility in an area, due to a high frequency of infertility among the families in the area.

e. Sterility refers to the absolute biological incapacity to reproduce.

f. A live-birth is usually defined as a birth where the child has cried after the delivery. The difficulty lies in the distinction of a live-birth, where the infant dies shortly after birth from a stillbirth, especially since mortality just after birth is very high. In many statistics the definition of a live-birth includes only those who survive the first 3 hours or 24 hours of life. And in many traditional rural East African communities, the child was not really considered alive until it had survived approximately the first 6—7 days, until the umbilical cord had dropped off. Comparisons of live-births in areas with different definitions and high infant mortality may therefore be dubious.

g. A stillbirth is a birth after at least 6 months of pregnancy, where the child does not cry, or does not survive the above-mentioned period, necessary to be classified as a live-birth.

h. An abortion or a miscarriage is any terminated pregnancy less than 6 months old. This is also called foetal mortality. The difference in time between a stillbirth and a miscarriage is put at 6 months, as the child has a chance of surviving after 6 months of gestation, whereas the chances are practically nil before that time.

i.   Multiple births are defined as deliveries where more than one child is born. These are often (in the statistics) classified not only as multiple children, but also as multiple births, even though the children are from the same pregnancy and delivery. However, the number of twins and other multiple births are limited to approximately 1% of the total births (most often twins), therefore the error in the statistics is not of major importance.

j.   The reproductive period or the childbearing ages for women. This generally falls between the ages 15—50 years for women. Most births occur within this age-limit. The biological capacity (fecundity) may start earlier, but the socially relevant ages are seldom below 15, and most often over 18 years due to marriage norms. The upper limit may also in certain cases be over 50, although very few births are related to these older age-groups, as biological as well as social factors seems to restrict fertility at older ages.

Factors affecting fertility

Just like mortality, fertility is affected by both biological and social factors. However the relationship here is more complicated, as fertility and changes in fertility are often a result of a decision, and therefore a sociological phenomenon.

The biological factors are mainly related to the fecundity and to the health of women and men. A diversified and protein-rich diet and general good health seem to have a positive effect on fertility, through increasing the capacity to carry a pregnancy through to a live-birth.

Certain diseases seem to be especially related to the prevalence of infertility and sterility. These are venereal diseases, malaria and plague. Some of the venereal diseases mainly tend to hinder conception whereas the other diseases affect the frequency of miscarriages and stillbirths. This is especially a problem as high fertility seems to be a major concern for most traditional African communities, and barrenness and low fertility are often negatively sanctioned.

The biological incapacity to have the number of births wanted may be reflected by the incidence of childlessness among women over 40 or 45 years. For example, in the Congo in 1956—57, 20% of all women over 45 years were childless. This varied from 5% to 35% in the different regions.[1] Another indication may be obtained from the proportion of the women having less than 4 children. A survey in a few rural areas in Western Nigeria with problems of subfertility, revealed that of all married women who had been married more than 15 years, half of the women had less than 4 children, and this is an area where the wanted number of children is well over 4.[2]

The main impact on fertility however, seems to be generated by social

[1] Brass et al.: *The Demography of Tropical Africa.* Princeton 1968, p. 331.
[2] Kwaku Adadevoh: *Subfertility and Infertility in Africa.* Ibadan 1974, p. 48 and op. cit., p. 325.

factors. These are listed and discussed below:—

a.   Age of marriage determines the length of time that women are exposed to the risk of childbearing within the reproductive period. The younger the age at marriage, the longer the period of a woman's reproductive capacity, and the more children she is likely to have. However, this tendency is not so clear for ages below 16 or 17. In India there are indications of relatively high post-partum sterility of very young mothers (aged around 16) and thus a lower total fertility for this group.

b.   Proportions ever married. The more the number of women who marry the higher the fertility in the area, (all other things being equal) as more of the "reproductive capacity" is utilized. In African as well as Asian countries the proportion of women who never marry is practically nil. In many of the tribal cultures of East Africa, the language does not cater for the concept of a spinster (adult unmarried woman). This is related to the widespread incidence of polygyny in most areas, and the high emphasis on marriage and fertility in these communities. In Europe and USA on the other hand the proportion of women who never marry is approximately 10—30% (the highest in Ireland).

Moreover divorced women seem to continue reproduction either outside marriage or within a new marriage, and often as a younger wives in polygynous unions.

d.   Polygamy *versus* monogamy: In all African countries it has been revealed that fertility is higher per woman in a monogamous union, than in a polygamous union. This means that although men are getting more children in a polygamous marriage, each woman seems to have a lower average number of births. This may be related to the following factors: 1) The frequency of polygynous unions is higher if the first wife has no children or only a few (especially if she has few children and no boys), 2) Divorced women often join polygynous unions, and these women often have lower fertility than women who have never been divorced. 3) The difference in fertility between the first wife in a polygynous marriage and a monogamous marriage is very little; it is mainly among the younger wives that the fertility is considerably lower. The first wife remains the single wife for some time, and the later wives are usually married when the husband is much older. 4) However, one important factor seems to be that the post-partum abstinence taboo appears to be more closely observed in a polygamous than in a monogamous union. This protects the woman lactating her child, until the child is weaned. This is a very common taboo in most East African tribes, even though the time periods of expected abstinence may vary. In some areas the period is quite short, as among the Luo, where abstinence appears to be limited only to the lactation period and is estimated around 8—9 months;[3] whereas among other tribal groups, the periods are quite long, e.g. among the Meru of Kenya, where husband and wife are prescribed not to sleep in the same hut until the child has lost its first milk-teeth (around 4—6 years)[4].

[3] A. Molnos: *Cultural source material for population planning in East Africa.* Nbi. 1973, vol. 3, p. 334.
[4] Ibid., p. 61.

e. The frequency of intercourse within marriage, may be affected by several factors: 1) migration of the men for employment in other areas, leading to a physical separation of spouses which may last for long periods. 2) abstinence due to diseases, 3) abstinence due to a woman lactating her youngest child. In many tribal groups the sperm was perceived as polluting the mother's milk, and thus poisoning the baby. 4) voluntary abstinence for the purpose of preventing a birth.

f. Voluntary factors affecting the exposure to conception or to the fulfilment of a pregnancy to a live birth—these are mainly the methods under family planning programmes emphasized in many developing countries. These include, first, contraceptive methods, namely, the mechanical (condom, diaphragm), the chemical (the oral pill or injections of same hormonal content), the intrauterine like IUD or the coil, and rhythm and coitus interruptus. The two last are not new to any society, though the rhythm method has shown only very little efficiency as many of the East African tribes had a wrong perception of the period of high risk of conception in the woman's cycle.[5]

Coitus interruptus seems to have been used to a large extent both in premarital sexual relations and in sexual relations during lactation. Another method is sterilization, which is deliberately induced sterility for women or men, usually in the older age groups, who already have the number of children they want. This is not legal in Kenya and is not a method used in many countries. However in the Indian programme, this was an important element of family planning and in fact some Indian States have tried to bring in compulsory sterilization. A third method to postpone or to hinder births is induced abortions. These are not legally permitted in Kenya, and only a few developing countries, in which illegal abortions have been a serious medical problem because of many side-effects from unskilled handling, have expanded the access to abortion due to a broad definition of socio-medical reasons, e.g. Uruguay, Costa Rica and Chile. In Europe and the USA, however, legal and free abortions have been introduced in several countries, and recently these programmes have been promoted by the women's organizations, wishing to establish the right of a woman to decide for herself how many births she wants.

Description of fertility level and trends in East Africa compared with other parts of the world

The fertility of East Africa is relatively high compared to other areas of the world. It is however not higher than that of most African countries. The trend in fertility shows that it has been increasing in the past decade. In Kenya in 1962 the crude birth rate was around 48—50 per thousand (the total fertility rate being 6.6 to 7.0), and in 1969 it had increased to a rate of 50 per thousand with a total fertility rate of 7.6. In the Demographic Baseline survey in 1973,

[5] Ibid. p. 16. The majority believed that the best chances for conception were just before or just after menstruation.

the total fertility was estimated to be 7.8, thus showing a further increase.[6] This trend is similar to that of other African countries and may be explained partly by an actual increase in fertility, and partly by a more complete coverage of data collection, therefore improving the validity of the data.

Table 30. *Crude birth rate and total fertility rate for selected countries in Africa.*

Country	Year	CBR per thousand	Total Fertility
Kenya	1962	48	6.6—7.1
Kenya	1969	50	7.6
Tanzania	1967	47	6.6*
Uganda	1969	44	5.4
Ethiopia	1970—75	45.1	5.8
Central African Republic	1970—75	46.6	6.0
Benin	1970—75	50.3	6.6
Senegal	1970—75	45.9	6.0
Gabon	1970—75	32.9	4.0
Nigeria	1970—75	49.7	6.6
Ghana	1970—75	46.8	6.4
Sudan	1970—75	48.5	6.8
United Arab Republic	1970—75	43.7	6.0

* On the basis of current fertility estimated to be 7.8 and on the basis of retrospective survey 5.3. Estimated to be most likely 6.6.

Source: S. H. Ominde: *The Population of Kenya, Tanzania and Uganda.* Nairobi 1975, pp. 11—39; B. Egero & R. Henin; op.cit. p. 201; *E. C. A. Demographic Handbook for Africa.* Addis Ababa 1975, pp. 66—68.

Table 30 shows the similarities in the fertility rates between the various African countries.

Fertility is one of the indicators used to distinguish the "developing" and the "more-developed" countries, as the fertility differentials are quite distinct between these two types of regions. Africa as a continent continues to have the highest fertility level, although several countries in the Latin American and South Asian continents have equally high levels of fertility (see Table 31).

The fertility in Europe and the other areas where it is now low, had previously been at a high level, although it was always lower than the level of fertility found at present in the high fertility areas. The CBR in Europe was around 30—35 per thousand and fluctuating. However, in France and Northern Europe it began declining in the late 19th century. In the beginning of the 20th century, the fertility continued dropping until 1933 during the economic depression, when it had reached a level of 15 per thousand. After the second World War (in 1946—47) the fertility increased in the so-called "baby boom" in all the countries, but dropped again to a low level in the fifties and sixties. Late in the sixties however, the fertility dropped still further due to the introduction of the oral pill for contraception, which seems to be more efficient than the other contraceptive methods to fulfill the desire for fewer children.

[6] *Demographic Baseline Survey Report 1973*, Central Bureau of Statistics. July 1975, Nbi., p. 24.

Table 31. *Crude birth rate per thousand and total fertility for continents of the world, 1965—70.*

Area	CBR per thousand	Total fertility*
Developing regions	41	5.4
More-developed regions	19	2.6
Africa	47	6.2
Western Africa	49	6.4
Eastern Africa	47	6.2
Middle Africa	45	5.8
Northern Africa	47	6.4
Southern Africa	41	5.4
Asia	32	4.0
Mainland region	33	4.2
Japan	18	2.0
Other East Asian countries	35	5.0
South Asia	44	6.0
Europe (excl. USSR)	18	2.6
Latin America	38	5.4
North America	19	2.8
Oceania	24	3.4
USSR	18	2.4

* Total fertility is defined as the average number of children a woman would have, if she experiences the set of current age-specific fertility rates at each age-group as she passes through her childbearing ages.

Source: UN. Determinants and consequences of population trends. N.Y. 1974, p. 64 and calculations.

In Southern and Eastern Europe as well as in the USA and Australia, fertility also declined in a similar manner from a high level of around 35—40 per thousand. The trend was faster, but showed the same deviations as described above. In Japan the fertility rate declined after the influx of the population from the previously occupied countries in the late 1940s. During the first part of the period the fertility increased, but the Abortion Law in 1948 gave way to a rapid fertility decline.

The demographic transition describes the trends in mortality and fertility decline as experienced in the developed countries. In graph 1 under "Historical Trends in the World Population", the decline in mortality and fertility experienced by Denmark is provided. This trend gave the basis for the "Transition Model", which is shown in graph 16, and is compared with the smoothened model for the developing countries, being very similar to the East African pattern.

The fertility decline in Europe as described, actually meant that the completed family size, or the total number of children born per woman in her generation throughout her reproductive ages, decreased from around 6 to around 2—3. The explanations of this trend and social change are many, as

Graph 16. *Development in crude birth rate and crude death rate. "The Model of the Demographic Transition", and the pattern from developing countries (Ceylon).*

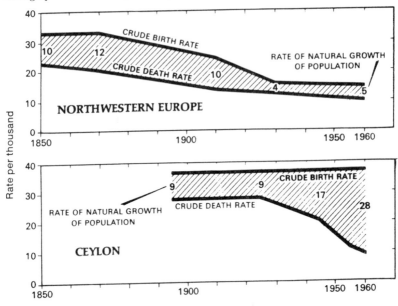

Source: G. Myrdal: *Asian Drama.* Mass. 1968. Vol. 2, p. 1400.

many variables changed in this period. The main variables associated with the decline were:

1. A very high decrease in fertility in older age groups, i.e. an earlier termination of reproduction.

2. The proportion of women who married was increasing, while the age at marriage declined, therefore the fertility decline had to be attributed to the limitation of the family size within marriage.

3. A concentration of fertility in the ages between 20—30 years.

4. A decline in fertility first among white collar workers in towns, with a certain level of education and medium income. The decline in fertility in these age groups was related to increased costs of children due to an urban way of life, fixed salaries, costs of schooling, no economic benefits from children, poor housing, the need for women's employment outside the home.

5. The decline in fertility spread to other groups in the urban areas, as these also experienced higher costs of having many children. The migration from rural areas resulted in more and more people living under urban economic conditions.

The fertility decline in Europe can thus be ascribed to changes in the social and economic conditions, and not to any biological factors, as a higher proportion of women who actually experience child-bearing. The change in family size resulted from a strong economic desire among both husband and wife for fewer children and the decline was managed by the adoption of simple contraceptive techniques such as abstinence, rhythm and coitus interruptus. There was no government policy to reduce the number of births. On the contrary, the policy in most of the European countries until recently was towards favouring high fertility and high population growth (especially in France).

The later decline in fertility in Japan and China and a few other small nations such as Puerto Rico, Mauritius, Singapore and Taiwan cannot be explained by the same variables. In all these countries there seems to have been a greater need for reducing family size and thus a motivation for trying the available methods to limit the number of births. But also in these countries government policy has very strongly favoured small families. However, in other areas where government policy strongly favours small families, success has been more limited due to the lack of the perceived need for these services among the population (e.g. in India and many parts of Africa).

Fertility differentials and explanations of these in Africa

Information on the differential pattern of fertility in Africa is very limited. There is only information on regional variations and on the large urban areas, but none on the general rural-urban differences or on the different status groups.

The regional differences in Africa seem to reflect mainly different biological capacities to reproduce, such as differential morbidity and nutritional status, which have an impact on fecundity. But there are also major differences among the tribes in the norms regulating fertility behaviour.

Norms exist in all societies to control fertility as well as sexual behaviour. No society uses the fecundity or capacity to reproduce to the fullest, and there are variations among the tribes in East Africa as to the restrictions laid on fertility. Table 32 shows fertility in Kenya. The table shows high fertility in Central, Western and in parts of Eastern Province, and low fertility in Nairobi, in the Coast Province and among the pastoral people in North Eastern and the Rift Valley Provinces. The highest fertility is found among the permanently settled agricultural population in the most densely populated areas.

In most African countries pastoral people have a lower level of fertility than settled agriculturalists. This lower level of fertility may be ascribed to health conditions as well as to voluntary control of births. The conditions of life for pastoral people are rough, and the poor health of mothers and infants may result in a higher frequency of miscarriages, stillbirths and early infant mortality than among settled agriculturalists. But many explanations for specific areas have been put foward, e.g. the narrow pelvic region of Masai women is considered an obstacle to giving birth. Venereal disease is widespread and less often cured, thus resulting in a higher frequency of sterility among both men and women.

Table 32. *Total fertility estimated for provinces and districts in Kenya, 1969 (unadjusted).*

Area	Total fertility rate	Area	Total fertility rate
Kenya	7.6	*Nyanza Province:*	7.9
Nairobi E. P. D.	5.5	Kisii	7.3
		Kisumu	5.7
Central Province:	8.7	Siaya	6.0
Kiambu	8.1	South Nyanza	5.7
Kirinyaga	6.9		
Murang'a	8.6	*Rift Valley Province:*	6.6
Nyandarua	9.7	Baringo	4.6
Nyeri	8.0	Elgeyo-Marakwet	5.4
		Kajiado	8.5
Coast Province:	5.6	Kericho	6.0
Kilifi	4.7	Laikipia	6.7
Kwale	4.8	Nakuru	6.8
Lamu	3.5	Nandi	6.6
Mombasa	4.2	Narok	5.6
Taita	5.4	Samburu	4.9
Tana River	4.2	Trans Nzoia	
		Turkana	3.3
Eastern Province:	7.6	Uasin Gishu	5.9
Embu	7.7	West Pokot	3.4
Isiolo	3.7		
Kitui	8.8	*Western Province:*	8.6
Machakos	7.6	Bungoma	8.1
Marsabit	5.8	Busia	6.5
Meru	6.8	Kakamega	8.1
North Eastern Province:	6.6		
Carissa	8.0		
Mandera	4.2		
Wajir	4.3		

* Unadjusted data differ from the adjusted data, e.g. the adjusted total fertility for Kenya is 7.0. The unadjusted data may also reveal several errors, e.g. the very high fertility of Kajiado District may reflect an immigration of other populations to the District, but also a poor quality of data (i.e. errors in the information). In 1962 the total fertility in Kajiado District was estimated to be 1.7 (S. H. Ominde).

Source: S. H. Ominde: *The Population of Kenya, Tanzania and Uganda.* Nairobi, 1975, p. 33.

The other group of explanations is related to voluntary birth control. Examples of advanced techniques for limiting births in periods of drought are revealed for the Bedouin of Sahara. In addition, in some societies in tropical Africa, children and calves compete for the same milk and norms exist to have children at least at 2 yearly intervals, which may lead to the limitation in the number of births. R. Henin has shown increasing fertility for pastoral people settled in an irrigation scheme in the Sudan. Thus the improved economic basis had a positive impact on fertility, increasing the number of children per woman, and lowering the level of childlessness among women over 30 years.[7]

[7] R. Henin: The level and trend of fertility in the Sudan. In *S. H. Ominde & C. N. Ejiogu* (eds): *Population Growth and Economic Development in Africa.* London 1972, p. 81—82.

The differential pattern of pastoralists *versus* settled agriculturalists shows variations with a combination of factors affecting the fertility level, and it is not possible to ascribe any explanations to only a few of the factors.

In 1962 in Kenya the urban areas could be separated from rural areas for the African population. This showed an average of 3.5 live births to African women 45—49 years old in urban areas, compared with an average of 6.0 births per every rural woman.

In 1969 the total fertility for Nairobi and Mombasa was 4.6 and 4.1, and it was characterised by a concentration of birth-giving in the younger ages up to 35 years.[8] This seems to indicate that this lower fertility is partly due to voluntary family planning. The same trends of rural-urban differentials are revealed for Tanzania, with a total fertility of 4.4 for urban women and 6.7 for rural women (1967). But this pattern of urban-rural differences is found in nearly all African and other developing countries, as well as in the industrial countries. The differences between rural and urban fertility seem to reflect some of the same traits everywhere, that the costs of children among middle-class families in urban areas are increasing rapidly.

In Tanzania 1967, the differential fertility by educational and socio-economic groups is also provided. Women's education seems to be an important factor for reducing the level of fertility. The total fertility of women with over 9 years of education was 2.0, while for those with 5—8 years of education, it was 5.0 and for women without any education it was 5.0—5.5.[9] The same differences are found for the countries of West Africa.

The fertility differentials by socio-economic status have been estimated in Tanzania, revealing that there was practically no difference for the country as a whole, but socio-economic differences appeared when the urban and rural areas were analysed separately (see table 33). This table also reveals why the differences did not show up on a country-wide scale, since the high status groups in the rural areas have a higher level of fertility than the lower status

Table 33. *Mean number of live-births after the reproductive period for women of different socio-economic groups, and distributed according to rural-urban areas in Tanzania, 1967.*

	Tanzania	Urban	Rural
Professionals, technical, administrative executives	4.8	3.7	5.2
White collar	4.4	3.9	4.7
Blue collar	4.0	3.2	4.5
Farmers, own-account workers or family workers	5.3	—	—
Agricultural labourers	4.6	—	—
No occupation	4.9	—	—

* The socio-economic groups are estimated on the basis of residence and occupation of the head of household.

Source: B. Egero & R. Henin: op.cit., p. 199.

[8] S. H. Ominde: *The Population of Kenya, Tanzania and Uganda*, Nairobi 1975, pp. 34—35.
[9] B. Egero & R. Henin: op.cit., p. 199.

groups. This may be due to better health and better nutrition, and no restrictions on fertility beyond those of other rural groups. In urban areas, on the other hand, the pattern is not clear, but the white collar middle groups appear to have the highest fertility. The differences however are so small that conclusions drawn from this material can only be tentative. For example, some of the differentials may be explained by the problems of classifying socio-economic groups. The main difference in the fertility levels then is between urban and rural areas, independent of the status groups.

In West and Central Africa, there are major differences in fertility between regions and tribes even though they may be close to each other. These fertility differentials may be ascribed to differences in the frequency of venereal disease. In the comparison of fertility however, other factors also vary and may distort the comparisons. An example from Nzakara in the Central African Republic shows that women over 45 years had an average of only 2 children, and 40 percent had never given birth to a child. Of all the pregnancies that occurred, 35 percent were never carried through to a live birth. In this area three-quarters of the women were found to suffer from gynecological infections, and serological syphilis seemed to be one of the major causes of the high rate of miscarriage since more than half the women (54 %) had syphilis. Two neighbouring areas were studied, one showing a serological syphilis rate of 35 %, and an average number of 3.3 children per woman and the other with a rate of syphilis of 16 % and an average of 4.6 children per woman. In all these areas the wanted number of children was higher than 5. One of the problems in the comparison is that the low fertility areas also show a much higher rate of divorce than the high fertility areas, thus many other social factors may also vary.[10]

In relation to sub-fertility, which is a problem in many sub-regions of Africa, it may be relevant also to estimate the proportion of miscarriages, stillbirths and the number of surviving children. Table 34 provides an estimate of these factors for the urban and rural sample areas in Nigeria.

Table 34. *Pregnancy outcome paradigm, rural Nigeria and metropolitan Lagos (1964).*

	Estimated no. of pregnancies	Estimated pregnancy wastage	Average no. of live-births	Child mortality (0—15)	Average child death	Average surviving children	Surviving children as % of pregnan...
Rural	6.4	12 %	5.6	370	2.1	3.5	55 %
Lagos	7.9	7 %	7.3	220	1.6	5.7	72 %

Source: R. W. Morgan and P. O. Ohadike: Fertility levels and Fertility Change. In eds. J. C. Caldw... al.: *Population Growth and Socio-economic Change in West Africa.* 1975, p. 199.

The table reveals that the estimated number of pregnancies in Lagos is a little higher than in the rural sample. However, the difference between the two areas becomes much larger in the number of children surviving to 15 years of age. Foetal and child mortality is much higher for the rural sample.

[10] B. Kwaku Adadevoh: *Sub-fertility and Infertility in Africa.* Ibadan 1974, p. 72—73.

Measures of fertility

One aspect of fertility makes it more difficult to measure than mortality. Whereas everyone in a population dies, and all persons die only once, not all women give birth, and many give birth several times, sometimes even to 2—3 children in one delivery. Due to this pattern, we have to work with only rates and not with life-tables in the measurement of fertility.

However, this does not imply that generation measures are not used. The best measures are in fact related to a generation or cohort of women, because births may be delayed for 1—2 years without changing the total family size. And in the cases where the delay is caused by external factors such as famines or economic depressions affecting a whole society, the measures based on calendar years may show great variations, without any change having occurred in the completed family size.

The childbearing ages are much more vague than the age limit for mortality and are both a function of biological development and of socio-cultural norms. Biologically we know that the lower limit of fecundity decreases from 15 years to around 12—13 years for girls of very good nutritional status. But as the norms and behaviour relating to age at marriage and age at first birth are not changing, it is not relevant to consider the ages below 15 years. Most groups actually do not begin reproduction before 18 years due to social norms in the society. Also the upper limit of reproduction seems to be flexible, and is a result both of biological capacity, i.e. improved health, and social norms. Fecundity may last up to 50—55 years, but most societies have norms against a woman giving birth after her oldest child has had children, i.e. against having children and grandchildren of the same ages. However, in the Tanzanian census contrary norms were reported for major areas; namely that it gave high status to women, if they were still considered fecund. In the Tanzanian Census, this gave an unusually high response of births during the previous 12 months even for women aged 65 years. This pattern reflects partly the above-mentioned norms and partly the perception of grandchildren as one's own children if the grandmother is taking care of them, as well as the perception of the 12 months as much longer, and finally it can be explained partly by an overestimation of the women's ages. The male reproductive period or ages of reproductive capacity are not considered important in demography, it is assumed to be longer than that of women, starting around the same age, but continuing to higher ages. However, it is not considered a limiting factor for fertility.

Crude birth rate (CBR)

This is one of the most frequently used indices of fertility and indicates the number of births per 1000 of the total population at risk in a year. It is thus comparable to the crude death rate.

$$\text{CBR} = \frac{\text{Total births in 1 year in an area}}{\text{mid-year population men + women all ages}} \cdot 1000$$

113

The mid-year population should estimate the "population at risk" as in the case of the crude death rate, but since everyone is not under the risk of giving birth, we may get distortions and often have to use another measure. For example, if a population has a skewed age distribution with many women in the reproductive ages, this alone may lead to a high CBR, even though the number of births per woman may not be high. In Kenya this would imply that we could expect a low CBR in Nairobi, because of the low proportion of adult women in Nairobi, in relation to other areas in the country.

The CBR usually varies between a minimum of 13 per thousand and a maximum of 65 per thousand. The average in low fertility areas is 16—25 per thousand, and in high fertility areas 35—40‰. In 1969, Kenya had an estimated CBR of 50 per thousand.

General fertility rate

Due to the limitations of the CBR, we often need a kind of standardization for the proportion of women of reproductive age. Instead of the standardization used for mortality, we use the measure General Fertility Rate, which provides the number of births per 1000 women in the reproductive ages in a year.

$$\text{General Fertility Rate} = \frac{\text{no. of births in 1 year in an area}}{\text{mid-year population of women 15–49 years in the area}} \cdot 1000$$

This improvement over the CBR gives a much better basis for comparison of fertility. The measure varies between a minimum of 70 per thousand to a maximum of 300 per thousand. Roughly it is approximately 4 times more than the CBR, as women in the reproductive ages usually make up approximately one-fourth of the total population. The average in low fertility areas is 100—200‰ and in high fertility areas 200—275‰. In Kenya in 1969 it was estimated to be 275 per thousand.

Age-specific fertility rate (ASFR) refers to the number of births in 1 or 5 year age groups for the mid-year population of women in the same age-groups, for women between 15—49.

$$_5f_{20} = \frac{_5B_{20}}{_5F_{20}} = \frac{\text{no. of births for women 20—24 years}}{\text{mid-year population of women 20—24 years}}$$

Similar to the age-specific death rate, this measure provides information on the age-pattern of fertility (graph 17).

Graph 17. *Age-specific fertility rates for Kenya 1969, Tanzania 1967 and Uganda 1969.*

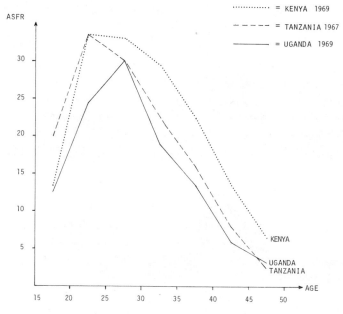

Source: S. H. Ominde: *The Population of Kenya, Tanzania and Uganda.* Nbi. 1975, pp. 19, 26, 31.

The graph shows that the high fertility is in the 20—24 and 25—29 year age groups. The lower fertility in the previous ages is related to the age of marriage, which is typically around 17—18 years of age. The declining fertility by age can be explained partly by declining fecundity with increasing age. Minor variations, especially regarding the age groups which have the highest fertility, may be explained by the quality of the data, especially the age data for the women.

The pattern of fertility in East Africa is fairly similar to that of the other countries of tropical Africa, but the fertility curves of the Arab, Asian and European countries vary both in level and shape, due to different social norms about age at marriage and limitations of fertility especially in the older ages. In countries with low fertility, fertility has been reduced in the higher age groups, and is mainly restricted to only a few years of the reproductive period, namely between 20—34 years. Examples from the different continents reveal this difference in graph 18.

Graph 18. *Pattern of age-specific fertility for selected countries in different continents and with different level and pattern of fertility.*

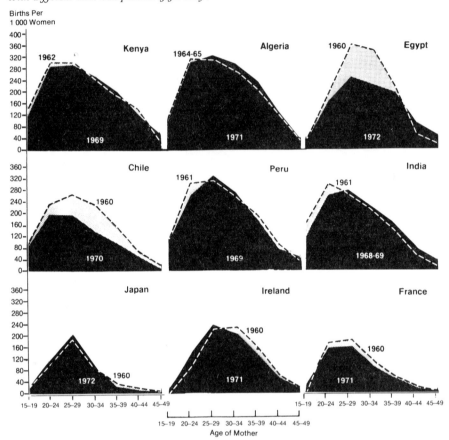

Source: R. T. Ravenhold & J. C. Chao: *World Fertility Patterns.* International Statistical Programme Center. U. S. Bureau of the Census. N.Y. 1974.

The general pattern in Europe during the demographic transition was the tendency for a high level of fertility to be associated with a high and broad peak in the curve, while low fertility showed a very narrow peak. However, while this pattern seems to hold for some areas during declining fertility, in other areas—as for example, in Egypt—the decline shows a totally different age pattern. Also, the present European pattern is not uniform and shows major variations.

The age-specific fertility rate is calculated on a calendar basis, often directly by data on the number of births per woman over 12 years of age in the 12 months preceding the census.

However, it may also be estimated by the number of births to a woman during her different age periods, based on her retrospective fertility experience.

This provides the age-specific fertility for 20—24 year old women, both for those women in this age group at the time of the census, as well as for those women who were 20—24 years old back in time, e.g. in 1940. In areas where fertility does not show any major changes, these may not be significantly different.

The problems of the "current fertility" registration in the 12 months preceding the census, are usually related to: 1) The reference period. It may be difficult both to avoid births occurring before this period, and to include all the births within the 12 months. 2) problems of exact age of women and 3) the registration of children who have died shortly after delivery. An adjustment of the data is therefore necessary, and it may be provided by using the retrospective data on parity. The retrospective data available in the East African censuses includes the total number of live births per woman (parity) for all women, and the age of the living children. The data for women under 35 years seems to be more reliable, as older women tend to omit births occurring a long time ago, especially if the child has died.

Total fertility rate (TFR) is a measure showing the average number of children a woman would have, if she experienced the set of current age-specific fertility rates at each age group as she passed through her childbearing ages.

This measure is a hypothetical generation measure, for women 15—50 years just like the life table, i.e. using the current (calendar) age specific fertility rates, and finding the total for a generation. It is, thus, not a true generation measure based on the experiences of actual generation. However, if fertility is constant this measure may well be used for a generation, and be comparable to the "completed family size". If the fertility is fluctuating as it may in relation to a famine or an economic boom, the total fertility rate will fluctuate also, and thus will not be valid for a generation which may have the same completed

Table 35. *Calculation of the total fertility rate in Kenya 1969.*

Age	Age specific fertility rate
15—19	0.1320
20—24	0.3305
25—29	0.3373
30—34	0.2942
35—39	0.2232
40—44	0.1351
45—49	0.0677
Total	1.5200

$$\text{TFR} = 5 \cdot \sum_{x=15}^{50} {}_5f_x$$

Total fertility rate = $5 \cdot 1.52 = 7.6$

Source: S. H. Ominde: *The Population of Kenya, Tanzania and Uganda.* Nbi. 1975, p. 31.

family size, even though the yearly fertility rates are fluctuating.

The total fertility rate is calculated by adding all the age-specific fertility rates for the different age groups, i.e. 15—19, 20—24, 25—29 etc, and multiplying by 5, because they are covering 5-year intervals. If we have the age-specific fertility rates for 1-year intervals, the total fertility rate would simply be the sum of these rates. The calculation of the total fertility rate for Kenya 1969 on the basis of the 5-year age-specific fertility rate is provided in table 35.

The total fertility rate gives an indication of the total number of children born per woman. This ranges between an average of 2—3 in low fertility countries, and an average of 6—9 in high fertility countries (see variations in Kenya, table 32).

Completed family size is a generation measure. This indicates for a woman at the end of her reproductive period, the total number of live births she reports to have had. A question on the number of live births a woman has had is asked in all East African censuses to all woman above 12 years of age. The average number of births per woman in the different age-groups (called parity) is thus revealed, but only the parity for women over 50 years measures the completed family size. Table 36 provides the parity for Kenya 1962 and 1969, and Tanzania 1967.

Table 36. *Parity or average number of live-births per woman in different age groups in Kenya 1962 and 1969 and Tanzania 1967.*

Age-groups	Kenya 1962	Kenya 1969	Tanzania 1967
15—19	0.36	0.35	0.52
20—24	1.65	1.88	1.97
25—29	3.01	3.65	3.18
30—34	4.20	5.11	4.16
35—39	5.07	6.00	4.79
40—44	5.61	6.44	5.04
45—49	5.90	6.69	5.22
50—54	5.62	6.40	*
55—59	5.94		*
60—64	5.14		*
65—69	5.21	5.78	*
70—74	4.76		*
75+	3.99		*

* No information available.

Source: S. H. Ominde: Demography and Ethnic Groups. In: Vogel et al: *Health & Disease in Kenya.* Nairobi 1974, p. 40. *Kenya Population Census 1962,* vol. III, p. 65, *Population of Tanzania,* p. 276.

This table reveals the increasing number of children through the reproductive ages, as well as the average number in each age-group. However, it also shows a declining number of live-births reported for women over the reproductive period in the Kenyan censuses. This could be a result of increasing fertility in the population. However it is more likely to be the result of "recall lapse" especially in those cases where the children have died during early childhood. These cases are often omitted, especially when a long time period has elapsed between birth and registration. Because of this "recall lapse" the evidence given by women 20—34 years old is considered the most reliable. The level of the measure follows the total fertility rate closely.

Gross reproduction rate

We usually measure births in relation to the female population, therefore the reproduction of the female population is also in focus. The Gross Reproduction Rate (GRR) measures the total number of female births a woman would have, if she experienced the current age-specific fertility and sex-ratio of children, at each age group as she passed through her reproductive period. It is assumed that all women survive to 50 years of age. The measure is comparable to the total fertility rate, and is calculated in the same way, taking into account only the female births. One therefore has to multiply the proportion of female births by the total number of births.

The calculation is:

$$GRR = \Sigma \ ASFR^f = TFR \cdot \frac{\text{female births}}{\text{male + female births}}$$

If the measure equals 1 the female population will not increase but remain stable. This means that if no deaths occur in the female population before the age of 50, the population will neither grow nor decline. However, the assumptions about mortality are unrealistic, and it is only a hypothetical generation, therefore some stability in the fertility must be reached, i.e. 30 years before the measure has any kind of predictive value for the growth or decline of the female population.

The measure varies between a little less than 1 and 1.5 in the low fertility countries, and an average of 3 to 4.5 in the high fertility areas. Note that a little less than half the births are female births, therefore GRR is approximately half the total fertility rate.

Net reproduction rate

A more realistic assumption for the prediction of reproduction of the female population is the Net Reproduction Rate (NRR). In this measure the average number of female births is calculated as under the GRR, but here under the assumptions about mortality conditions as in a life-table at the time of the calculation.

If this measure is 1 the female population can exactly reproduce itself—but on a generation basis will neither increase nor decline. Usually the measure is over 1 showing increasing population, however, in a few countries, (Denmark, Sweden, Hungary, Japan) the measure is now under 1, indicating a decline in the population in the long run, if the trend continues.

Child-woman ratio

The child-woman ratio indicates the number of children between 0 and 5 years per 100 women in the reproductive ages. This indirect measure of fertility which is calculated on the basis of a census, gives an indication of the level of general fertility during the previous 5 years. But mostly, the ratio is used as the basis for estimations of other fertility measures.

$$\text{child-woman ratio} = \frac{\text{no. of children in a census 0—4 years}}{\text{no. of women in a census 15—49 years}} \cdot 100$$

Proportion of childless women

Hitherto, the measures of fertility have been covering all women in the reproductive ages. However, the proportion of childless women in different age-groups indicates the distribution of birthgiving within the female population. This is important for the comparison of different low fertility areas, as low fertility may either be the result of few children per family, but with many women giving birth, or it may be the result of few women giving birth and many births per fertile woman. The first pattern is predominant in low fertility countries of the West, while the latter characterizes low fertility in many rural areas of Africa.

Table 37. *Percentage of childless women in selected areas of Cameroon.*

Age-group	Central, South & East 1962—64	North 1962—64	Bamilike country 1965	NW & SW 1964	Divorced women Cameroon
15—19	72	73	64	56	76
20—24	29	27	18	10	39
25—29	28	20	11	7	40
30—34	30	19	14	6	37
35—39	33	17	14	8	39
40—44	29	13	19	7	45
45—49	29	11	17	7	42

Source: B. K. Adadevoh: *Sub-fertility and Infertility in Africa*, pp. 66—67.

Table 37 shows how childlessness varies in the different ages and by regions. It is important to note, that high childlessness among women under 30 years may just reflect those who have not yet delivered their first child, and they may still experience a birth. Therefore the percentage of childless women drops during the ages 15—35. Over the age of 35 years, the chances of birthgiving, if no previous birth has occurred, are minimal, and the percentage childless at this age is an indicator of the frequency of total infertility in the area. An average of between 4 and 7% infertility seems to be normal in a healthy population. An increase in childlessness above this level indicates poorer health and lower capability of giving birth.

For a comparison, the proportion of childless women is provided for the 1967 Tanzanian Census (by regions), for 1962 Kenyan Census, and for 2 samples from a survey within Machakos District 1973.

Table 38. *Proportion of childless women in 5-year age-groups for regions of Tanzania 1967, Kenya 1962 Census and the sample surveys in Machakos District, 1973.*

Age-group	TANZANIA (mainland)				KENYA		
	Urban	Arusha	Coast	Total 1967	Census 1962	Machakos Distr. sample A	sample B
15—19	67.2	72.9	55.4	65.6	34.1	86.1	86.0
20—24	30.0	25.3	21.5	20.5	11.7	23.0	33.6
25—29	20.6	13.6	16.8	12.1	7.2	2.6	12.6
30—34	19.4	10.3	15.8	10.9	5.9	3.8	7.0
35—39	19.2	8.6	16.4	10.3	4.8	2.9	3.3
40—44	20.8	10.5	17.3	11.3	4.8	1.8	6.4
45—49	21.5	10.1	16.2	10.9	4.9	2.4	3.8

Source: B. Egero & R. Henin: op.cit., p. 191, P. G. Blok: *Report on the Demographic Studies of the Joint Project Machakos.* Nbi. 1975, p. 55—56 and *Kenya Population Census 1962.*

This table shows that the incidence of childlessness is much higher among women in Tanzania than in Kenya. This may be one of the explanations for the fertility differentials in the two countries. The regional pattern shows that childlessness is especially high in the urban population and in the Coast Region. In Uganda, fertility differentials showed a similar pattern of variations, with low fertility areas in Teso and Bunyore.[11] But even with the low level of infertility in Kenya, it is estimated that 20% of couples or approx. 300,000 women are affected by infertility problems.[12]

Sources of information and the quality of data

In East Africa the registration of births is not complete. In all the East African countries efforts to introduce registration have resulted only in a low proportion of registered births, the highest being around 70% in the major cities. This results in a high dependency on population censuses and surveys for the fertility data, as the data is seldom valid or directly applicable.

In the Kenyan Census 1969 the following information was collected:
1. Age-distribution in order to calculate the child-woman ratio.
2. A question was posed to all women above 12 years on the total number of

[11] S. H. Ominde: *The Population of Kenya, Tanzania and Uganda.* Nbi. 1975, p. 26.
[12] Y. Eraj: *Family Planning.* Seminar on Population Growth and Economic Development, 1969, Nbi.

live-born children they had had. This provided the parity for each age-group of women and the average completed family size (retrospective data).

3.   The date of birth of the last-born child. This gave the basis for estimating the general fertility rate, CBR and age-specific fertility for the previous year (calendar-based data).

In Tanzania the last question was replaced by a question on the number of births in the previous 12-month period. This however created problems of defining the boundary for the time period, i.e. to ensure that all the births within the 12-month period were recorded, and that none outside the period were reported. Among older women especially, many births which occurred earlier than 1 year before the census were recorded within the reference period.

A survey carried out by the Central Bureau of Statistics in Kenya in 1973 supplemented the census information on births. The sex of the child and whether he/she was alive or dead at the time of the survey was checked carefully for all births to women over 12 years. Furthermore, each birth interval over 2 years was probed in order to identify children who had died or left the household.

The resulting pattern of fertility showed only very little difference from the census data. The main difference was that the peak of fertility was in the 20—24 age-group, while in the census the peak was in the 25—29 age group.

None of the methods of fertility estimation provides totally reliable data. There are problems of age-misreportings, especially if the age is not known and the interviewers tend to estimate the age from the number of children a woman has. Moreover the problem of recall lapse may be quite high, especially if the infant mortality is high, as it is usually children who have died who are not reported. An improvement of the age-data, registration of fertility or the expansion of hospital deliveries would improve the basis for the fertility estimations.

Implications of different levels of fertility

Implications for the age structure

The impact of fertility on the age structure can be shown by the set of age-structures chosen to illustrate the process of declining fertility as in the demographic transition.

a.   The graph for Mexico 1965 shows a result of a stable high level of fertility, which is very similar to that in East Africa. Mortality has declined, but this is not revealed in the pyramid. The CBR is approximately 45 per thousand.

b.   In the age structure for Singapore 1965, the fertility has declined a little, but not drastically. The CBR is 31 per thousand, and mortality is low.

c.   The population pyramid for Japan 1965 shows the effect of a rapid decline in the fertility, following the Eugenic law in 1948. This is typical for a population in the early phase of rapidly declining fertility. The CBR has dropped to 18.6 per thousand.

122

Graph 19. *Age-structures of selected countries with different levels of fertility (1965).*

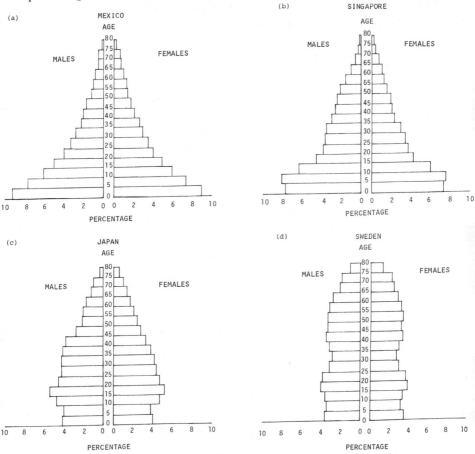

Source: UN. Determinants and Consequences of Population Trends. N.Y. 1974, p. 267.

d.   The age structure for Sweden shows a more stable situation with low fertility, though the fertility is still declining. The fertility was very low in the 1930s (see the age-groups 25—35 years), but increased a little after 1945. Fertility has been declining since the 1950s, and in 1965 it was 16 per thousand.

It may be concluded, that fertility has a very high impact on the age structure of the population. Small bulges and gaps in the structure may be due to the fertility trend but these have to be analysed in relation to the specific historical conditions, as they may well stem from wars or migrations.

Implications for the health of women and children

Medical surveys show that many births and especially many frequent births create a strain on the woman's health. This strain is increased if the nutritional conditions and general health are not very good. This is likely to result in greater risk for the mother and also much more frequent incidences of miscarriages and stillbirths.

In relation to the health of the children and infants, it is quite clear that the better the health conditions for the mother and the longer the lactation period, the greater are the chances of survival for the child. The crucial factor in this respect, seems to be the interval between births, as a new pregnancy during the lactation period tends to dry up the milk. Actually, it seems likely that the earlier the weaning of the child, the higher its mortality risk. This may be the case if the change of diet is to cereals, though it may not be the case for pastoral people, among whom the main content of the diet for children is milk.

Intervals of 2 years between pregnancies protect the health of the children, and the social norms of all East African tribes prescribe intervals of at least that length. Some groups however have norms for longer intervals of 3—4 years (i.e. the Gusii), and some of the Meru tribes appeared to have a sexual taboo between spouses until the child has lost its first milk teeth (i.e. up to 4—6 years)[13] but this is an exception.

The mother's health condition also appears to have a clear impact on the health of the children. This may be one of the reasons for higher infant mortality among children from parities of higher numbers, than among those of lower number. A study in Burundi and Zambia, revealed a child mortality for children from parity 1 and 3 of 23% and 12% respectively. While the child mortality for children from higher parity, i.e. born as number 4, 5 etc., was 32.5% and 26% respectively.[14]

Social implications of high versus low fertility

The African families traditionally emphasized and needed a large family for reproduction of the family under conditions of high mortality. The children did not only ensure continuity, but also provided highly needed family labour for the household and agriculture, as well as constituting the only form of old-age security.

Under these conditions the childless woman was considered a social deviant, the chances of divorce or that the husband might take another wife in the household were very high—since reproduction had to be ensured. Childlessness for a woman (irrespective of who is the sterile partner) was considered a reason for divorce, and traditionally in most of the East African tribes it gave the husband the right to return the wife to her father. Her only chances would then

---

[13] A. Molnos: *Cultural source material for population planning in East Africa.* Nbi. 1973, vol. 3, p. 61.

[14] H. E. Polak: *Problems of Malnutrition in East and Central Africa in Planning and Coordination in the Field of Child Welfare in East and Central Africa,* Nbi. August 1971.

be to become part of the family labour in her father's household, or be married into a polygynous household where she would also constitute a form of cheap labour. However, she never got the prestige attributed to a mother, and was considered an outcast or a "tree without leaves".

The emphasis on reproduction is still so high that in some African tribes (examples from Nigeria) the fiancee has to prove her fertility by getting pregnant before marrying, and the girls who do not get pregnant relatively soon are likely to take on several sexual partners and therefore have a probability of contracting venereal diseases, thus making it even more difficult to conceive.

Several groups or tribes in Kenya, e.g. the Akamba, provide a kind of "solution" to such a problem: thus the infertile wife may "marry" a young woman and the children of this young woman legally become the children and heirs of the infertile wife.

Infertility and subfertility is a serious problem for those women and couples who experience it. No modern medical assistance has been offered to overcome the problem, if any help was possible, and as this and not high fertility has been of concern for women in rural areas, the sudden interest in women's reproduction in order to limit it (birth control) has evoked reasonable suspicion of the programmes.

In a society where children have specific functions and obligations in the production and in the family development cycle, infertility is not only a problem for the women who experience childlessness, but also the household and agriculture will suffer from lack of labour, and both husband and wife will have no old age security. Children in rural East Africa provide an important part of the household labour like fetching water and firewood, herding cattle, assisting in the house, and working in agriculture.

Recent studies of the importance of children's contributions in rural households in Kenya reveal that the children still play an important role of providing labour in the families, even when they go to school. However, the total economic benefit of having many children has changed considerably, with the increased school enrollment, as the payment of school fees is one of the major cash burdens of rural families.

In some areas, the women respond to the changed economic conditions for large families, and to the declining child mortality by wanting smaller families,[15] but this varies a lot according to status and region. In areas where many factors increase the economic burden of many children, and where land is scarce, the women tend to want smaller families of around 4—5 children, for example in Kisii[16] and Kabete[17] in Kenya. The study of Kabete close to Nairobi, showed that the husbands did not want any family planning, and only the women stressed the importance of limiting their family size.

[15] Research project "The relationship between family size, division of labour within the family and family economy in rural areas of Kenya", by Mette Monsted, 1975.
[16] Mette Monsted: Conditions for a regional family planning policy. Working paper. Dept. of Sociology. Nbi. 1976 (Mimeo).
[17] A. Thairo: An Evaluation of the Use of Family Planning in Kabete. B. A. Dissertation. Dept. of Sociology. Nbi. 1976.

However, in areas where the economic costs of many children do not prove a constraint for the family, or are balanced to a certain extent by the need for their labour, the women still want or desire large families.

The issue about the importance of children in family labour and in providing the only possibility for expanding economic conditions for a poor family, is not only of relevance for areas of East Africa, but has also been raised and supported by some evidence from India. There it was found that among poor peasants and landless labourers, a large number of sons constituted the only chance for a family to improve its situation by increasing the number of hands to work, not only in agriculture on the peasants own farm, but also as income earners from a young age on other farms.[18]

Also at the clan or tribal level there has been a lot of emphasis on high fertility, as this has been necessary during periods of high mortality for the survival of the group. When land was sufficient, the number of people in the working ages determined the amount of land which could be cultivated, and for a clan or a tribe, it also determined the possibility of expanding land frontiers and protecting good and fertile land in the fight with other tribal groups, for example the fights between the Gusii and the surrounding tribal groups, especially the Luo.[19]

Supplementary reading

1. B. Egero & R. Henin (eds): *The Population of Tanzania.* An analysis of the 1967 Population Census. Census Vol. 6. Dar es Salaam 1973. Chapter 12, pp. 186—201 and pp. 246—252.

2. S. H. Ominde & C. N. Ejiogu (eds): *Population Growth and Economic Development in Africa.* London 1972.
   pp. 77—83 R. Henin: The level and Trend of Fertility in the Sudan.
   pp. 193—197: S. H. Ominde: Migration and Childbearing in Kenya.

3. Angela Molnos: *Cultural Source Materials for Population Planning in East Africa.* Nbi. 1973. Vol. 3: Beliefs and practices. pp. 7—24,

4. J. C. Caldwell and C. Okonjo (eds): *The Population of Tropical Africa.* London 1968, pp. 214—224, Romaniuk: Infertility in Tropical Africa.

5. *Kenya Population Census 1962.* Vol. III, African Population. Central Bureau of Statistics. Nbi. 1966. pp. 58—70.

6. *UN. Determinants and Consequences of Population Trends.* N.Y. 1974. Chapter 4, pp. 64—107.

7. G. Hawthorn: *The Sociology of Fertility.* London 1970, pp. 18—119.

---

[18] Mahmood Mamdani: *The Myth of Population Control.* N. Y. 1973.
[19] W. Ochieng: *A Pre-Colonial History of the Gusii of Western Kenya C. A. D. 1500—1914.* Nbi. 1974.

Chapter XI

Migration

Problems of definition

In contrast to mortality and fertility, which are both influenced by social and biological factors, migration is exclusively a social phenomenon. The change of residence is a result of decisions taken by those migrating in response to their economic and social conditions. As such the emphasis here will not be purely on the description of migration processes and its quantitative measurements, but more on the sociological aspects of migration and its implications for the country's overall social and economic development.

First of all, migration may conventionally be defined as a movement from one permanent residence to another. This implies that a permanent residence must be defined. This definition leaves nomads and semi-nomads out of the conventional migration analysis, although in some cases they may be considered a special case of rural-to-rural migration. Moreover, due to certain constraints within their areas, the nomads might cause changes in distribution and density in some regions. These changes would have the same implications as other rural-rural migrations.

Definition problems in relation to time period

How long should a movement last before it may be considered a migration? Or in other words, when does a residence become permanent? For instance, would seasonal labour migrations be considered a change in permanent residence? If so, how long should the season be in order to be considered permanent change in residence and thus a migration?

This is a serious problem because of the kind of information available on movements of population. In East Africa it would imply frequent surveys to check on the population movements, and we do not have that kind of information. Information on migration is usually collected in a census, asking the head of household on the movements of the members of the household.

Because of the varying perception of temporary migrations in different countries, comparisons are difficult to interpret as in some cases the labour migrations to plantations or to urban areas will be registered as migrations, while in other cases they will not. In the case of the temporary movement the person is perceived to belong to the household and only temporarily out of the household. This is especially the case with young men seeking employment in other areas.

The registration period for migration is determined by the kind of questions on the census questionnaire. It may relate the migration to a definite or an indefinite time period as indicated below:

Place of birth statistics. Information on place of enumeration and place of birth is the most frequently used for classification of migrants vs. non-migrants. People who live in the same location as they were born are called "non-migrants" and people enumerated elsewhere are "migrants". This gives rise to several problems: *The time period is indefinite*, as old people will refer to migrations over a long time period, and young people per definition refer to a shorter time period. In the Kenya 1969 census, migration will thus cover labour migrations in the 1960s, the movement of families from the "white highlands", movement of people away from the land during the last part of the colonial period (punishment for taking part in the Mau-Mau fighting) wives' movement to the husbands residence at marriage, movement of pupils to boarding schools, etc. But the data do not include any information on the dynamics of migration, i.e. the different kinds of migration at different times, and the life-history of migration for the individuals. Neither does it include the migration of persons who have moved back to their home areas (birth-place).

However, information on people's birth-place and where they are at present seems to be the type of information which is possible to get and to be the most frequently used.

Residence at a specific time, e.g. 5 or 10 years before the enumeration. This kind of information covers a definite period of time, but there are other problems of boundary and recall-lapse errors. Unless it is a time period of very definite significance for the whole population, it will be difficult to remember the residence of all the members of the household during that period. Independence may be used to limit such a time period as the head of household will recall precise information, but again this causes problems in areas where a fight may have been going on, and where the movements of people were very intense, e.g. from "protected villages".

Place of last residence. This kind of information usually only supplements the above information. It may check the last movement of the population, and for those who have migrated back to their place of birth, this information may reveal that a person has migrated during his life time even if the place of residence and place of birth are the same.

The duration of residence at the place of enumeration. This information is also supplementary, and points out the time period involved.

Regular check-up of actual residents. Inquiring about the people staying in the household the previous night is one of the ways of determining migration. Though a time-consuming method, this is probably one of the best as it is a follow-up analysis and is not based on retrospective data.

These different kinds of information give both different definitions of migration as well as varying volume of migration. If the place of birth statistics are used, all the persons who have moved through their life-time are registered as migrants, except those registered in the same place as they were born. But this will not give information on the number of migrations since these people may move several times during their life-time. On the other hand the information on migration within the last 5 years provides a definition of migration which registers a smaller number of migrants, and only in a very limited period. The number of registered migrations will thus depend on the time period used.

Administrative boundaries

Another important problem is the definition of boundaries. What boundaries have to be crossed for migration to occur? Urban and rural border lines, division, district, provincial or national boundaries are usually the relevant units considered.

The larger the enumeration areas, the lower the number of migrants, whereas the smaller the enumeration units the larger the volume of migrations that have to be considered. For example, the Kenya 1969 Census showed that 1.4% were born outside Kenya and were considered international migrants, while 12.7% were born outside the province in which they were registered.

In relation to a long registration period, i.e. one based on birth-place statistics, some of the administrative boundaries may change, and may thus influence the volume of migration to be considered. The crossing of administrative boundaries may not reflect the distance of the movement. The importance of administrative boundaries is illustrated by the following example: a movement from Vihiga to Lugari settlement within Kakamega district may not be considered a migration, as it does not pass over a district boundary, whereas a movement from Vihiga to Siaya does (a much shorter distance). As migration must be related to the administrative units for which information exists, there is no way of using distance as a criterion for defining migration.

Another boundary problem arises in relation to cities and towns. How is the boundary determined and what happens to the boundary when the town grows? Even where the boundary is sufficient and covers an expanding area, some of the areas in the urban centre are of a rural nature and a movement across the boundary, although rural in character, may still be registered as a movement to an urban centre. On the other hand, if the boundary covers only the urban area, then in the case when the town grows, the population expands beyond the boundary and this may thus be registered as a "false" urban-to-rural migration.

Usually however in the census interview, people do not perceive the administrative boundaries so clearly and tend to give more emphasis to the urban or rural characteristic, or whether the people have moved away from the community. People who are interviewed tend to emphasize the "socially relevant units" and the main traits instead of the strict administrative units. This may create problems of using them in relation to administrative boundaries, but may be more relevant for the description and especially for an explanation of the substance of migration.

We are considering the following types of migration, where internal migration will involve the crossing of either a division boundary, a district boundary or a provincial boundary.

1. Rural to rural migration
2. Rural to urban migration
3. Urban to rural migration
4. Urban to urban migration
5. International migrations across national borders.

The different types of migration must be explained in different ways, and are thus important as a preliminary typology.

Theories of migration

Theories on HOW people migrate have been developed by demographers, sociologists, and geographers. These are descriptive theories, or models. Theories on WHY people change their residence, i.e. explanatory theories, are however very poor. One reason for this may be that only a few migration researchers have been really concerned with the migrants as individuals or groups of individuals. Migration has, instead, been looked upon as a mass phenomenon resulting from changes in the physical or social environment to which human beings are anticipated to react as a group in a certain prescriptive way. We may group the theories of migration under these two headings mentioned, i.e.

1. Descriptive generalizations regarding the patterns of migration.
2. Theories trying to explain migration as a result of different economic and social opportunities in areas experiencing out-migration *vis-a-vis* areas of in-migration.

Descriptive theories basically deal with the volume of migration and its relationship to distance. As far back as 1885 Ravenstein published his "Laws of Migration" in which he argued that migration tends to be of short distances and that the volume of migration diminishes as the distance from the "centre of absorption" increases.[1]

Where long distance migration does occur it tends to gravitate toward the great centres of commerce and industry. Most of the models of generalizations developed in the 20th century are basically derivates of Ravenstein's "Laws", and have often been expressed in refined mathematical terms, being part of the so called "social-physics". Zipf thus said he found strong evidence that migration is directly proportional to the product of the population of places of origin and destination, and inversely proportional to the distance between the two

[1] Ravenstein: *The laws of migration.* 1885.

places. (The so-called P_1P_2/D hypothesis).[2]

These theories have been expanded with different factors of correction especially related to the economy, e.g. GNP, number of workplaces, etc. But the main problem seems to be rural-urban migration as the distance is very difficult, if not impossible, to define, especially in the rural areas.

The laws of migration may provide some basic features of certain migration trends, but they do not explain any causes, and so far they have not been able to predict migration in specific areas.

Theories for explaining migration are much more difficult to work out as the same trends of population movements may have many different explanations, and a combination of factors influences a person's decision to move. These decision processes have been discussed and elaborated by a variety of researchers, from demographers, economists, geographers, sociologists to social-psychologists.

Most of these theories are related to the main trend of migration from rural to urban areas which implies a change of living conditions for the migrants. One of the initiators of these theories, Adna Weber,[3] in the analysis of the growth of cities in the 19th century observed the tendency towards a geographical concentration of the population, and argued that this concentration of urbanization was caused by the changing economic "organization" of the society. The population distribution is adjusted to these changes by migration from areas with less opportunities (push tendency) to areas with more opportunities (pull tendency).

The push-pull hypothesis may be considered an off-spring of the neo-classical economic theory that "man is rational". Rationality in this respect is however, often reduced to the economic sphere alone, and only to marginal benefits in the labour market. Moreover, everybody is supposed to be able to evaluate the marginal profit of migration. In these theories, it is anticipated that individuals as well as groups will move where the best economic opportunities are found. This implies, therefore, that everyone is considered a potential migrant whether migration materializes or not. The size of migration and the direction of migration depends on the knowledge of economic opportunities elsewhere, and on the opportunities relative to the prospects of economic welfare at the present location.

Migration theory could be seen as a part of neo-classical economic theory according to which labour and capital will tend to move from areas with a relatively ample supply to areas with a relative deficit. That is, people must move to those areas where capital is concentrated because whereas people are scarce in relation to capital in the cities they are in surplus in the rural areas.

The push-pull hypothesis is basically associated with 19th century European economic development. In England, for example, the consolidation of small farms into large ones, and the prohibition of subdividing farms, "drove la-

---

[2] G. K. Zipf: *Human behavior and the principle of least effort.* 1949, chapt. 9–10.
[3] Adna Weber: *The Growth of Cities in the Nineteenth Century.* 1899.

bourers off the land depriving them of their vital rights of pastorage for sheep and geese on common land," and hindered all sons in a family to take over land. Also the declining conditions for the rural craftsman and rural industries due to increasing competition from large scale urban industries contributed to the decrease of rural employment and therefore created a push from the rural areas. On the other hand, the urban centres sheltered large-scale industries as well as many small-scale industries typical of the early stages of industrial capitalism. Both large and small industries were labour intensive. Also, due to the laws protecting industries from competition and the international division of labour established by colonialism, these early industries had a large enough market to absorb the labour of the rural migrants. Only some of the rural migrants went overseas to capture "virgin" lands in America or in the colonies. Thus the pull of the cities was established as an economic attraction produced by industrialization.

Later the push-pull hypothesis has been applied to explain international migration, especially the movements from Europe to North America of landless poor peasants, craftsmen and workers who were squeezed by land shortage in their local areas or by unemployment in urban industries. Thus economic pressure in the place of origin generated a push-factor, while for the 50–60 million Europeans who went to North America during the 19th and early 20th century, "the virgin" (i.e. the Indian) lands of the big plains were an economic opportunity and a pull factor, which the potential migrants responded to in a rational manner. The trend in the flow of population has been closely related to the relationship between the economic pressure in the place of origin and to the opportunity in the migration area, e.g. the failure of the potato harvest in Ireland 1845–46 pushed migrants from Ireland to North America in very large numbers.

In the long run this tendency of the migration flow is expected to result in the levelling out of wages and profits in different areas. This may in a few periods have been the outcome of migration in Western Europe and North America. But generally, rural-urban wage differentials are still high and have not levelled out. Also, in the developing nations, the push-pull theory does not seem to be valid for explaining rural-urban migration. In these countries peasants and craftsmen are being "pushed" out of the rural areas to seek employment and better economic opportunities in urban areas, but since no labour intensive mass industrialization is visible, the "pull" element of the hypothesis may be invalid as an explanatory variable of migration today.

Other sociological variables affecting migration may be the background variables of the migrants themselves such as the kind of training or education gained, as well as "perception of better economic opportunities". The problem with the migration theories is not only their severe limitations in relation to developing countries and the absence of the predicted disappearance of wage-differentials, but also their focus on the masses of migration flows. They do not explain why some people migrate, and why others do not migrate. This is

[4] *UN. Determinants and Consequences of Population Trends.* N.Y. 1974, p. 202.

because the economic characteristics are only limited to area-characteristics and not to any social differentiation even if it may be suggested that people do not move unless they are economically forced to. Thus there is no explanation as to why under the same economic conditions certain occupational and educational groups migrate and others do not, or why some men migrate alone, while others move with their whole family.

Because of these features of migration theory, only labour migration from rural to urban areas seems to be described while all other migration trends still need to be analyzed within a sociological framework, even though some rural-rural migration seems to be linked to the same economic area characteristics, especially availability of land and employment, as the rural-urban migration.

Determinants and social consequences of internal rural-to-urban migration in East Africa

Explanations of rural-urban migration in East Africa are practically only related to labour and employment possibilities. Even though we cannot determine the causal variables, we can specify the variables which are associated with the migration trends.

The following variables are found to be related to rural-urban migration in surveys carried out in the major Kenyan towns on the analysis of the motivations for migration.

Landlessness. Around 70% of the rural-to-urban migrants seem to have no land and no possibilities to inherit land in their own area.[5]

School education. Even little school education and/or training seems to increase the inclination to migrate to the urban areas, especially for males. The higher the education however, the higher the migration rate.[6] But this is measured for the migrants who are already settled in urban areas and who have not returned. The trend may not be as clear for all of those moving to urban areas, as the more educated may be more likely to get a job and remain in urban areas, while some of the poorly educated may be forced to go back to rural areas, when they do not succeed in getting a job.

Employment. Employment opportunities seem to be important both in place of origin and the place of destination. This seems to be especially related to the kind of employment, as the educated may not find relevant employment possibilities in rural areas.

If the actual availability of job-opportunities in the cities was to create the "pull" factor, then migration may be expected to level off due to the increasing unemployment in the urban areas. But the relationship is more complicated as

[5] Rempel & Todaro: Rural-to-Urban Labour Migration in Kenya. In: *Ominde & Ejiogu (eds): Population Growth & Economic Development in Africa*, London 1972, pp. 230—31.
[6] Ibid, pp. 221—27.

it involves the potential migrants perception of the job-opportunities relative to those of the home area. Especially among the school educated the expectations of job opportunities in towns seem to be very high.

It is important in this analysis to distinguish the type of employment available. The status differential is an essential explanatory variable as an area may have a seasonal or even permanent deficiency of farm labourers and yet be an outmigration area for the educated youth.

Income differential. The discrepancy between incomes in urban and rural areas is supposed to be one of the causes for migration. Farm and non-farm incomes from self-employment as well as employment in rural areas are much lower than urban salaries.

The difference is apparent even with the much higher cost of living in the urban areas. These differentials in income are perceived by the migrants to be high enough for them to accept unemployment for several months during the job-seeking period.

Income differentials however are not very clear in all types of jobs. The high-salaried modern sector jobs for the highly educated are more available in the urban areas. But incomes in the "informal" sector from small-scale trade, crafts, etc. may not show the same major income differentials. The main questions are, therefore, which differences of income do the migrants focus on when they decide to migrate and what are the realistic chances of getting the highly paid jobs?

Sex. Rural-urban migration in East Africa consists mainly of men. 65% of the migrants to the big cities in Kenya are men.[7] The school attendance among males may cater for most of this difference. The high male migration to the urban areas implies a very great surplus of young men in urban areas.

However, in Ghana where rural-urban migration increased at an earlier time, young women appear to form an increasing part of the migration stream.[8] In Ethiopia, rural-urban migration is predominantly a female phenomenon, resulting in a large scale female surplus in the big cities, the largest being in Addis Ababa.[9]

Age. Rural-urban migrants in East Africa are young. Over 65% of the migrants are less than 25 years old.[10] This pattern is related to the high frequency of migration of school-leavers.

Marital status. The majority of the migrants, i.e. 56%, are unmarried. Of those married, however, most (approx. 60%) had their wives residing outside the

[7] W. Elkan: Is a Proletariat Emerging in Nairobi? Disc. Paper IDS No. 168, Nairobi.
[8] J. C. Caldwell: *African Rural-Urban Migration.* N.Y. 1969, p. 38.
[9] L. Bondestam: Urbanization in Ethiopia. Its Pattern, Causes and Effects. Addis Ababa, June 1972. (Mimeo).
[10] Rempel & Todaro, op. cit., p. 220.

town.[11] This means that less than half were married with the wives staying with them, while the other half had wives in their home areas—usually cultivating the land for subsistence.

Relatives and friends in town. The contact with relatives or friends already staying in town tends to increase the tendency to move. These are essential for providing information, housing and food during the first period of jobseeking. It has been estimated that around 50 % of the migrants have these contacts when they come to town.[12] The contacts increase migration and knowledge about the possibilities in the urban areas. This can clearly be seen in areas with similar poor agricultural conditions but different levels of contacts in towns, e.g. Vihiga and its surrounding areas towards Lake Victoria.[13]

The social consequences of the migration may be analyzed for the nation as well as for the urban and rural areas. Out-migration from the rural areas can be seen as a relief on the land-pressure, as was the case in Europe. But in Kenya we know that many of the migrants do not own any land, and those who have land or access to land maintain their rights to it as security, even if the migration is perceived as permanent.

Education and vocational training in the planning phase often have been seen as incentives for the rural economy helping to promote the technical knowledge for development of the rural areas. However, because migration is higher for people with some education or training, the rural areas are deprived of an essential part of the potential for technical knowledge and innovation. The out-migration of men may also in certain areas drain the labour force, which is so essential during peak seasons away from agriculture and generally it tends to transfer the male tasks within farming to the women.

For other kinds of problems, i.e. social problems in raising children without the father and older brothers, there is not much evidence from surveys, neither do surveys on migration cover anything on the implications of women's migration, e.g. in case of divorce. We know that social security in marriage is breaking down and since divorced women do not have any right to land, which leaves them without the traditional means of supporting their children, they may have to migrate. This is illustrated in a study of buzaa brewing in Mathare Valley, where all the women were unmarried or divorced with children to support.[14]

Another problem of getting information is difficulty in reaching all the migrant groups, thus migrants who get jobs and are permanently living in the destination areas are more likely to be interviewed, giving a biased picture. Whereas those migrants staying temporarily with families or friends, or mi-

[11] Ibid., p. 220
[12] J. C. Caldwell: *African Rural-Urban Migration*, N.Y. 1969, p. 81.
[13] S. Nyaoke Owuor: Primacy of Determinants of Rural Urban and Reverse Urban-Rural Migration in Kenya. M. A. Thesis, Dept. of Sociology. Nairobi 1974, p. 44.
[14] Nici Nelson: Buzaa Brewing in Mathare Valley. Staff Seminar Paper, Dept. of Sociology, Nairobi 1973.

grating back because of failure to find jobs, or those who have become criminals, or the women brewing *chang'aa* (local liquor) or engaging in prostitution, will be almost impossible to trace for sampling and will therefore be under-represented.

Determinants and social consequences of urban-rural migration in East Africa

The urban-rural migration is much less common than the rural-urban migration, and mainly consists of the following groups:

1.   Rural-urban migrants who have given up finding a job in the towns and have returned home.

2.   People who have accumulated money in the urban areas and go back to invest in land and/or business in the rural areas. These are especially the older people above 50 years.

Among the latter we find many rural businessmen and they tend to become a part of the entrepreneurial class. But the first group is a "problem group". Rural-urban migration itself tends to be selective with respect to education. The urban-rural migration also tends to be selective and will tend to include those with:

a.   Very little school education, i.e. up to Std. 6, where the migrant may not even be able to read and write, and has no technical training. The lower the school-education and amount of training the more difficult it is to get a job in urban areas.[16]

b.   No employment experience.

c.   No contacts in town; resources decline quickly when the migrant has no housing, food and contacts. Also, the longer the unemployment the more likely that the migrant loses support from friends.

In the Nairobi survey the average unemployed job-seeking period was three months for those who were still staying in Nairobi.[17] It may be even more, since people who have given up and gone back may have had even longer periods of unemployment.

The rural-urban as well as the urban-rural migration, especially of the young men, tends to drain the community of the best youth potential. The migrants who are less successful come back after having drained their resources, but they have not solved the problem of employment experience or obtained adequate training. This group thus may become a burden for the family.

---

[16]   Phillip Mbithi: Employment Problems of Youth with Special Reference to Policy Issues. March 20, 1975. Paper for Pan Commonwealth Workshop on National Service and National Youth Programmes, April 1975, Accra.

[17]   Rempel and Todaro Survey. Personal communication with Rempel.

Determinants and social consequences of rural-rural migration in East Africa

The rural-rural migration is very different from the rural-urban movement. We may distinguish 3 different types of migrants according to the main "pull" factors related to the migration.

    a.   Migrants who move to newly acquired land, i.e. to settlement schemes, newly developed areas or to low density areas where land is bought.

    b.   Migrants who move to settle on land they do not own, i.e. squatters who take up trust land, forest land or uncultivated farmland for their own cultivation.

    c.   Migrants who move for wage-employment in the rural areas, i.e. in plantations like tea estates, sugar estates and in associated factories.

    The factors influencing or related to rural-rural migration are:

Landlessness — too little or too poor land for supporting a family. Access to grazing land may be of crucial importance in some areas. Non-availability of land to supply the family with important and basic food-stuffs may be pressing people into a migration.[18]

Drought and famines in the home area seem to be factors pushing many people to migrate. An example of this kind of migration can be seen in the movement from Eastern Province towards the Coast Province.[19]

Lack of employment opportunities or of possibilities to earn an income to supplement agriculture may increase the tendency to move.

Age. The rural-rural migrants tend to be much older than the rural-urban migrants. In the squatter group the head of household was around 40 years,[20] and the study of landowners who have migrated shows an average in the early thirties.[21]

Education. The rural-rural migrants tend to have very poor school education and training. Among squatters and labourers, the illiteracy rate is very high, estimated to be more than 60%.[22] But also among the rural migrants who are land-owners, very few have school education, only 50% had any schooling at all, and more than 60% had less than 4 years of school education. This characteristic was also common for the non-migrants, thus education does not discriminate rural migrants from non-migrants in the rural areas.[23]

[18] Mary Matingu: Rural to Rural Migration and Employment: A Case Study in a Selected Area of Kenya. M. A. Thesis, Sociology, Nairobi 1974, p. 82—83.
[19] Philip Mbithi & C. Barnes: *Spontaneous Settlement Problem in Kenya.* Nairobi 1975, p. 83.
[20] Ibid., p. 160.
[21] Mary Matingu, op. cit.
[22] Mbithi & Barnes, op. cit., p. 160.
[23] M. Matingu, op, cit., p. 171—172.

Family structure. The migration of squatters or land-owners to other rural areas is primarily a family migration. The women and the children constitute the main labour force to develop and cultivate the land, and are therefore necessary partners in the migration process. Little is known about land labourers, but they seem to be more often single males.

The "pull" factors, or the factors related to the place of destination will vary for the different groups involved in migration and therefore these groups will be treated separately in the analysis. The migrants who have acquired new land in settlement schemes or in newly developed areas, clearly see the prospects of larger landplots, which would make it possible to increase the income from agriculture.

Availability of land for cultivation and grazing is mentioned as the most important motivation for migrating. The people have larger and better pieces of land after migration and much better output.[24]

Migration between the districts of Kenya is quite high. In 1969, 15.4% were born outside the district in which they were registered. From comparisons of the 1962 and 1969 census population flows between the provinces may be estimated, though some migrants may have moved more than once. Also the 1962 census is not equally valid in all areas. From this comparison (see table 39) Central Province, Eastern Province and Western Province seem to be the main out-migration areas, while Rift Valley and Coast Provinces are the main receivers of migrants.

Table 39. *Inflows and outflows of population in the Kenyan provinces up to 1969 (rounded figures).*

Province	Outflow	Inflow
Central	332,600	151,400
Coast	27,700	155,200
Eastern	161,900	33,500
North Eastern	10,300	8,900
Nyanza	186,000	169,300
Rift Valley	88,800	428,400
Western	200,900	58,700

Source: P. Mbithi & C. Barnes: *Spontaneous Settlement Problem in Kenya,* Nairobi 1975, p. 82.

Within Central Province the major out-migration districts are Nyeri and Murang'a. In Western Province out-migration is high from all districts and in Eastern Province the outflows are primarily from Machakos, Isiolo, Marsabit and Kitui Districts. Net out-migration is much lower for Nyanza, though it is high from Kisumu and Siaya Districts.[25]

[24] M. Matingu, op. cit., p. 114—115 and Liyai, Vacation research, Dept. of Sociology 1975 on migrations from central to Eastern Isukha location (Kakamega).
[25] P. Mbithi & C. Barnes, op. cit., p. 82.

The migration areas were receiving a different combination of migrants. The migrants to the Coast region mainly came from Machakos, Kitui, Kisumu, Kakamega and Siaya Districts, while those in the Rift Valley mainly came from Kiambu, Nyeri and Murang'a Districts and a smaller proportion from Kakamega, Bungoma and Nyanza Districts.[26] The migration to the Rift Valley was historically a labour tenant migration, while now it is both to acquire land as well as a labour migration.

The implications of rural-rural migration seem to be a redistribution of the population from heavily populated areas to areas with a relative surplus of land, without much distortion in the population structure in the affected areas, as this in a family migration. Rural-rural migration toward new agricultural land thus seems to increase the potential for rural agricultural production. However the migrants are not educated and the groups are not what we usually identify as "change agents" or "entrepreneurs". Instead, these groups seem to be relatively traditional and very closely attached to the land. The characteristics of these groups show great discrepancy from the characteristics of the urban migrants.

Determinants and social consequences of urban-urban migration in East Africa

This is one of the migration patterns we do not know much about. The traditional theories from Europe and USA anticipate that the urban-urban migration is a part of the rural-urban migration and urbanization process as this is expected to be a stepwise migration from rural areas to small nearby towns and later further on to more distant larger towns. This would imply, for example, that the migrants from the rural areas around Kakamega went first to Kakamega, or to Kisumu and later migrated to Nairobi. We cannot confirm this for East Africa. We only know that among the migrants to the urban areas a lot of them move between the different towns in order to find jobs, but how systematic this is in relation to movements from smaller to larger towns, we do not know. The effect will mainly be a redistribution of the urban population. However, in Kenya a higher growth in Nairobi and Mombasa than in the other towns appear to be the result.

International migration in Africa

These migrations should be seen in the historical context in which they have taken place. Here we will just list the major types of migration trends in the different periods.

---

[26] Ibid.

Precolonial migration in East Africa

Migration is not a recent phenomenon in Africa. The history of the different tribal groups shows that most tribes of East Africa have come from other areas of Africa, and that major flows of population have dominated the time period up to around 1700 A.D. Examples from the history of East African tribes reveal some of these migration patterns:

1. Kikuyu land was originally settled by the Dorobo (Athi), but was invaded by Bantu-speaking families in three stages and from three directions: From the east (Tharakaland), the south-east (Kambaland) and from Meru or from the Mt. Elgon area. The first flow came around the 14th century and the last and major group arrived in the 16th century. The Kikuyu, the Gusii and the Kuria are supposed to have come from the Mt. Elgon area and thus claim to have the same origin.[27]

2. The Akamba appear to be originally from the area around Mt. Kilimanjaro and in the period before 1000 A.D. they moved north to the Tana River area, then south again, out to the coast, to Kilimanjaro and finally around 1450—1550 A.D. they settled in their present area, which was then uninhabited.[28]

3. The Meru people are said to be close to the Kikuyu, and may have come in the distant past from around Mt. Elgon. However, most Meru trace their origins to the coast.[29]

4. The Abaluyia of Western Kenya seem to have settled to the south of the present Abaluyia areas around the end of the 15th century, coming partly from the northeast and partly from the northwest. The oral history of the Abaluyia refers to their ancestors as having originally come from Egypt, a country of scarcity of rain, poor sandy soil and constant starvation. The area however is more likely to be either Northern Kenya (the Turkana area) or a part of the Sudan. The area now settled was previously grazing land for the Masai and the Kalenjin people with whom relations were usually quite friendly.[30]

5. The Luo of Nyanza and Uganda appear to have moved from eastern Equatorial and a part of the Sudan. (The Nilotes most likely had evolved as a distinct group by 1000 A.D.). The Luo people split into two in the migration southwards, one group moving east of Lake Nyanza (Victoria) and the other moving west of Lake Nyanza and round the lake to the eastern shore. The Luo arrived at their present country between 1450—1600 A.D.[31]

These major migrations of the peoples of East Africa have often in the early stages of migration been difficult to distinguish from the regular seasonal movements, mostly of the pastoral people. The reasons for leaving an area and moving much further are usually related either to a severe drought or to

---

[27] W. R. Ochieng: *Eastern Kenya and its invaders.* Nairobi 1975, pp. 27—33.
[28] Ibid, pp. 33—36.
[29] Ibid, pp. 36—41.
[30] G. S. Were: *A History of the Abaluyia of Western Kenya, 1500—1930.*
[31] B. A. Ogot: *History of the Southern Luo.* Vol. 1: Migration and Settlement 1500—1900 A.D. Nairobi 1967.

overpopulation and overgrazing of an area. At different stages of migration, contact with the surrounding groups of people (or tribes) has led to adjustment to assimilation and trade with the people of the land occupied. A high population increase in one group may restrict another tribal group from expanding their areas. In western parts of Kenya especially the Luo, Gusii, Masai and Kipsigis seem to have checked each other's territorial expansion.[32]

Pre-colonial and mercantilistic period in Africa

1.   The Arabian expansion along the trading routes involved movements along the east coast of Africa and towards West Africa. It was mainly a migration along the coast line, where trade routes to the Middle East were established and also to a few inland towns, such as Tabora in Tanzania, which were focal points for trade. The Arabs remained in these places and specialized in trading.

2.   With the introduction of Islam in West Africa, a travel route for pilgrims across the continent to Mecca began. Considerable numbers from this stream settled along the route, mainly in the Sudan.[33]

3.   The slave-transports from West and Central Africa towards the plantations in North and Middle America. Approximately 20 million people were captured, and even in the more heavily populated areas the population was reduced seriously. The prosperous trade in these regions suffered from these captures, and the economy and agricultural production declined as the remaining population consisted mostly of old people and children in a few isolated areas. The slave trade stopped around 1800.

4.   Slave transport from East Africa, mainly organized by the Arabs. This was on a much more limited scale, but the area at that time was already thinly populated, and so the population declined. Agricultural productivity was seriously affected by the loss of population. The slave trade was very limited until around 1860–1880, when the beginnings of plantations at Zanzibar, Reunion, and Mauritius created an increased labour demand. Zanzibar functioned as the main centre for this transport of people.

Colonial patterns of population movements

1.   The colonization and the inclusion of West Africa into close trade with Western Europe led to changes in the economy, and created a large-scale labour demand in the coastal regions. This demand led to labour migration and a draining of labour from the hinterland, which seems to have continued.[34]

[32] W. R. Ochieng: *Pre-colonial History of the Gusii of Western Kenya.* C.A.D. 1500—1914. Nbi 1974.
[33] W. T. S. Gould: International Migration in Tropical Africa. In: *International Migration Review.* Vol. 8, No. 3 1974, p. 353.
[34] Samir Amin: Underdevelopment and Dependence in Black Africa—Origins and Contemporary Forms. *Journal of Modern African Studies.* Vol. 10, no. 4 1972, pp. 503—524.

2.   The colonization of South Africa, Rhodesia (Zimbambwe), Zambia and Kenya by the white settlers. Most of the settlers went to South Africa and Rhodesia. In all, settlers to Africa south of the Sahara numbered 4.5 million, of whom 3 million went to South Africa and 200,000 to Rhodesia.[35]

3.   The movement of Asian contract labourers from India to build the railway in East Africa. Following the initial migration, there was heavy in-migration of Asian craftsmen, traders and bank clerks to the newly "opened" area. This migration was supported and protected by the British colonizers.

Post-independence movements

The impact of colonialism on migration patterns is still significant. The independent African states are still characterized by the economic structure and centres of economic activity created under colonialism. The large scale labour migration across boundaries follows the colonial pattern especially toward the mining areas in South Africa and Zambia. The international labour migration in Africa has been estimated to involve 5 million people per year from around the middle of the 1950s. The areas still under colonialism, South Africa, Zimbambwe and Namibia or those at the dawn of independence (Mozambique and Angola) have other problems of migration, namely those related to political refugees.

1.   The most important type of migration today seems to be the labour movement toward the mines of South Africa and to a smaller extent to Zambia. In South Africa in 1971 there were 500,000 foreign labourers (only males) who were not allowed to bring their families. Recruitment of these labourers was carried out through labour recruitment offices, most of which were to be found in Mozambique, Malawi and in Southern Zambia (see map of Labour Movements to South Africa). Of the 500,000 migrants in 1971, 200,000 came from Lesotho, 160,000 from Mozambique and 60,000 from Malawi. Tanzania and Zambia prohibited the recruitment in 1966. As a result of labour migration the economies of Malawi, Lesotho and Swaziland became extremely dependent on the income of these foreign workers. In Malawi, the income from migrant workers constituted the third most important source of foreign currency (after tobacco and tea). As much as 20% of the total adult population is working outside the country and as much as 75% of the population at some time works abroad (1971).[36]

Labour migration is not only directed toward South Africa and the mines, but also to a large extent to other centres of employment such as industries and plantations in Uganda, Kenya, Tanzania and Rhodesia. In Kenya, such centres are the Mumias and Chemelil Sugar estates, Kericho tea estates, plus the industrial centres in Nairobi. Uganda has the cotton plantations in Jinja and Tanzania has the sisal estates in the Tanga region, all these employ both local

---

[35] UN. Determinants and Consequences of Population Trends. N.Y. 1974, p. 236.
[36] R. Mansell Prothero: Foreign Migrant Labour for South Africa. In: International Migration Review, Vol. VIII, no. 3, p. 389.

Graph 20. *Foreign migrant labour for South Africa*

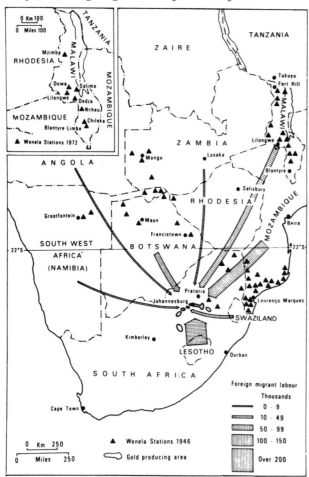

Source: R. Mansell Prothero: Foreign Migrant Labour for South Africa. In: *International Migration Review*, vol. 8, no. 3 1974, p. 387.

and foreign labourers.

2.   In West Africa, Ghana has been the large scale immigration area, where migrants have come from Asia, Lebanon and from the neighbouring African countries. Many of the migrants were working in trade, but also some of the migrants who came from the neighbouring African countries were farmers. In 1960, 12% of the total population was born outside Ghana.

A reverse migration of these people started in 1970, just after the passing of the "compliance order" in Ghana. This law implied that all non-residents should obtain residence permits within 14 days or leave the country. 200,000

143

people left the country. Many of the Asian and Lebanese population sold their businesses and left Ghana permanently.[37]

3. The movement of the population due to drought is usually a local or internal migration. However, the migration due to the large scale drought and famine in the Sahel zone from around 1972, has involved a movement of the population from Mali, Niger, Chad and Sudan toward Upper Volta and Nigeria. Also the nomads often cross borders between Ethiopia, Somalia and Kenya during the seasonal variations, looking for water in these areas.[38]

4. Refugees constitute a major portion of those who move across the borders in Africa. It is estimated that in 1972/73 there were around 1 million refugees in Africa. This is very high in relation to the population size and the number is only surmounted by the number of Palestinian refugees (approx. 1.5 million) and the number of refugees between Pakistan and India. A refugee is defined as an individual who owing to well-founded fear of being persecuted for reasons of race, religion, nationality, membership of certain social groups, or political opinion is outside his country of nationality and is unable or owing to fears, unwilling, to avail himself of the protection of that country.[39]

Table 40. *Estimated total number of refugees in Africa in December 1972 distributed by country of origin, and the four main receiving countries, as well as total out-migration, from the country of origin (to all African countries).*

Country of origin	4 main countries of reception				Total refugees from the country to other Afr. countries
	Tanzania	Uganda	Zaire	Zambia	
Angola	—	—	400,000	17,200	421,000
Burundi	23,000	—	31,000	—	58,000
Mozambique	58,000	—	—	6,400	64,400
Namibia	50	10	—	900	1,000
Rwanda	14,000	72,800	23,000	—	152,000
South Africa	100	30	20	300	900
Sudan	—	59,400	36,000	—	128,000
Zaire	1,400	34,500	—	—	43,800
Zambia	—	—	750	—	750
Various African countries	1,450	—	—	200	144,200
Total	58,000	166,500	490,000	25,000	

Source: W. T. S. Gould: Refugees in Tropical Africa. In: *International Migration Review*, Vol. VIII, No. 3 1974, p. 415.

[37] W. T. S. Gould: International Migration in Tropical Africa. In: *International Migration Review*, vol. VIII, No. 3, p. 356—57.

[38] Ibid., p, 359.

[39] W. T. S. Gould: Refugees in Tropical Africa. In: *International Migration Review*, Vol. VIII, No. 3, p. 413.

144

This kind of migration thus occurs mainly in areas where there have been severe fights between different groups of the population, or especially in areas where the liberation struggle against the colonial regimes has pushed people out to the surrounding countries.

Most of the refugees come from Angola, Mozambique (close to 500,000 in Dec. 1972), and from Burundi and Rwanda (a total of more than 200,000 in 1972). The number of refugees in West Africa has been much lower in number, mostly from Guinea Bissau to Senegal (around 80,000) and a few from the Sudan. In 1972/73 around 150,000 Sudanese were repatriated to the Sudan, and the number of refugees in the neighbouring countries declined.

The above table reveals the main refugee streams in Africa. It appears to be mainly from colonized areas, where a war is going on, to the border regions. The main flow from Angola to Zaire has resulted in a severe pressure on land in the border regions. The refugees seem to settle mostly in the rural areas, either in spontaneous settlements (squatters) or in organized refugee settlement schemes. The latter have been organized both in Tanzania and Uganda for the refugees from Rwanda and Burundi, who seem to be considered more permanent settlers. In Rwanda and Burundi, however, the stream of migrants does not only comprise of refugees. There is also intensive migration of labourers, thus providing Uganda with 72,800 Rwandan refugees, but a total of 150,000 migrants including the migrant labourers. Other major migration streams were from Guinea Bissau to Senegal in December 1972, estimated to be 80,000, and from Ethiopia to Sudan, estimated at 50,000. Refugee flows, however, may be considered temporary and the migrants will tend to move back when conditions in the home country improve.[40]

5. A special flow of refugees is that of the Asians expelled from Uganda in 1972. This is not registered as a refugee problem in Africa, as most of the expelled Asians went to England, Canada and other countries outside Africa. The few Asians who settled within other countries of East Africa settled as businessmen who could support themselves and were not a problem group of refugees needing support. In Kenya and Tanzania, Asians have not been expelled, but many non-citizen Asians have migrated to other countries outside Africa, trying to find work and business possibilities in countries which seem to have fewer restrictions for business.

6. For an overall indication of the migration flows across the borders to Kenya and Tanzania, we only have information from the censuses, i.e. from Kenya 1969 and from Tanzania 1967. These figures show the distribution by birthplace for the people born outside the two countries and also indicates the very different nature of the international migration in the two countries.

If other criteria such as the "place of birth" were utilized for Tanzania then the migration flow would be even larger. A total of 400,000 in Tanzania were born in the neighbouring countries, 8,000 in other African countries, 13,000 in Europe and 23,000 in Asia. This implies that 1.5% of the population in Kenya

[40] Ibid., p, 416.

10 – A demographic...

Table 41. *Place of birth for foreign-born in Kenya, 1969 and those with foreign citizenship in Tanzania, 1967.*

Place of birth/citizenship	Kenya 1969	Tanzania 1967
Tanzania	39,000	—
Uganda	33,000	(see other Afr.)
Kenya	—	40,000
Rwanda	500	26,000
Burundi	500	30,000
Somalia	1,600	(see other Afr.)
Ethiopia	4,600	(see other Afr.)
Mozambique	(see other Afr.)	61,000
Other African countries	4,000	28,000
United Kingdom	19,000	17,000
Other European and USA	11,000	(Other)
India and Pakistan	38,000	11,000
Other countries	5,700	17,000
Total	160,000	240,000

Note: The definition of international migrations is different.

Source: Egero & Henin: op. cit., p. 60; *Kenya population Census 1969*. Vol. III, pp. 53—54 and calculations.

and 3.7 % of the Tanzania population were born outside the country.

The analysis of international migration shows that the patterns seem to be related to the following factors:

a. Lack of employment opportunities in the home area (country) and possibilities to move to other areas for employment. The area of destination will tend to be the one perceived as providing the best possibility for improved employment. The major outmigration areas are the very poor regions which depend on this employment of their nationals.

b. Civil war or liberation wars in colonial areas. Refugees are often just moving across political boundaries where they have a chance to remain at least during the period of conflict.

Legislation creates an important regulation on international migration, e.g. the policies of Ghana and Uganda, and the regulation of labour recruitment in Tanzania and Zambia. It is therefore much more regulated and there are more valid estimations of this migration than of internal migration. However in census data, refugees will tend to give wrong information on place of origin, and the number of foreigners may be underestimated.

The migration of highly educated people from African countries to Europe and USA. This "brain-drain" however does not yet seem to be a widespread phenomenon though it is increasing. This pattern seems to be more widespread for Latin America, North Africa, Asia, where the highly educated people remain in the country where they have had their education and training.

146

Urbanization and Migration

The treatment of urbanization in this section will not be too detailed and only the salient features which are pertinent to the migration process will be covered. Urbanization refers to a concentration of people under certain occupational and economic conditions. It is a concept which has been closely related to the industrialization in Europe, even though old cities and towns have existed before industrialization in Europe, Asia, Latin America and in Africa. These towns were administrative centres with many people in non-farm activities, such as service occupations.

The basic condition for having an urban population is the existence of a surplus in agriculture to feed the extra people, who are not producing any food.

The development of the urban pattern or the spatial distribution of the population in Europe, however, was different from that in other continents, especially Latin America and Africa. Roughly, the development of the cities in Europe was integrated with agricultural development. Small centres and towns grew up with linkages between them, building up an integrated transport pattern between the interlinked villages and the major centres. Around 1800 some cities along the coast increased their size not only due to contact with the hinterland, but also because of the inflow of goods and export to the other continents.

Contrary to this, in Latin America and Africa only a few "primary" cities developed which functioned as administrative centres for the colonial government and as control centres for export of raw materials to the colonial powers. The cities therefore grew up at strategic points, e.g. at the important harbours and where they could be connected with the hinterland to bring out the goods. The networks were not interrelated, but made clear patterns of transport routes and cities along the export roads.

The major growth in urbanization in Europe followed industrialization, whereby the peasants and local craftsmen were pushed out of the rural areas into urban industry which was labour intensive and could provide employment possibilities for the rural-urban migrants. The change therefore involved an occupational change mainly from agriculture to industry.

In Europe the pattern of employment in the city centre is illustrated by the percentage of working population in different sectors of employment:

1. Primary sector: agriculture, mining, etc. less than 5 %.
2. Secondary sector: industry, manufacturing 40—50 %
3. Tertiary sector: service, trade etc. 40—50 %.

The service sector changed during the industrilization to become less of a domestic service group to one, with a higher extent administration and trade.

In developing countries the pattern of the occupational structure is different. In the big cities, even those above 50,000 people, the typical distribution of the population in the different sectors is:

1. primary sector 5—15 %
2. secondary sector 10—15 %

3.   tertiary sector 60—75%

The tertiary sector also has a lower percentage of the employed in adminis-tration and trade and a higher proportion of domestic servants and under-employed petty traders.

This structure of the cities forms the economic basis for the fundamental differences in the migration and employment—unemployment patterns be-tween the industrial and developing nations.

The large scale flow of migrants to urban areas and the growth of big cities resulting in a structure where the major part of the population lives in big cities is a relatively new phenomenon. Even though there were ancient cities, around 1800 only about 3% of the total world population was estimated to live in urban areas. In 1970 the urban population was estimated to be 35% of the world population.

Table 42 shows the percentage of the urban population in the different continents. This table shows great variations, from over 50% in the industrial countries and in Latin America to as low as 20% in Africa. The lowest levels of urbanization are found within East Africa.

Table 42. *Urbanization of the major areas of the world in 1965**

Developing regions	23 %				
More-developed regions	61 %				
1. AFRICA	20 %		4. LATIN AMERICA	52 %	
West Africa	18 %		South L. A.	73 %	
East Africa	8 %		Lowest: Caribbean	39 %	
Central Africa	14 %		5. NORTH AMERICA	72 %	
North Africa	32 %				
South Africa	44 %		6. OCEANIA	67 %	
2. ASIA (excl. USSR)	22 %		Highest: Australia		
Highest: Japan	48 %		New Zealand	82 %	
Lowest: Middle-South	18 %		Lowest: Melanesia	3 %	
3. EUROPE (excl. USSR)	61 %		7. USSR	53 %	
North-West	72—75 %				
South-East	51—52 %				

% Percentage of population in each area living in urban areas. Urban areas defined as "densely inhabited districts" according to the census.

Source: UN. Determinants and Consequences of Population Trends, N.Y. 1974, p. 185.

The definition of cities, towns and urban areas, however, varies according to the subject discipline, and another problem is the difficulty in interpreting the work of researchers engaged in this sector. A combination of the criteria often used is based on: physical structure, concentration of population, social way of life, occupational pattern, size of the agglomeration and administrative func-tions.

The size of agglomeration is usually not sufficient as a classification criterion. For example, in Nigeria there are agglomerations of 20,000 people which are still completely rural in character and occupation pattern. The definitions and criteria used for East Africa are presented below:

a.   Kenya 1962: The intention was to use the administrative centres: 1) Municipality, 2) Grade "A" township, 3) Grade "B" township, 4) Trading centres.

However, the last two categories were found to be extremely small, and the size criterion alone was used. Urban centres were then defined as centres having more than 2,000 inhabitants. In 1962 there were 34 such centres.

b.   Kenya 1969: Urban centres were still defined as having more than 2,000 inhabitants. There were 44 urban centres in 1969.

c.   Tanzania 1967: The urban centres were defined in relation to the ad-ministrative townships. In 1967 there were 27 such centres of which 25 had over 1,000 inhabitants.

In India and in many European countries, the criteria of size and adminis-trative functions of the urban centre were supplemented by a criterion de-manding that over 50 %, or in some cases two-thirds, of the population en-gaged in non-farm activities.

In the evaluation of the history of urbanization in East Africa, it is important to note that the dominant pattern of settlement is dispersed homesteads. Urbanization in East Africa is a relatively recent phenomenon, mostly domi-nated by the populations which have invaded the country from outside. The coastal cities were old trading centres dominated mostly by the Arabs. The large cities in the interior of the countries were built up as administration centres and Nairobi was also a supply centre for the construction of the railway.

Exceptions to this pattern can be seen in the development of Kampala as a centre for the centralized and densely populated Buganda Kingdom and in the centres and towns of more recent origin.

Although African rural-urban migration has increased the proportion of the African urban population, the other ethnic groups, mainly the Arabs, Asians and Europeans, are nearly totally urban and thus still form a relatively large

Table 43. *Urbanization percentage of population living in towns in Kenya, Uganda, Tanzania (national definitions of township).*

Country	Year	% urban
Kenya	1962	7.8 %*
,,	1969	9.2 %
Tanzania mainland	1957	4.1 %
,,	1967	5.7 %
Tanzania, including Zanzibar	1967	6.2 %
Uganda	1959	4.3 %
,,	1969	7.0 %

* 5.3 % of the African population

Source: S. H. Ominde: *The Population of Kenya, Tanzania and Uganda.* Nairobi 1975, pp. 89—90.

149

proportion of the urban population. For example, according to the 1969 census 82 % of the non-African population were living in the major towns; Nairobi and Mombasa contained the majority (71 %).

Urbanization in East Africa is oldest in the coastal region and in Zanzibar, and these regions are by far still the most "urbanized", i.e. 30% of the population of Zanzibar lives in urban centres. In the other areas the level of urbanization is generally low and shows only little variation, with the same rapid increase in urbanization in all the East African countries (see table 43).

A comparison with other African countries, with urbanization defined in a standardized way as the population living in agglomerations with more than 20,000 inhabitants, is provided in table 44.

Table 44. *Percentage of urban population in cities over 20,000 inhabitants in selected African countries.*

Countries	Year	% urban
Kenya	1962	5.9 %
Kenya	1969	7.7 %
Tanzania (Mainland)	1967	4.7 %
Uganda	1969	5.1 %
Burundi	1965	2.6 %
Zambia	1969	26.8 %
Ethiopia	1970	5.7 %
Malawi	1966	2.7 %
Senegal	1960—61	22.5 %
Benin (Dahomey)	1961	8.3 %
Ghana	1970	17.7 %
Nigeria	1963	14.0 %
U. A. R.	1966	38.2 %
Morocco	1971	30.6 %
South Africa	1960	35.4 %

Source: ECA. Demographic Handbook for Africa, 1971 and 1974, pp. 50—54.

This table illustrates the differences within the African continent, showing the highest levels of urbanization in North Africa with its large focal points of trade and in South Africa. West Africa in general has a higher proportion of the population living in cities than Central and East Africa. The exception is Zambia because of the high percentage of the population in the mining areas.

Most of the data available on the urban population in Kenya is based on the 1969 census. The census shows that 9.2% of the total population lived in towns of over 2,000 people. However, most of the towns in Kenya are small in size and the urban population is mainly concentrated in the two big cities of Nairobi and Mombasa. These have 55.0% and 27.0% respectively of the total urban population in the 11 major towns. Table 45 shows the percentage of the urban population in the major towns. The concentration of such a large proportion of the population in the two cities implies that the migrants must be travelling great distances to the larger cities. One might conclude that in most provinces it appears as if the larger the city the longer the distance over which the migrants come, whereas in the very small urban centres, the migrants seem to have travelled short distances, usually coming from the same district.

Table 45. *Distribution of urban population in the major towns of Kenya, 1969 (percentages).*

Town	%
Nairobi	55.0
Mombasa	27.0
Nakuru	5.1
Kisumu	3.5
Thika	2.0
Eldoret	2.0
Nanyuki	1.3
Kitale	1.3
Malindi	1.2
Kericho	1.1
Nyeri	1.1
	Total 100.6*

* Rounding errors.

Source: Kenya Population Census 1969 (calculated).

The available information indicates that the tendency of the migrants to move outside their districts varies with the different regions. In Central and Nyanza Provinces, most people have moved within the same district and the same province, whereas towns in the Rift Valley Province seem to have a large proportion of the people from outside the province, thus making it a heavy in-migration area for the other provinces. It is difficult to indicate the pattern for Coast province since the information is distorted by the very high percentage of non-response.

Measures of migration

Direct measures

If we have information on the number of migrations or migrants to or from a certain area, we can estimate migration rates similar in nature to the mortality and fertility rates. These may be crude rates or specified for different age-groups.

$$\text{Immigration rate } m_i = \frac{\text{Immigration in a year}}{\text{Population at risk}} \cdot 1,000$$

This is a measure equivalent to the crude birth rate and crude death rate. There is however one major problem with this measure; at the national level the population at risk is the total population outside the nation, therefore what we take instead of the population at risk, is the total population in the area of the in-migration. This tells us something about the impact of immigration in an area, especially when used in areas of heavy in-migration.

$$\text{Out-migration rate } m_o = \frac{\text{Out-migration in a year}}{\text{Population at risk}} \cdot 1{,}000$$

In relation to out-migration the concept of population at risk is more meaningful in an area and should be used if possible to measure the net-migration rate.

$$\text{Net-migration rate } m_n = \frac{\text{Net-migration in a year}}{\text{Population at risk in this year}} \cdot 1{,}000 = m_i - m_o$$

These measures may be used for more than one year, or even for life-time migrations where the time-period will be varying.

Also migration rates may be specified for age, sex, occupational groups, and by type of migration. For example, the age specific net migration rate or:

$$\text{Net-migration rate for the age group 25—29 years} = \frac{\text{Net-migration for age-group 25—29}}{\text{Population at risk 25—29 years}} \cdot 1{,}000$$

These measures, however, are based on the counting of persons who change their residence across certain boundaries. This information is usually only available for international migrations, or may be based on imprecise indications such as place of birth and place of enumeration, which is not a direct measure.

Indirect measures

If however we have good censuses or surveys, indirect measures of migration trends may be obtained.

Table 46 gives an indication of the amount of migration for the total Kenyan population: 1.4% were immigrants or those who have migrated across the national border, 12.7% were internal migrants across provincial boundaries, and 15.4% were internal migrants across district boundaries.

Table 46. *Migration according to place of registration and place of birth in Kenya for the different ethnic groups 1969 (absolute population in thousands and percentages).*

	Total	Place of birth				
		Same district	Province elsewhere	Kenya elsewhere	Outside Kenya	Not stated
Total pop.	10,943	9.036	444	1,234	149	80
Kenyan African	10,674	8,924	437	1,203	33	77
Other African	59	17	1	5	36	*
Non-African Kenya	88	57	4	12	14	1
Non-African Non-Kenyan	122	39	1	14	66	2
Percentages:						
Total pop.	100	82.6	4.1	11.3	1.4	0.1
Kenyan African	100	83.6	4.1	11.3	*	0.1
Other African	100	28.8	1.7	8.5	61.0	*
Non-African Kenyan	100	64.8	4.5	13.6	15.9	1.1
Non-African Non-Kenyan	100	32.0	0.8	11.5	54.5	1.6

* too little to register, i.e. less than 1,000.

Source: Kenya Population Census 1969, Vol. III, Table 3.

Age-specific census survival ratio method. If we have 2 population censuses and estimated mortality by age for a place we can calculate how many people in each group will survive to the next census, e.g. 10 years later. The difference between the projected number of survivors in each group and the actual census numbers will indicate net-migration. An example is provided in table 47.

Table 47. *Example of survival ratio method in Bombay, 1941—51 (pop. in thousands).*

Age	Census 1941 pop.	Census 1951 pop.	Expected no. of survivors	Net-migration estimate
0— 4	77			
5— 9	85			
10—14	79	133	70	+ 63
15—19	83	170	82	+ 88
20—24	126	264	75	+ 189
25—29	155	254	77	+ 177
30—34	139	195	116	+ 79
35—39	109	151	142	+ 9
40—44	82	118	126	− 8
45—49	47	76	97	− 21
50—54	37	66	70	− 4
55—59	15	32	38	− 6
60 +	25	42	48	− 6
Total over 10 years	897	1.501	941	+ 560

Source: UN. Manual VI. Methods of Measuring Internal Migration. 1970, p. 26.

This method is in principle a projection of the population, but the 0—9 year-olds are not taken into consideration as very young children do not play a major role in the migration flow. In table 47, the population 0—4 years old in

Table 48. *Sex-ratios among adults in towns in Kenya 1969.*

Central Province		Coast	
Thika	187	Kilifi	118
Kiambu	176	Malindi	138
Fort Hall	160	Kinangop	77
T. Falls	151	Lamu	86
Nyeri	185	Mombasa	161
Karatina	179	Voi	177
		Wundanyi	89
Eastern		Galole	84
Embu	202		
Isiolo	128	*Rift Valley*	
Kitui	183	Eldama Ravine	116
Machakos	169	Kericho	179
Athi River	222	Lumbwa	130
Marsabit	127	Londiani	109
Meru	202	Nanyuki	134
		Nakuru	150
		Gilgil	167
Nyanza		Naivasha	165
Kisii	193	Elburgon	113
Kisumu	160	Njoro	122
Homa Bay	189	Molo	132
Migori	185	Kapsabet	151
		Narok	184
		Wamba	98
Western		Maralal	123
Bungoma	168	Baragoi	69
Kakamega	153	Kitale	161
		Lokitaung	110
Nairobi	*186*	Eldoret	164

Source: Kenya Population Census 1969. Vol. II, Table 2 (calculations).

1941 census (77 thousands) are going to be 10—14 years old in 1951. Some of the 77 thousands have died and 70 thousand are expected to survive. The comparison between the expected number of people in this age-category and the actual enumerated number makes up the estimated net-migration. Likewise with the other age-groups, e.g. of the 79 thousand 10—14 year olds in 1941, 75 thousand are expected to survive to 1951 when they will be 20—24 years. Actually not 75 but 264 thousand were enumerated, estimating an inmigration in this age-group of 189 thousand. Total net-migration is found by summing net- migration in the single age-groups., (excepting the young children). This method is also an indirect method, using residuals for estimation and is therefore highly dependent on the quality of the data.

Estimations on the basis of the age-sex structure. This method is based on the differential age-sex migration pattern, which implies that bulks and gaps in the urban or rural age-structure may be a result of migration. The existence of large numbers of young men in urban areas, and their absence in rural areas, provides some evidence of the amount and pattern of migration. However, the

Graph 21. *Age-sex pyramids for Nairobi E. P. D. and Nyanza Province. 1969.*

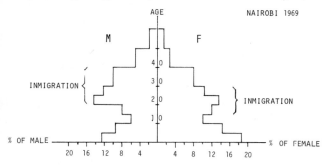

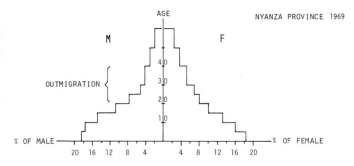

Source: Calculations of *Kenya Population Census 1969*, Vol. 1.

bulks and gaps may also result from changing fertility if it is equal for the two sexes. If migration to the urban areas includes an equal number of men and women, then sex-ratios are not valid for measuring rural-urban migration, and this method will also be invalid for measuring rural-rural migration. Table 48 illustrates the use of sex-ratios as indicators of migrations for towns in Kenya 1969. The problem of interpreting them is that low sex ratio may either indicate little or no in-migration, or in the case of the very big cities it may indicate a relatively higher female migration flow than to less important cities.

Examples of different age-structure are provided in graph 21, indicating in-migration (especially of young men) to Nairobi, and out-migration of men from Nyanza Province.

Supplementary reading

1. S. H. Ominde & C. N. Ejiogu (eds): *Population Growth and Economic Development in Africa*. N. Y. 1974.

    E. V. Engmann: *Some Consequences of Population Movements*, pp. 173—187.

    H. Rempel and M. P. Todaro: *Rural-to-Urban Labour Migration in Kenya*, pp. 214—234.

2. J. C. Caldwell & C. Okonjo (eds): *The Population of Tropical Africa*. N.Y. 1968.

    R. M. Prothero: *Migration in Tropical Africa*, pp. 250—263.

    S. H. Ominde: *Some Aspects of Population Movements in Kenya*, pp. 264—269.

3. B. Egero & R. Henin (eds): *The Population of Tanzania*. An Analysis of the 1967 Population Census. Census Vol. 6, Dar es Salaam, 1973.

    C. F. Claesson & B. Egero: *Migration*, pp. 56–75.

4. P. M. Mbithi & C. Barnes: *Spontaneous Settlement Problem in Kenya*. Nairobi 1975, pp. 82—87.

5. W. R. Ochieng: *Eastern Kenya and its invaders*. Nairobi 1975, pp. 27—41.

6. G. S. Were: *A History of the Abaluyia of Western Kenya, 1500—1930*. Nairobi 1967.

7. W. T. S. Gould (ed): Migrations in Africa (special topic volume). In: *International Migration Review*. Vol VIII, No. 3 1974.

    W. T. S. Gould: *International Migration in Tropical Africa*, pp. 347—366.

    R. Mansell Prothero: *Foreign Migrant Labour for South Africa*, pp. 383–394.

    W. T. S. Gould: *Refugees in Tropical Africa*, pp. 413—430.

8. S. H. Ominde: *The Population of Kenya, Tanzania and Uganda*, Nairobi 1975, pp. 40—58.

9. I. L.O.: *Employment, Incomes and Equality*, Geneva 1972, pp. 45—50.

10. R. M. A. Zwanenberg with Anne King: *An Economic History of Kenya and Uganda 1800—1970*. Nairobi 1975, pp. 253—274.

11. Samir Amin (ed): *Modern Migrations in Western Africa*. Oxford 1974, pp. 84—115, Introduction by Samir Amin.

Chapter XII

The Labour Force

Most countries need information on the size and composition of the working and non-working members of the population. This reflects the social and economic conditions of the country, and as a base for economic planning one needs to know the dimensions of the country's manpower supply and structure. Only part of the population is involved in the labour force as some are only consumers while others are both consumers and producers. In the study of the labour force, it is however important to analyse also the nature and extent of employment and unemployment in the population. For example, how many people are in wage employment and how are they differentiated into occupational and industrial patterns at a given time? How do shifts occur over time in the composition and distribution of the labour force? Why do some participate in economic activity and others do not? etc. Labour force analysis involves a variety of demographic factors such as fertility, mortality and migration, but the analysis also has to be closely related to economic factors. The following questions become significant: (1) How does the age-sex structure of the population affect the size and composition of the labour force? (2) How is the fertility pattern related to women's participation in the labour force? (3) What determines the choice of occupations for both men and women and how do these affect social position and child-bearing patterns? (4) How is migration and population distribution affected by the occupational structure and how do these processes in turn influence the occupational structure? (5) What implications do wage control policies, and differences in wages and work conditions across industries and in rural and urban areas, have for the movement of labour within the labour market? These seem to be major influencing factors on migration patterns and unemployment within a country. (6) What is the impact of the educational level on women's labour force participation and, therefore, on fertility?

On the whole then, fertility, population growth and distribution, occupational and industrial composition, income distribution and manpower utilization are closely inter-related. Knowledge of the age-sex structure of the labour force as well as the projected or perceived growth of it, is necessary in order to identify differential participation levels by skills, occupation, industry and location. One has to take account of all this when adopting strategies for dealing with problems of unemployment and underemployment, manpower training, the creation of new jobs, etc. Some of the relationships between the various factors determining the size and supply of the labour force are illustrated by a flow diagram:

Flow diagram of basic determinants of labour force size.

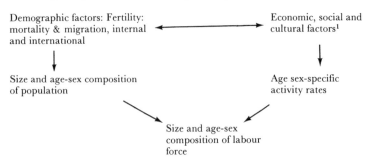

Source: Ghazi M. Farooq, "Population growth, manpower and employment". In: *Population and Development Planning,* ed. W. C. Robinson, p. 46.

Not only does one look at the labour force, but also at dependency ratios as indicators of the proportion of consumers in the population, and the level and nature of expenditure and investment on services. The two concepts are therefore considered to be indicators of social and economic development in a country.

Problems of definition

In relation to sociological and economic research as well as planning, the labour force concept may be used in a variety of ways using different definitions, thus mixing the demographic and economic approaches.

The conventional Western definition of labour force is limited to the strict demographic variables. The standard definition classifies all people between ages 15—64, i.e. the working ages, as the labour force in the strict demographic sense. These groups of the population are considered "mainly producers" while those below 15 and above 64 years are perceived as consumers or dependents only. This does not mean that all people of 15—64 years are working or employed, but that these are the potentially economically active population. However, the concept must not be confused with the group of "economically active" which is always a smaller share of the population than the total labour force. One must however question the relevance of a conceptual framework and

[1] According to Farooq—Economic factors: per capita GNP, average earning level for workers, employment opportunities and their geographical distribution, industrial and occupational structure, organisation of production, etc.

Social factors: Educational opportunities and attainment, urbanization, marital laws and characteristics.

Cultural factors: Traditional attitudes toward participation of different groups, particularly women in economic activity, religious influences on attitudes to work etc.

age limits developed on the basis of the socio-economic structure of developed societies when dealing with East African economic structures. The minimum age is set at 15 years, because education is widespread in the developed regions and it is assumed that most persons enter the labour force only after finishing school around the age of 15 (even if this is not valid in these countries any more). However, for the developing countries with rural based economies, this age is probably too high. It seems clear that in many developing societies children start contributing to the family production from the age of six onwards. Examples from some African censuses show that the age limit has tended to be lower than 15 years, e.g. 6 years in Libya and Algeria, 10 years in Ethiopia.[2] One must also note that for the formal and urban sector in the developing countries, for example Kenya, the minimum age may in fact be higher, probably due to late entrance into school as well as longer periods spent in school. Therefore, the established minimum age for labour force definition is questionable.

The upper limit of 64 years may also be too high or too low. In the developed societies social security schemes and pension schemes determine the age at which older people stop working. But in African countries there are usually no such schemes; in the rural areas old people may continue working until they are very old. Census and survey data prepared by John Durrand for 27 developing countries shows high labour participation rates for older males in the rural areas.[3] Even in the age group 65—69, over half of the countries show participation rates above 80%. These data are consistent with some U. N. data where it appears that the reported male participation rate for various countries is above 90% among the 55—64 years old males and around 70% for older males.

One must also consider differences in mortality levels: in countries of relatively high mortality, the expectation of life at birth (e_o) is usually approximately 50 years, compared to the developed nations where $e_o = 70$ years. Kenya has modified the usual international assumption of 64 years as the upper limit for determining the labour force to 59 years. The argument for this modification is the lower life expectancy in the country.[4] However, the minimum age still remains 15 years and considering the socio-economic context of the country, the criteria used for establishing these limits need to be discussed.

Another problem in labour force analysis lies in defining economic activity. The usual definition of the economically active population is: the number of persons in some form of employment plus those seeking employment. Therefore the economically active population = those employed + those unemployed in the working ages. This creates problems, as not all those who do not work are unemployed, e.g. housewives are not considered employed, and neither are students. Another way of defining economic activity is by asking what is a person's usual occupation (gainful work). For more steady statuses, gainful

[2] "Demographic Problems of Growth and Data Collection in Africa", Population Programme Centre, ECA, p. 5

[3] John Durrand: *Economic Development and Dimensions of the Labour Force.* 1975

[4] *Kenya Statistical Digest.* Vol. IX, No. 2, June 1971, p. 4.

occupation is a better reflection of the situation, but in places of frequent change of occupation, numbers actually employed might be a better measure of the volume of employment. It is clear from the above that the definition of economic activity implies a standard of judging what activities are productive and by what degree of performance to classify a person as being active. The problems may not be as great for industrialized countries where the majority of the people are in wage employment, or for the formal sector of the economies of developing countries, as it is for the subsistence sector where the concentration is on agriculture and the many part-times jobs.

One of the problems of estimating the economically active population in East Africa is related to the problem of many casually employed as these estimations have to be made during the peak seasons. For example, the numbers employed on small farms and settlement schemes in Kenya were estimated in 1969 for one day during the long rains and one day during the short rains. This gave an indication of 186,000 permanently and 192,000 casually employed.[5]

The entire concept of the economically active population has been questioned with respect to its usefulness in developing countries. The traditional definition of production tends to include only activities which contribute to the GNP. Such activities as housework, unpaid family work, childcare and such activities that women and children normally perform in the rural areas are not considered production. Childrearing, for example, is considered an economic activity if performed in an institution or by an employee, but not if the mother or other members of the family rear the child. However, the separation between producing marketable or economic goods and services, and producing non-market or "home services", such as those of a subsistence farmer or a housewife, becomes imprecise in developing countries. This point about the serious limitations with the usual concept of labour force is well illustrated when one considers family enterprises. As Mueller points out,[6] "children and women in rural areas are largely unpaid family workers. They may work regularly anywhere from one to ten or more hours per day. Or they may work occasionally, i.e. on some days, in some weeks, during some seasons." Thus in subsistence economies every family member may contribute to some extent to the production of commodities for the family. Surveys with questions on children's labour contribution have shown that most young children are engaged in jobs like herding, fetching water, collecting firewood and other household tasks.

A study by J. Caldwell in the rural areas of Ghana shows that the labour contribution of children is quite substantial. He observed that "the value of children for farm work declines as subsistence agriculture is transformed into cash cropping. But as the economy becomes more market-oriented, petty trading, especially by daughters, assumes greater significance. In traditional societies the work of children has been chiefly of four kinds: farming, housework, water-carrying, and the undertaking of errands or the delivery of mes-

[5] I. L. O., *Employment, Incomes and Equality*, Geneva, 1972, p. 39.

[6] Eva Mueller: "The Economic Value of Children in Peasant Agriculture"—Conference on Population Policy, sponsored by Resources for the Future, February 28—March 1, 1975, p. 15.

sages. Often farming was further defined as weeding, hoeing, or looking after animals, while household tasks were explained as cooking, cleaning, lighting fires and looking after babies. Obviously not all work listed above is equally productive of saleable goods but in a subsistence economy, no meaningful line can be drawn between farmwork and housework.[7] The table below shows some of Caldwell's findings:

Table 49. *Percentage of children performing different work tasks in the family. Regions of Ghana 1963.*

	Division 1 (n = 312) %	Division 2 (n= 201) %	Division 3 (n = 196) %
Farm work	67	57	46
Housework	33	31	56
Water-carrying	14	14	25
Petty trading	1	22	17
Running errands or taking messages	21	13	11

Source: Caldwell: Fertility Attitudes in Three Economically Contrasting Regions of Ghana, *Economic Development and Cultural Change.* Vol. 15. No. 2. 1967, p. 229.
NB. Division 1 to division 3 reflects a transition from subsistence farming to the cash economy respectively.

A preliminary analysis of case study data on children's labour contribution collected in Kangundo (Machahos District)[8] also shows that children make significant contributions as regards activities, similar to the ones Caldwell mentions like cultivating the shamba, herding, fetching water, collecting firewood, childcare and additional household tasks. Interviews with the women indicated that the youngest ages at which children take part in household tasks are between 4 and 5 years. The major contribution appears to come from the younger children between 6 and 16 or even 18 years, who are still in school and therefore staying at home with the parents. These children help the parents both after school hours and during vacation. The older children tend to be away earning an income and therefore make their contribution only during their leave. Most of the women consider their children's labour contribution important and useful. Sometimes especially in the case of business women, the children may be doing as much work on the shamba as the mother does.

Other studies indicate the same pattern, although it appears that while the contribution of girls towards household work does not change when they start schooling, other work such as farming becomes more limited to week-ends and vacation work in the peak seasons.[9]

[7] J. C. Caldwell, "Fertility Attitudes in Three Economically Contrasting Regions of Ghana". *Economic Development and Cultural Change,* Vol. 15, No. 2 1967, p. 229.

[8] The sample comprised of 15 women and their husbands. The case studies concentrated on getting detailed information on the type and amount of contribution of all the family members to the household enterprise, especially that of the children. The fieldwork was done during January and February 1976 by P. Walji.

[9] Mette Monsted: "The Changing Division of Labour in Rural Families in Kenya". Centre for Development Research, Copenhagen, Oct. 1976. (Mimeo).

The pattern of child labour in many farm families may not be considered "economical" or contributing to the production, because it is mainly a part of the family labour engaged in subsistence. But children also assist in the cash-crop areas, and among some farm labour families more children above 6—7 years means more hands to work. In the coffee plantations and during maize harvests the children's help is important as the payment is based on piece rates.[10] Also children sell their labour mainly as herdsboys from around 8 years of age.[11]

The conclusion on children's labour therefore is, that limiting the evaluation of economic activity to a minimum age tends to underestimate their contributions.

Another important problem in measuring economically active population is the role of women's work. In all societies, women contribute to the reproduction of the labour force, by giving birth, feeding and preparing children to become fit workers in the society. In the economic calculations of GNP this area however is considered "the private sector" and is not included in the GNP estimates unless non-family members do the job.

In the African agricultural society the errors and under-estimations of the economically active population are even more serious, it is the women who tend to be the daily labour force in agriculture. They are responsible for food-crops, but also labour inputs towards the cash crops. Therefore they should also be included within the conventional economic definitions. In the Kenyan statistics the economically active population is estimated to be 95% of males 15—59 years old and 45% of females in the same ages.[12] This measure may become realistic in urban areas, where the women's employment rate is lower than that of the men. But in rural areas practically all the women are working. Most of them remain the labour force for weeding and harvesting, but they also in many cases have more than one job, thus supplementing farming with trade, brewing or as casual farm labourers. Neither in the Kangundo survey[13] nor in other studies could any of the women be considered not working—yet their work is only to a very limited extent considered as economic activity.

These critical remarks have to be kept in mind when the statistics on employment and activity rates are presented.

A look at the figures in tables 50 and 51 for different countries on male and female activity rates will show the divergence for females, thus reflecting different definition practices in reporting women's economic activity.

---

[10] Abdul Rahman: Employment Problems in Kenya Plantations with special reference to seasonal labour recruitment—ILO, JASPA, Addis, July 1975.

[11] Mette Monsted: op. cit.

[12] *Kenya Statistical Digest*, op. cit.

[13] Kangundo Case Studies: op. cit.

Table 50. *Economically active population for selected African countries: 1960.*

Country	Crude activity rate* %		
	Males	Females	Both sexes
Nigeria	51.9	34.2	43.1
Benin (Dahomey)	57.1	45.5	51.2
Ghana	49.5	31.0	40.3
Niger	59.9	5.9	32.2
Kenya	54.5	28.2	41.2
Uganda	60.0	31.1	45.6
Tanzania	57.7	33.2	45.3
Ethiopia	61.3	32.6	46.7
Algeria	51.3	1.7	26.7
Morocco	52.1	4.2	28.2
Libya	51.0	2.7	27.5

* The crude activity rate or the crude participation rate is the proportion of economically active persons to the total population.

$$Thus\ CAR = \frac{\text{Economically Active Population}}{\text{Total Population.}} \cdot 100$$

Source: ILO. Employment in Africa: Some critical issues; Geneva, 1973.

The crude activity rates are usually computed separately for males and females and by the different age-groups because of substantial age-sex variations. Table 50 clearly shows how activity rates for the whole country are significantly lowered because of the lower rates estimated for the females.

Table 51. *Percentage economically active of male and female labour force in selected countries**

Country	Male	Female
Tanzania	88%	72%
Ghana	89%	57%
Iran	93%	9%
Indonesia	89%	31%
Ethiopia	93%	7%

* The percentages are arrived at by calculating the proportion of the male and female population in the labour force ages who are recorded as economically active. i.e.:

$$\frac{\text{Economically active pop.}}{\text{Pop. in labour force ages}} \cdot 100$$

Source: B. Egero & R. Henin (eds.): *The Population of Tanzania:* An Analysis of the 1967 Population Census. Census Volume 6. Dar es Salaam 1973 p. 139.

The Tanzania census uses the population 15 and over in the denominator while Ethiopia uses the population between 10—59, but the difference in

163

countries with a young age structure (i.e. few people in the old age groups) is minimal.

From the above tables it is clear that variations in the activity rates are less considerable in the case of men than in that of women as definitions of male work are more uniform. Some countries include females who work as unpaid family labourers in household or family enterprises as part of the economically active population, others do not. More important however is the definition for women in agriculture, which engages the bulk of the female population. Some studies in Nigeria[14] and Tanzania[15] showed higher female economic activity in rural areas as compared to males: In the 1967 census analysis, Tanzania used time or hours spent by females on household enterprises as a criteria for classifying the employed—the time criterion was one-third of the full time spent on household, farming and other enterprises, which gave quite high rates. In all the Moslem countries we find very low female participation rates, as women are less involved in activities outside the home. One must therefore be careful in interpreting the reported level of female activity. The reporting of female participation in economic activity is mostly influenced on the one hand by cultural and social factors and on the other hand by differences in concepts, definitions and enumeration procedures of the economic definitions of productive work, thus rendering a contextual analysis very important.

Additional problems in classifying the economically active population also arise because of difficulties in defining unemployment. Given that the economically active population comprises of the employed as well as the unemployed, it is important to know what categories to include in statistics on the unemployed. Problems arise because of the differing nature of the unemployment problem in different countries and the lack of adequate data. The following considerations are important in the classification:

a. If one refers to open unemployment, does one include active as well as passive job-seekers? What about those who choose to be jobless because they have certain expectations about the type of work they perform and the levels of income acceptable to them, which are at variance with the work opportunities available?

b. What about those who are under-employed in terms of the number of hours they put into productive work? Also, what about nomadic tribes who may be producing far less than they might as a social group with other production patterns.

c. Does one include those who are working very hard but receive very limited incomes which are below any acceptable subsistence level? The ILO classifies these as the "working poor".[16]

d. How does one treat those irregularly employed or in part-time occupa-

---

[14] FAO: The Socio-Economic Role of Farm Women in Agricultural and National Development in West Africa. Dec. 1971.

[15] *U. N. Country Report on Tanzania.* Gabon 1971.

[16] ILO. *Employment, Incomes and Equality*, op. cit. p. 9.

tions? The numbers vary as a result of seasonal variations, but are generally large in Africa.

The easiest and most conventional method is to include only those registered as unemployed in official labour offices. This may explain the very low figure for some countries. The volume of this problem may be illustrated by the following table produced by the ILO team in 1970 (see table 52):

Table 52. *Proportions registered as seeking employment out of employed in the modern sector and of population at working age, Dec. 1970. Kenya.*

Province	Registrations as % of 1969 no. employed in modern sector	Registrations as % of pop. in working ages	Employment as % of pop. in working ages.
Nairobi EPD	31.8	17.4	54.6
Central	43.1	5.8	13.6
Nyanza	86.4	4.1	4.8
Western	142.7	4.8	3.3
Coast	47.9	8.0	16.1
Rift Valley	33.3	4.9	17.1
Eastern	71.2	3.3	4.6
North Eastern	157.1	3.3	2.1
Total	46.4	5.8	12.4

Note: special Tripartite Agreement on expansion of employment.
Source: ILO. *Employment, Incomes and Equality.* Geneva 1972, p. 531.

Here the limitations of basing an evaluation of the economically active on the formally registered employed and formally registered unemployed is clearly shown. The rate of formal employment is especially high in Nairobi, but very low in most other provinces.

P. M. Mbithi[17] shows in his paper on wage policies, industrial relations and employment, that for Kenya the openly unemployed were estimated at 10% in 1970, the working poor at 13.6% and the total unemployed at above 23%. This compares with only 3.8% unemployment for Ethiopia which does not make this distinction between openly unemployed and the working poor. It is apparent that the figures will vary with different classification criteria.

The above shows the difficulties involved in arriving at appropriate definitions of employment, unemployment and the labour force especially in subsistence economies. Most of these countries have good records of permanent employment in the "modern" or formal sector (Kenya for example has fairly detailed statistics on the number of employees by sector, industry, province, town, nationality, sex, occupation, etc)[18] but not on the informal sector which engages the bulk of the population, nor on the unemployed.

[17] P. Mbithi, "The Impact of Government Wage Policies On Industrial Relations and Employment". E. A. Countries Research Symposium On Industrial Relations and Employment. Zambia, 1976, p. 30.
[18] *Statistical Abstract 1971*, Republic of Kenya, Ministry of Finance and Planning, Statistics Division, and Economic Survey, 1972.

Sources of data

There are many conceptual problems and errors involved in the study of the labour force as mentioned above. This makes it very difficult to get reliable and accurate data and valid comparisons between countries. An ECA paper summarizes the availability and reliability of labour force statistics in Africa.

Actually, not enough attention has been given in the past to collecting adequate and reliable information on the economic activity of the population of Africa. Statistics related to this present special problems, which arise from the fact that the methods and concepts commonly used elsewhere are difficult to apply in an economy where the non-monetary sector is still very important and the division of labour is much less advanced. As the conditions are now, it is often difficult to ascertain whether women are economically active in society, nor is it easy to apply the same minimum age for employment in most African censuses as obtained elsewhere.[19]

Most of the data on the economic characteristics of a population are supplied by censuses, sample surveys by industry and occupation, and in some cases registration data (for example, in labour exchange offices). Most of the comments about the limitations of the statistics will refer to the census data, though some of them could also apply to survey data.

The census classifies people according to economic activity (by asking questions on occupation and employment), and secondly it provides total population figures by age and sex, against which to measure the size of the economically active population. However, the reliability of the data is affected by the usual errors in the census, i.e. errors in estimates of the total population and therefore the population in working ages, age mis-statements; omissions of certain groups of individuals, false statements about occupation and employment; errors in the description of the type of economic activity. It is also important to consider length of the reference period to which the census relates (the longer the period, the higher the economic activity rate), and the time at which the census is taken–if it is a peak season then a higher proportion will be in employment. Major problems also arise from the definition of various types of employment. One must therefore be aware of the constraints and limitations of censuses before using data on the labour force.

A look at the census data in the East African countries shows that only Tanzania has gone into the analysis of the data on economic activity collected in the last census.[20] Kenya did not include economic characteristics of the labour force in the 1969 census, and most of the information for the country is based on the ILO estimates and labour force surveys.

Classification of the labour force: By sex and age

Having discussed the definitional and methodological problems involved in labour force analysis, one can now examine the existing data on the labour

[19] Demographic Problems of Growth and Data Collection in Africa, op. cit.

[20] B. Egero and R. Henin: op. cit., chapter 8.

force. At present, for lack of a better definition as well as inadequate data on the subsistence and informal sectors, one has to adopt the conventional definition of labour force, and examine its composition pointing out the various constraints and limitations.

First, the labour force has to be classified by age and sex, because of the differences in participation rates at different ages as well as by sex. From table 53 on age specific activity rates, it is clear that for both developed and developing regions the economic activity is concentrated in early and middle adulthood, usually between 15 and 64 years, although both the minimum and maximum ages vary in different countries. Participation rates for different age groups are however closely related to the type of economy and the predominant level of education within the country.

Table 53. *Estimated age-specific activity rates—by sex for the world, developing and more-developed regions, 1960.*

Age	Male			Female		
	World	Developing regions	More-developed regions	World	Developing regions	More-developed regions
All ages	56.0	55.0	58.0	29.8	28.3	32.8
10—14	20.2	26.3	4.2	13.0	16.7	3.3
15—19	68.2	71.3	59.7	44.7	42.9	49.5
20—24	90.0	90.5	88.8	52.4	48.3	61.7
25—44	96.8	97.1	96.4	49.7	49.1	50.8
45—54	95.2	96.0	94.2	48.5	47.8	49.3
55—64	86.0	88.5	82.9	35.2	36.4	34.1
65 & over	49.0	64.6	34.7	16.6	19.6	14.4

Source: International Labour Office, Labour force projects, 1971. Part V, Table 2.

Note that although age-specific activity rates for the males are higher in the developing regions compared to the more-developed regions, the overall rate is higher for the developed regions because of the difference in the population structure.

Table 54. *Regional male activity rates by age group for Africa, 1960*

Age group	Total	Region of Africa (percentages)				
		Western	Eastern	Middle	Northern	Southern
10—14 years	32.8	33.4	42.2	32.1	26.9	12.0
15—19	74.9	69.3	85.2	72.7	72.4	68.4
20—24	92.7	89.8	96.6	93.6	90.9	94.6
25—44	97.8	97.5	98.6	97.5	97.4	98.1
45—54	97.2	97.5	98.2	95.4	96.4	97.6
55—64	92.8	93.0	95.1	92.2	90.8	91.7
65+	71.1	75.2	77.0	75.7	64.3	56.2

Source: ILO: Employment in Africa, Geneva 1969, Table III.

Almost all adult males are considered economically active. The common profile of male activity rates by age for the African regions shows a peak between ages 25–45 years, when virtually all men (98 %) belong to the active population (see table 54) There is a slow decline after age 45, becoming sharper for the age groups above 55 years. However there are major regional differences especially in the 10–14, 15–19 and the 65+ age groups, showing especially low activity rates for young age groups in Northern and Southern Africa.

For the females however, the picture is rather different. As has been previously discussed, there is considerable variation between the different regions because of social, cultural and institutional factors which govern the roles and expectations of women in any society and condition the attitudes of the society toward female work participation and because of the different criteria used to define and calculate the female labour force.

The curves in graph 22 show increasing rates between ages 10–54 and then a moderate decline up to age 64, after which there is a sharp drop. In most

Graph 22. *Female activity rates by age group for African regions.*

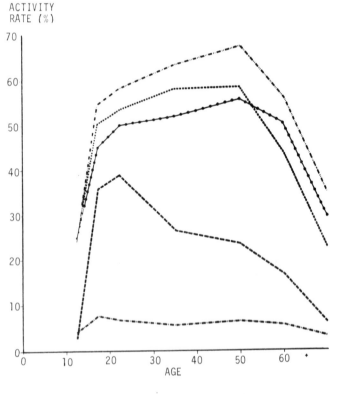

ACTIVITY RATE (%)

AGE

......Western Africa   •••Central Africa.........Eastern Africa
----Rep.of South Africa ---- North Africa

Source: ILO: *Employment in Africa.* Geneva 1969, p. 25.

168

countries, female rates are much lower than the male rates, and so the curve is much flatter. This is especially so for the Moslem countries.

It can be seen that the female economic activity rates appear to be relatively uniform for Western and Eastern Africa, indicating a female activity rate of 50—70% in the 15—59 age categories. The definitions and the patterns are relatively similar. The pattern for the Republic of South Africa however tends to be more "urbanized" and could be a result of the effort to keep the labourers in special cities, while the families, i.e. the wives and children remain in the "reserves", where they are not considered economically active.

The pattern for North Africa reflects the norms in Arab and other Moslem societies to confine the women to housework, and much more limited female participation in agriculture, trade and other economic activities outside the household.

The dependency ratio

The most utilized measure derived from the narrow demographic labour force concept is the dependency ratio or dependency burden.

The dependency ratio is defined as the number of dependents, i.e. the population, below and above the working ages per 100 persons in the labour force, i.e. population in the working ages.

$$\text{Dependency ratio} = \frac{\text{Pop. } 0\text{—}14 \text{ years } + 65 \text{ and over}}{\text{Pop. } 15\text{—}64 \text{ years}} \cdot 100$$

The dependency ratio is important as it is often used as a measurement of economic potential, determining surplus investment capability (i.e. savings) and development. The measure is, however, only a reflection of the age-structure and is used in the neo-Mathusian arguments that high fertility leads to high dependency ratio and that the "non-working" thus "eat up" the surplus generated by production.[21]

The argument is based on the following assumptions:

1. No persons below 15 or above 64 years work. They are only consumers or dependents. The previous arguments on child labour, however, contradict this.

2. All those within the 15—64 age categories work. This depends on the type of economy, whether there is high employment and how well the human resources in the country are utilized in the production process. There might be large numbers in this category who are really dependents. For example, what about those unemployed in the Kenyan context who stay with their kin till they

[21] See A Coale and E. Hoover: *Population Growth and Economic Development in Low-Income Countries: A case study of India's prospects*, Princeton University Press, Princeton 1958, for a discussion of the disadvantages of high dependency burdens for economic development.

can get jobs? In areas of out-migration of the men, higher dependency ratios are found, but this gives a false picture since the dependents are supported from elsewhere, and often have to rely on their own labour.

It is therefore clear that the ratios do not necessarily reflect the level of economic development. Other factors are much more important.

Table 55 gives dependency ratios for the different provinces in Kenya based on the 1969 census. The overall ratio for the country is estimated to be 116. Kenya has a very large proportion of her population in the young age-groups reflecting her high level of fertility. An example of the percentage distribution in the different age groups is given below. The estimated figures for the USA in 1967 are provided for comparison of an old age structure to Kenya's young age structure:

Age group	Kenya 1969	USA (1967)
0—14	48.3%	30.1%
15—59	46.3%	56.4%
60 +	5.4%	13.5%
Dependency ratio:	116	78

The type of age distribution in Kenya gives a high dependency ratio. However one must also take account of the dynamics of the age structure. Thus those who are in the dependent ages (or the young consumers) are also future producers, and the changes in the economic value of a man during his life have to be considered. Sauvy [22] makes estimates of the costs of maintaining persons in various age groups, showing that the cost of supporting a dependent child may be different from that of an aged dependent. A shift in the age structure of a population whereby the proportion of older persons in the population has risen rapidly and more than in the USA as a result of declining fertility, may also cause an increase in the dependency burden, where the society will still have to incur great costs in supporting the old-age dependents.

Table 55. *Dependency ratios for the provinces of Kenya (1969).*

Province	D.R.*
Kenya	116.2
Nairobi	58.5
Central	138.6
Coast	92.6
Eastern	123.0
North Eastern	99.0
Nyanza	120.0
Rift Valley	111.4
Western	136.5

$$*(D.R. = \frac{Pop. <15 \text{ and } 60 +}{Pop. \ 15—59} \cdot 100)$$

Source: Calculated from Kenya 1969 Census.

[22] Alfred Sauvy: *General Theory of Population*, New York 1969, pp 248—253.

Note that Nairobi's very low dependency ratio can be attributed to the high rate of in-migration of the men between 20—40 years; whereas Western province, an area of heavy out-migration of men of working ages, shows a high dependency ratio, as the children constitute a relatively larger proportion of the population.

Rural-urban differentials and economic sectors

The percentage of the labour force varies by residence. The Tanzanian census shows that especially the female participation in the labour force is much higher in the rural as compared to urban areas, 74% and 20% respectively. This wide divergence between the two sectors appears to be due to the large numbers of women in agriculture being classified in the employed class in the rural areas. The figures for the males do not vary widely, being 89% for the rural areas and 85% for the urban areas. In general, the proportions in the two sectors will vary in the different countries according to the type of production pattern and the definition of urban areas, as well as the extent of urbanization.

Dependency ratios, especially in the African countries, tend to be higher in rural than in urban areas. This can probably be attributed to the fact that the age structure in both sectors is very much affected by the migration of men in working ages from the rural to the urban areas.

The distribution of the economically active population by type of activity is related to the economic organization of the country. Shifts in population structure as related to the main activities give an indication of the direction of economic development. A structural shift in the economy wherein the preponderance of agriculture gives way to a more balanced economy, in the form of growing commercial, industrial and service sectors, indicates economic development. There are two ways of distinguishing the type of economic activity:

1. By asking questions on the occupation of the individual.
2. By asking about the industry and the number of employees as well as the sector of production. This does not necessarily indicate the work the individual does, and therefore the two types of questions do not yield the same information.

Over half the world's population is heavily dependent on agriculture. This is shown by the proportion reporting farming as the type of work they do. Within Africa, the proportion of the labour force in agriculture is highest in East Africa (a little over 85%) and lowest in South Africa (41.3%).

Table 56 shows the distribution of the labour force by sectors for selected African countries.

The proportion of the female labour force in agriculture is higher than that of the male labour force. The vary low proportion of women working in agriculture in North Africa may be ascribed to the combination of 1) male-dominated agriculture, where women are mostly expected to be responsible only for household work and 2) underestimation of the agricultural work carried out

171

Table 56. *Distribution of labour force by sector in 1960 (percent).*

Country	Agriculture	Manufacture Mining	Services	Total
Ethiopia	88.0	4.5	7.5	100
Tanzania	89.4	3.8	6.8	100
Kenya	85.8	5.1	9.1	100
Malawi	92.4	2.8	4.8	100
Sudan	85.7	6.2	8.1	100
Zambia	78.6	7.0	14.4	100

Source: Labour Force Projections 1965—1985. Part II, Africa, Geneva, 1971.

by women as family labourers. For the majority of the regions, the proportion employed in industry is fairly low and more so for women. In general, the participation of the economically active population in the agricultural and non-agricultural sectors in developing countries is strikingly different from that of the more developed countries. Usually a measure of the level of economic development and the degree of industrialization is reflected in the degree of participation of the economically active population in non-agricultural sectors.

Data on economic characteristics is one of the more complex sets of demographic data. The two basic problems are: (1) The degree of ambiguity of the concepts for the African countries. This arises from applying a Euro-American conceptual framework to the study of demographic data, and the lack of a contextual analysis of different social, cultural, institutional and economic factors. (2) The inadequacy of the data as well as the existence of systematic errors in the recorded results.

However, the census and survey data, though crude, do provide some kind of an overall picture of labour force composition, which may give a basis for formulating and evaluating social and economic policies. There is, however, need for a lot of research on economic activity in different populations, and especially on the contribution and participation of children and women as regards economic activity.

Some of the research issues that could be considered are:

- detailed age-sex specific data on hours worked, during different seasons and within different agricultural patterns.
- time budget studies, covering all household members over 6 or 8 years of age.
- need for comparative data within the different regions of the country.
- sector by sector analysis of participation ratios by specified groups e.g. age, sex...
- analysis of mobility of labour across sectors.
- operational re-definition of economic activity.

On the basis of such data, perhaps a relevant definition of an economically active population could be aimed at. If the research indicates results along similar lines to some of the findings illustrated in this paper, then Kenya should redefine the labour force, perhaps by lowering the labour force ages including a larger proportion of women in the economically active population. The present 45 % of women in the labour force appear too low considering that in some areas women are now heading households and taking over male tasks in agriculture because of heavy male out-migration.

But using the traditional definition of production only as that which contributes to the GNP does not appear relevant for the Kenyan context and can lead to a very misleading picture of the country's composition of the economically active population.

Supplementary reading

1. B. Egero & R. Henin (eds): *The Population of Tanzania*. An Analysis of the 1967 Population Census. Census vol. 6. Dar es Salaam 1973, pp. 131—148 and 243—244.

2. I.L.O. *Employment, Incomes and Equality*. Geneva 1972, pp. 33—43 and 51—60.

3. E.A.T. Abdel-Rahman: Employment Problems in Kenya Plantations with Special Reference ot Seasonal Labour Recruitment. I.L.O. JASPA Addis July 1975.

4. *U.N. Determinants and Consequences of Population Trends*. N.Y. 1974. Chapt. 9, pp. 293—337.

5. Lars Bondestam: *Some Notes on African Statistics*. Research Report, No. 18. Scandinavian Institute of African Studies, Uppsala 1973, pp. 26—30 and pp. 40—42.

6. P. Mbithi & C. Barnes: *Spontaneous Settlement Problem in Kenya*. Nbi. 1975, pp. 107—126.

# of Population

What is growth?

Already under the previous chapters on theories, evaluation of data, fertility, mortality and migration, the growth of population has been used as an important indicator of the other demographic phenomena.

a. Growth of population is the annual increase in the population due to births, deaths and migrations.

b. The above can be distinguished from natural growth, which only refers to the increase in population due to an excess of births over deaths. That is, natural growth = births minus deaths, or r = CBR—CDR.

Table 57. *Annual rate of growth in selected African countries 1960—70 (%).*

Country	Annual rate of growth	
	1960—65	1965—70
Kenya	2.9	3.1
Tanzania	2.5	2.5
Uganda	2.5	2.6
Ethopia	1.8	2.6
Reunion	3.2	3.2
Zambia	2.9	2.9
Angola	1.8	2.0
Mozambique	2.3	2.4
Rhodesia	3.2	3.5
South Africa	2.3	2.4
Rwanda	2.6	2.9
Gabon	0.5	0.8
Cameroon	1.8	2.0
Benin (Dahomey)	2.3	2.6
Ghana	2.7	3.1
Guinea	2.7	2.9
Liberia	1.5	1.8
Guinea Bissau	0.8	1.4
Senegal	2.3	2.9
Tunisia	2.9	3.1
Sudan	2.8	3.1
Marocco	2.7	3.4
U.A.R.	2.7	2.8

Source: ECA. Demographic Handbook for Africa, 1971.

Patterns of growth in East Africa compared with other regions.

The growth rates for selected African countries can be seen in table 57. These are compared with the growth rates for the "developed" countries at different points in time in table 58.

The increase in growth rates over time in most of the countries has been mainly due to the improvement of health and the decline in mortality. Therefore, countries with very high rates of growth seem to be those where the health programme has been most successful, since fertility in these countries does not seem to vary as much as mortality does.

Table 58. *Estimated natural growth, birth and death rates for developed and Third World Countries from 1750 to 1970 (per thousand).*

	Developed regions			Third World countries		
	CBR	CDR	r	CBR	CDR	r
1750—1800	38	34	4	41	37	4
1800—1850	39	32	7	41	36	5
1850—1900	38	29	9	40	38	2
1900—1910	34	21	13	41	34	7
1910—1920	26	23	3	40	37	3
1920—1930	28	16	12	41	31	10
1930—1940	22	14	8	41	29	12
1940—1950	20	15	5	40	28	12
1950—1960	22	10	12	43	22	21
1960—1970	20	9	11	41	17	24

Source: U.N. Determinants and Consequences of Population Trends. N.Y. 1974, p. 518

Comparison with the developed countries shows that the growth pattern for the developing countries is different. Originally in Europe, the rate of natural increase was low on the average due to high fertility and a high mortality level. Mortality was fluctuating thus leading to large fluctuations in population growth, with high growth occurring in the good harvest years and low rates of increase or even declining rates in the years of epidemics and famines. However, these figures are for major areas, and must be taken with some caution. Fluctuations in the different countries and in smaller regions within countries were much greater. Also, the movement of population from Europe to America, Oceania and Africa relieved some of the pressure from the natural growth rate in Europe. The table does not take this into account. The major flow of slaves from Africa to America is not covered either, because of the concentration on the natural growth of the population through births and deaths.

Composition of growth

Low growth or negative growth may be a result of the following combinations of demographic variables:—

1. high fertility, high mortality, and low migration
2. high fertility, high mortality, high out-migration
3. high fertility, low mortality, high out-migration
4. low fertility, high mortality, low migration
5. low fertility, low mortality, low migration
6. low fertility, low mortality, high out-migration

These different types of growth are qualitatively different and have different implications for the composition of the population. The first type was the one found in Europe in the period before 1800 and in Africa before the slave trade. This reflected low internal natural growth.

The second type did not occur in major areas of Europe, although groups of people migrated across boundaries. However, this was the type found in Africa during the heavy slave-transportation resulting in a serious decline in the population which affected the total economy and production.

The third type was found in the out-migration areas of Europe in the late 19th century where the high natural increase resulting from the decline in mortality was directed towards other continents.

The fourth type has only been found for short periods in small areas. This is often the case in areas with a very high level of sterility and infertility. It can also occur when fertility is low during periods of war, and can lead to a very unstable situation. A case in point is Ireland during the 19th century famine.

The fifth type is the one most highly appreciated and desired as a stable harmony. This is the only type of low growth of population referred to in discussions on the benefits of a low rate of population growth.

The sixth type is a very recent phenomenon in areas of Europe where declining economic growth is pushing people toward areas with higher chances of employment.

High growth may be a result of the following combinations of demographic variables:—

1. high fertility, low mortality, low migration
2. high fertility, high mortality, high in-migration
3. low fertility, low mortality, high in-migration

The first type was the pattern found in Europe during the first stage of the Demographic Transition, and is the type of high growth rate prevalent in most developing countries today. This is the type of growth referred to by economists when they argue that the population growth is "eating up" the economic surplus.

The second type was found in the settler areas of Africa and during the initial period of settlement in America and Oceania. It was also found in the slave based plantation economies in Middle America.

The third pattern reflects the trend during the major period of in-migration of Europeans to America. This pattern is also found today in the European countries which are "importing" labour from other countries, e.g. Switzerland, where nearly half of the manual labour force is made up of foreigners, mainly from Italy, Yugoslavia and Turkey.

This description of national population growth refers to the development of nations and major regions. If smaller areas are taken into consideration then the patterns with high migration rates become much more important, especially between regions in a country and between rural and urban areas. On a national basis those patterns based on migration do not seem to be very stable. The most stable for the moment seems to be the pattern of low fertility and low mortality, which maintains a balance. However, we do not know how stable the pattern of high fertility and low mortality in the developing countries seems to be.

What part of the population is growing?

The different patterns of growth also result in a different composition of the population in terms of sex and age. High fertility results in high population growth in the young age-groups and a high dependency burden; whereas high in-migration leads to large increases in the adult labour force, mostly among the men. These two patterns are very different in nature. Therefore, when we are concerned about the implications of population growth, we often have to specify what part of the population is growing: is it mainly the school age population, the labour force, or the old age population?

In relation to the implications of population growth for school expenses the increase among the pre-school and school age children is of importance. This group is also significant, together with the proportion in the labour force, in determining dependency burden. As regards employment, the increasing size of the labour force becomes important but this is just one of the factors, and the creation of jobs within the economy must also be taken into account. However, although a high increase in the labour force is seen as a threat to the economy of the developing nations, it has been perceived as an attribute for the developed economies because they could use the additional labour force since they had enough jobs available (until around 1974). Also, in the USA during the period of mass migration, the increasing labour force was seen as a significant contribution to the development of the economy, as the labour came ready for work and there was enough land available, while the costs of raising these people had been carried by other countries.

In the economies based on foreign labour, such as in Germany, USA (to a certain extent), Switzerland, Zambia, South Africa, the importation of labour is a clear benefit, as these people can be used as a labour reserve, available when labour is needed, yet the country has no obligation to feed, educate or assist them during unemployment or in old age. In addition to this, the position of the

177

labourers is flexible, they can be used when there is a boom in the economy, and thrown out when the economy is stagnating, thus the country does not have to carry the burden of supporting them. Therefore the growth of the labour force is important in relation to the structure and growth of the economy and it is not the growth of the labour force per se which determines the economic implications of population growth.

Why are we so concerned about population growth?

Population growth is used in the economist's calculations of economic development. During the 1960s, there appeared to be a negative correlation between population growth and economic development. This has led to concern about the retarding effects of rapid population growth. This relationship has largely been used in the classification of "developed" versus "underdeveloped" economies, where many of the other characteristics are different. The correlation does not imply that the same trend will be found under other conditions, or that there is any causal relationship between these factors. As we have seen, the large increase in the population of the USA did not result in low economic growth during the 19th century. Also, we know from Ester Boserup's research that in Africa high population growth was linked to high economic growth. Her argument is that in the thinly populated areas of Africa, a high population growth and high densities are necessary for the development of new technology and for expanding the infrastructure necessary for the development of the market system. Some of the relationships between population growth and economic growth are outlined below:

Population growth and land resources

This is an important issue in Kenya, where it is argued that there is enough land but that most of the land is privately owned and not free for expansion. Also, most of the discussion on policies is related to the possibilities of introducing irrigation in the dry areas or dry land farming technology, and of expanding the potential of the land, in order to cater for the growing rural population. It is therefore clear that policies on land adjudication, land ownership and land use, and type of technological use have to be taken into account to determine the impact of the population factor on land resources and the carrying capacity of the land.

Population growth and gross domestic product per capita

The argument that the lower the population growth, the higher the per capita income is widely used in the neo-Malthusian approach to population. Thus, if the economy is growing at a rate of 3%, a population growth rate of 3% will "eat up" the whole surplus of the economy. A higher rate of population growth will depress the real per capita income, whereas if the rate of growth is checked, then progress on a per capita GDP basis will be accelerated, all other things being equal. The last assumption, however, does not hold. With a bigger population GDP also has to increase, since there are more producers and consumers in the economy, thus creating a larger market for goods. Besides, this measure is of little relevance as an indicator of development in a country like Kenya where all the subsistence production is not included as part of the GDP, whereas the population in subsistence is all included in the GDP/population equation.

Population growth and unemployment

It has been stated that of the factors that have contributed to the unemployment crisis, population growth is one of the most important. A high rate of growth would mean a very large labour force and therefore the need for more jobs. However, employment is closely related to the types of production, patterns of land use, land distribution, choice of technology etc. The unemployment problem therefore goes much deeper than the population argument would imply. In most cases, where the comparison is made, only the formal sector employment is evaluated in terms of the labour force, and in countries where only a fraction of the labour force is engaged in the formal sector, this can give a distorted picture of the employment situation.

Population growth and education

A high rate of increase of young people, and at the same time an increase in the school enrollment as is the case in Africa, implies a very heavy increase in expenditure for the educational sector. If the population increase is curbed, the expenditure would be much lower, but also expenditure can be seen as an investment into the future labour force.

In relation to this, the arguments by E. Boserup and Samir Amin should be mentioned. Historically a high increase in population has created the basis for the development of new technology, which again provided a higher surplus in agriculture and thus a capacity for more people. Especially for the scattered populations, in the thinly populated areas, all kinds of services are lacking, and it is actually too expensive to provide these for such small populations as the per capita expenditure will be much too high.

Therefore areas with small population, especially nomadic areas are underdeveloped with respect to roads, health services, educational facilities, marketing for their products, and thus are also limited in their economic growth potential. However, if the population is larger, or at least more concentrated in a few focal points, it becomes cheaper and/or easier to build out the infrastructure to cater for this population as is the case in the population policy of Tanzania. It is therefore important to critically examine the relevance of the various arguments used about the implications of population growth for socioeconomic development.

Measures of growth

a. Annual increase = Births—Deaths + Net-migration per thousand of the
    population, or

    Annual inrcease = Natural increase + Netmigration per thousand of the
    population.

Annual increase may be estimated on the basis of two population censuses.

b. Natural increase = Births—Deaths per thousand of the population, or
    Natural increase = r = CBR—CDR, or
    Natural increase = relative surplus of births to deaths in a population.

c. Doubling period for a population = number of years for doubling the size
of the population, if the annual increase continues at the same level. If the
annual increase is approx. 3.5%, then a doubling of the population will take
approximately 21 years. If the annual increase is approx. 1.0%, then the
population will double in about 70 years. If the annual increase is approx.
0.5%, then the doubling period will be 139 years.

One of the problems of measuring growth is the same as the one mentioned
previously under the migration measures, namely that it is measured by the
residual of other factors and not directly. Also, if growth is measured as the
difference between censuses, then both the censuses have to be correct and
complete. If the last census is the most complete, then the resulting increase is
going to be too high. For example, if the Kenya population census of 1962 had a
10% omission rate and the 1969 census had a 4% omission rate, then the
difference is going to be counted as the increase in the population resulting from
fertility, mortality and migration regardless of the errors in the census counts.

Supplementary reading

1. Simeon Ominde: *The Population of Kenya, Tanzania and Uganda.* Nbi. 1975, pp. 115—123

2. Lars Bondestam: *Population Growth Control in Kenya.* Scandinavian Institute for African
Studies. Research Report, No. 12. Uppsala 1972, pp. 10—27.

3. S. H. Ominde & C. N. Ejiogu (eds): *Population Growth and Economic Development in Africa.*
London 1972.
    pp. 285—290 Igun: Social and Economic Effects of Rapid Growth Rates;
    pp. 304—312 M. D. Veitch: Population Growth and the Health Services;
    pp. 332—335 Y. Komora: Population Growth and Educational Planning in Kenya.

4. National Academy of Sciences: *Rapid Population Growth. Consequences and Policy Implementation,*
Vol. 2. Baltimore 1971.
    pp. 368—402 Leslie Corsa & D. Oakley: Consequences of Population Growth for Health Services
in Less Developed Countries;
    pp. 245—272 Theodore Schultz: The Food Supply-Population Growth Quandary;
    pp. 148—174 T. Paul Schultz: An Economic Perspective on Population Growth.

Chapter XIV

Population Projections

Methods of projection

One of the reasons for the interest in the growth rate of the population is the need in economic and social planning for a kind of "prediction" or projection of the population some years ahead. In order to make the projection of the population we have to take into consideration the previous trends in the population growth.

The projection of population does not necessarily mean a prediction of the population; rather, it is an estimate of the population some time in the future, based on certain assumptions about changes in mortality, fertility and migration.

The possibility of making relatively correct projections for a short time period is based on the fact that there is a lot of inertia in the changes of population size and structure. For example, the people projected to be in Kenya in 1985 are for the major part already born and are likely to survive to that time.

Projections however will not be very reliable if drastic changes, occur, for instance, changes in mortality through drought, famine, war or major changes in the fertility or migration pattern. For example, the projections for the population of Uganda, could not have anticipated the 1972—73 population development and the migration pattern in relation to the expulsion of the Asian population. Therefore these changes made most of the projections for the urban population useless.

The assumptions for a projection are always based on "qualified guesses" about the possible and likely changes in the different population variables. Therefore there are different methods of making projections, and these will be briefly covered in the next section.

Linear extrapolation

This just uses the size of the population until the last census. The curve after this census is simply extrapolated linearly based on an addition of the same absolute number of people each year. In the Kenyan cases, for example, this would mean that the absolute annual increase of the population is added each year to extrapolate the curve (graph 23 a).

Exponential extrapolation

In this curve the population size during the period until the last census is given

181

Graph 23. *Extrapolation of populations.*

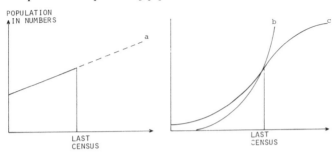

(as above). This time there is a difference since the population is perceived to grow each year with the same *relative growth rate*. This gives *exponential growth*, since the same percentage increase each year of a larger and larger population will give a higher and higher absolute number each year. (graph 23 b). In Kenya this would imply projecting the population with a rate of 3.5% a year up to say around 2000.

The logistic projection.

This is based on the experience in Europe during the demographic transition. In this "model" the growth is perceived to initially follow the curve as in graph 23 b, but then there is levelling out of the growth rate as a new balance between births and deaths is obtained, with low fertility and low mortality (graph 23 c).

For Kenya the two last methods could be applied, as no one yet knows whether population growth will decline, when it will decline and by how much. Kenya and most of Africa is in the phase where rapid growth is taking place and any one method may be as good as another for projections up to the year 2000.

However, the three methods mentioned here have a limited application as they only provide projections of the total population, i.e. the total absolute number of the people in the country. Moreover if the projection does not hold when it is checked after a new census, then there is no basis for correcting and adjusting it since single determinants of change cannot be identified or measured.

Component method.

The most important and most applied method of projections is the component method, whereby all the age-groups of the population are projected for the next 5, 10, or 15 years, on the basis of specific assumptions about fertility, mortality and sometimes migration in the different ages.

This method however also involves making "qualified guesses" about the development of the demographic variables, i.e. whether major changes are going to take place in these variables and if so, in what direction the change will occur. Therefore the type of assumption we make becomes extremely important for each projection.

Assumptions about mortality: Projections in Kenya on the basis of the 1969 census, suggest an increase in life-expectancy of 0.5 years per year, due to the decline in mortality. This gives the following life expectancies for the future.

for 1970—75: e_o males = 50.3 years e_o females 53.7 years
    1975—80   ,,   5.9 years   ,,   55.4 years
    1980—85   ,,   53.6 years   ,,   57.0 years

According to the 1967 Tanzanian Census mortality was projected to decline to a CDR of 22 per thousand between 1967—70; to 20 per thousand between 1970—75 and between 1975—1980 to 18 per thousand. This trend in mortality is mostly based on the Kenyan trend, where the mortality has declined faster than in Tanzania. But further declines in these countries will of course be related to social, political and economic development. This will determine the number of rural health centres to be built; the development in the nutritional status among the different groups of the population; improvements in the production of food crops, etc. With short term projections there is a good chance of reaching a relatively accurate prediction as the population components do not usually change that drastically.

Fertility assumptions are much easier for short term projections but much more difficult for projections in the distant future. Alternative projections are often made giving both high level projections and low level projections together with an evaluation of the likelihood of these two. These alternatives also help the planners to evaluate the maximum and minimum numbers in each age-group and year, and thereby to establish certain limits in planning for the population.

In Kenya two alternative projections have been made: 1) one with a constant fertility until 2000, i.e. with a total fertility rate of 7.6, 2) the other with a decline in fertility from 1975 onwards giving a total fertility rate of 4.0 in 2000.

In Tanzania two levels of fertility rates were also used in the projections. The high level projection was based on slightly increasing fertility, i.e. from a CBR of 48‰ in 1967—70 to a rate of 49‰ in 1970—75 and 50‰ in 1975—80. This is a continuation of the trend of the fertility increase in Tanzania between 1957 and 1967. The low level projection was based on the assumption that fertility remained constant throughout the period with a CBR of 47‰. The assumptions about the trend of demographic variables in Tanzania is based on the recent trends in demographic factors in Kenya.

The assumptions are "qualified guesses" based on the perception of the most likely development of the variables, and a certain stability in this development. In Kenya the assumption about the decline in fertility from 1975 onwards is based on the anticipated effect of the large scale family planning programme.

However, at present this seems to be unlikely and a slower decline in fertility starting at a later period, around 1980 or 1985, seems to be a better basis for projections on the size and composition of the population.

Population projections provide a method for a quantitative estimate of the population in future periods. However, these are based on assumptions related to the perception of a country's social and economic development and the success of different aspects of development. The most important aspect of the projections will be this evaluation, and the assumptions therefore will be the main basis for discussion of the relevance of certain projections.

But any government body has to plan both on the basis of certain political principles, and on the knowledge about the size and structure of the population. If a political decision on free education is taken, for example, then the Government has to know how many school-children can be expected and how many schools and teachers would be needed for them. Therefore projections have a lot of implications for actual economic planning. The component method helps to clarify the quantitative implications of certain mortality and fertility assumptions.

In the component method the principle is to find the mortality level which is going to be used for the calculation of survival ratios. In graph 24, a life-table is presented with an indication of what survival ratios are.

If a population of those "exactly 5 years of age" (at exact birthday) should be projected 5 years, then the survival ratio in the life-table would be the number of survivors at their 10th birthday = l_{10} divided by the number of survivors at their 5th birthday = l_5. However we are not trying to project a population exactly 5 years old, but a population in the different age-groups, i.e., we have to estimate what proportion of those 5—9 years old will still be alive 5 years later,

Graph 24. *Life-table and survival ratios.*

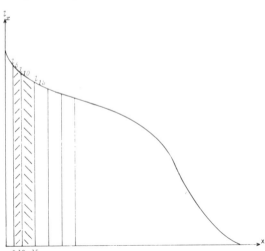

thus reaching the 10—14 year age-group. The survival ratio for this group is thus defined as the area under the life-table from 10 to 15 years divided by the area under the life-table from 5 to 10 years. This is the survival ratio for the 5—9 year old group for a 5-year period. The general formula is:

$$_nL_{x+n}/_nL_x \text{ or for the example } _5L_{10}/_5L_5$$

By using the life-table and survival ratios we can make projections for all the age-groups and see what proportion of the population can be expected to survive for the next 5 or 10 years. The only age-group that we cannot project by using survival ratios is the age-group 0 to 5 years old, as this group is determined not only by mortality, but also by fertility in the period.

Table 59. *Life-table and survival ratios for females and survival ratios for males in projecting the Kenyan population, 1970—75*.*

Age	Life-table females (1)	$_5L_x$ females (2)	Survival ratios females (3)	Survival ratios males (4)
0—4	100,000	438782	.961	.957
5—9	84,756	421850	.992	.990
10—14	83,984	418435	.991	.989
15—19	83,390	414607	.991	.982
20—24	82,453	409103	.987	.978
25—29	81,188	402298	.983	.974
30—34	79,731	394578	.981	.968
35—39	78,100	385600	.977	.956
40—44	76,140	374598	.971	.938
45—49	73,699	360373	.962	.908
50—54	70,450	341338	.947	.868
55—59	66,086	315383	.924	.819
60—64	60,068	279900	.887	.762
65—69	51,896	234338	.837	.686
70—74	41,843	176493	.753	.619
75+	28,754	110705	.589	.436

* see assumptions above.

In a 5-year projection, the whole population from ages 5—100 can be projected based only on mortality assumptions by applying the survival ratios selected (using col. 3 and 4 table 59).

The fertility assumption is in the form of age-specific fertility rates, i.e., the risk of giving birth per year in the different 5-year age-groups. But we have to find out the number of women under the risk of giving birth, and the number of years under risk for these women. The measure is the same as the "population at risk" covered earlier. Thus, we calculate the average number of women in the 5-year period and multiply by 5. For example, in table 60 the number of years under risk for women 20—24 years old between 1970 and 1975 will be:

Women 20—24 years 1970—75 $= ({}_5\text{Women}_{20}^{70} + {}_5\text{Women}_{20}^{75}) \cdot 5/2$

or $\dfrac{483+584}{2} \cdot 5 = 2667.5$

This then forms the basis for calculating the number of births in the population—the number of births for women between 20 and 25 years old in the 5-year period, can therefore be found by multiplying the women under the risk of giving birth by number of years for which the population is being projected, and multiplied by the age specific fertility rate for women 20—24 years old. For the Kenyan example the number of births for women 20—24 years $= 2667.5 \times 0.33 = 420$. The total number of births (both male and female) will be the sum of column 7 in table 60 or the sum of births for each age group of women.

Having found the total number of births, we have to estimate the total number of female births and the total number of male births, by using the expected or usual sex-ratio at birth. For example, if the total number of births is 3109, then female births will be: $0.49 \cdot 3109 = 1523$. Male births will be: $0.51 \cdot 3109 = 1586$ (or $3109{-}1523$). We now have the number of births for the 5-year period. However, as some of these births have taken place long before, up to nearly five years before 1975, some of the newborn have also died before 1975, and we have to reduce the number of births according to the risk of dying, in order to find the actual number of children 0—4 years old in 1975.

Graph 25. *Survival ratio for 0—4 year olds.*

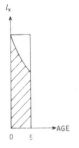

The proportion of the newborns who will survive to the 0—4 year age-group in 1975, will be calculated by using the survival ratio, which will equal the area in the life-table between 0 and 5 year olds divided by $l_0 \cdot 5$.

Survival ratio is therefore:

$$\frac{{}_5L_0}{l_0 \cdot 5}$$

Then the female population between 0 and 5 years old in 1975 will be the female births multiplied by the female survival ratio for that group i.e.

$$1523 \cdot \frac{438{,}752}{500{,}000} = 1523 \cdot 0.878 = 1337$$

The last figure in the projection is thus found, being 1337 for females and

1359 for males, and the projection is completed. The full calculation for the females' projection is given in table 60 and the full calculation for males in table 61.

Table 60. *Projection of the female population in Kenya from 1970 to 1975, based on mortality assumptions of $e_0 = 53.7$ and total fertility rate = 7.6.*

(1)	(2) Survival ratios $_nL_{x+n}/_nL_x$	(3) Females 1970 (thous.)	(4) = (2) = (3) Females 1975 (thous.)	(5) = (3) . (4) · 5/2 Women-year of risk of birth 1970—75	(6) ASFR	(7) = (5) · (6) number of births 1970—75
0—4	.961	1,083	1,337			
5—9	.992	859	1,041			
10—14	.991	709	852			
15—19	.991	589	703	3230.0	0.13	420
20—24	.987	483	584	2667.5	0.33	880
25—29	.983	393	477	2175.0	0.34	740
30—34	.981	324	386	1775.0	0.29	515
35—39	.977	263	318	1452.5	0.22	320
40—44	.971	218	257	1187.5	0.14	166
45—49	.962	176	212	970.0	0.07	68
50—54	.947	141	169			
55—59	.924	117	134			
60—64	.887	88	103			
65—69	.837	65	78			
70—74	.755	49	54			
75 +	.589	56	70*			
Total		5,612	5,775		1.52	3109

TFR = 5 · 1.52
= 7.6

Column notes

(2) Survival ratios, e.g. for group 0—4, what proportion of these will survive 5 years later, and reach the age-group 5—9. Based on estimated life-table from the mortality assumptions.

(3) Females from Census (or estimated 1 year after census)

(4) The number of females in 1975 will be the proportion of the females in 1970 who have survived the 5 years. This means that for all age-groups except the 0—4 in 1975 the projected population will be: $_nF_{x+n} = _nF_x \cdot$ survival ratio $(_nP_x.)$. E.g. females 5—9 in 1975 = females 0—4 in 1970 multiplied by survival ratio from 0—4 to age 5—9, = 1083 · 0.961 = 1041.

(5) The women-years under risk of giving births, i.e. women multiplied by years under risk, is calculated on the basis of column (3) and (4). Women-years $= [_nF_x^{70} + _nF_x^{75}] \cdot 5/2$ i.e. the average in the period multiplied by the length of the period. For example, Women-years for 15—19 year old group = (589 + 703) · 5/2 = 3230.

(6) Age-specific fertility gives the risk of giving birth for these women under the assumed fertility assumptions.

(7) Number of births in the 5-year period for each age-group of women, is the number of women-years under risk in each age-group multiplied by the age-specific fertility rate. Thus for women 15—19 years old the number of births = 3230· 0.13 = 420. The total number of births is the sum of column (7).

(8) Stage 8 is then to find the female births which equals 0.49 · 3109 = 1523.

(9) Stage 9 is to find the surviving children of these births, survival ratio = 438782/500000 = 0.878.

(10) Stage 10 is to find the number of children between 0—4 years of age = number of females 0—4 in 1975 = female births · survival ratio = 1523 · 0.870 = 1337 which is then added in column (4).

* See * to table 61.

Table 61. *Projection of male population in Kenya 1970 to 1975, under the assumption of mortality of $e_0 = 50.3$ and total fertility of 7.6.*

(1) Age	(2) Survival ratio $_nL_{x+n}/_nL_x$	(3) Males 1970 thousands	(4)=(2)(3) Males 1975 thousands
0—4	.957	1,099	1359
5—9	.990	865	1051
10—14	.989	716	856
15—19	.982	598	708
20—24	.978	493	587
25—29	.974	404	483
30—34	.968	334	393
35—39	.956	270	323
40—44	.938	220	258
45—49	.908	175	206
50—54	.868	137	157
55—59	.819	110	119
60—64	.762	79	90
65—69	.686	57	60
70—74	.619	40	39
75+	.436	40	41*
Total		5,635	6,730

Column notes to table

(2)   Survival ratios calculated on the basis of the assumed life-table.

(3)   Males calculated at census, (or estimated one year after census).

(4)   Males in 1975 are calculated on the basis of the males in 1970. Males, e.g. 20—24 in 1975 = males 15—19 in 1970 multiplied by the survival ratio for males 15—19 for the 5-year period = $598 \cdot .982 = 587$.

The first age-group 0—4 yeras old, is based on the male births in the period. This is taken from table 60 as the males = total births—female births or $0.51 \cdot$ total births $= 3109 - 1523 = 1586$ or $0.51 \cdot 3109 = 1586$.

The number of births has to be reduced according to the survival ratio for this group $= _nL_0/l_0 \cdot 5 = 0.857$. This leaves $1586 \cdot 0.857 = 1359$ in the 0—4 year category.

* Males 75 and over are calculated as: survived members of 70—74 year category + survived members of those 75 and over $= .619 \cdot 40 + .436 \cdot 40 = 24 + 17 = 41$. This is because the age-group is over 5 years, and those who are 75—100 in 1970, will be 80—100 in 1975. The new group 75—79 is coming from the survivors of age group 70—74 $(= 24)$.

Projections of special populations

In relation to economic planning the projection of the total population in Kenya only provides part of the relevant material. The projection of the total population in an area may provide the basis for estimating the need for food in an area, especially in relation to production, i.e. an evaluation of the surplus and its trends.

But the significance of projections for planning purposes lies in the projection of special parts of the population in relation to the resources available, e.g. projection of labour force in relation to employment possibilities, the projection of number of school children based on assumptions both about the number of children in school-going ages and on enrollment rates. Apart from this, for smaller areas like districts, locations or even sub-locations, a projection of the population and its structure is fundamental for estimating developmental needs. For example the number of health service facilities needed, or the decision on whether to build a hospital, health centre or dispensary will depend on population density and structure in the surrounding area, and what trend this is expected to follow. In the former "white settler" areas of the Rift Valley the need for educational and health facilities has changed tremendously with the subdivision of farms in settlement schemes and the development of companies or cooperatives which has led to a large inflow of people into the area. The increase in the population should be the basis for projecting the need for investment into expanding the existing health and educational facilities.

The projection of population for planning purposes will therefore always have to be based on the demographic components which form the basis of the projections, as well as on evaluation of the existing social and economic factors. Assumptions about the rate of investment into generation of employment activity rates, school enrollment rates etc. may however, be even more important for the actual planning than the actual projection of the population.

Population projections are also useful in the pre-planning stages in evaluating what the relationship between population and resources will be if no changes are induced. For example what would happen if the Government were to practice a laissez-faire policy and the pravailing tendencies were extrapolated 10—20 years ahead? This kind of population projection, especially in relation to employment generation, will often underline the need of planning in certain sectors of the economy.

Projections of the school-age population

A projection of the population of school children will involve a projection of the total population for about 10 to 15 years, to find the total number of children and thereafter a reduction of this number by the proportion enrolled in school in the different ages.

The number enrolled in school has increased tremendously from 1963 to 1970 (see table 62). Assuming the same system and trend in educational enrollment for the projected period, there will be 3.9 million children in primary and 350,000 in secondary school education.

Table 62. *Enrollment for primary and secondary education*

	1963	1970	1985 projected
Primary	900,000	1,400,000	3,900,000
Secondary	35,000	145,000	350,000

Source: ILO; *Employment, incomes and equality*, Geneva 1972.

The figures in 1970 are based on the finding or estimate that in 1969 about 64% of the children between the ages of 6—11 years were in primary school, though this enrollment varies with the different districts.

The enrollment in primary schools as projected in the 1974—78 Development Plan is shown in the table 63.

Table 63. *Projected enrollment in thousands. Primary schools**

Year	Std. 1	Std.2	Std.3	Std.4	Std. 5	Std. 6	Std. 7	Total
1974	450	382	334	270	234	216	230	2116
1975	504	428	374	327	248	248	242	2371
1976	565	479	419	367	263	263	278	2672
1977	582	537	469	411	319	319	295	2951
1978	600	553	526	460	358	358	357	3232

* Assumptions: annual growth of standard 1 enrollment in 12% per year until 1978, when the total enrollment is approaching the total number of children 6—12 years. From 1977 the annual increase is projected to be 3% per year (= natural growth of pop.), the rest of the classes are based on the survival ratios from one class to the next, which is due to 1) number of repeaters 2) drop-outs 3) number of passes 4) number of new entrants.
Source: Development Plan 1974–78, Republic of Kenya. Nairobi 1974, p. 440.

This table is therefore more based on estimations derived from the existing pupils in primary education and the trend of development over time rather than on the actual percentage in school in each age-group. However the number of entrants and enrollers must be based on the number of people aged about 6 years.

In projections like these on school-children there has to be some evaluation of the possibilities of expanding government economic support to the schools, especially in the projections of the secondary school population. This is very important as no expansion of secondary schools seems to be planned after 1974.

Table 64. *Projected secondary school enrollment**

Year	Form 1	Form 2	Form 3	Form 4	Form 5	Form 6	Total
1973	23,400	21,700	20,400	18,200	3,970	3,320	90,990
1974	24,600	22,800	22,200	19,800	4,450	3,830	97,680
1975	24,600	23,900	24,210	21,700	4,450	4,300	103,160
1976	24,600	24,600	26,120	23,520	4,450	4,300	107,590
1977	24,600	24,600	26,930	25,440	4,450	4,300	110,320
1978	24,600	24,600	27,740	26,260	4,450	4,300	111,950

* This projection is based on a consolidation of the already aided schools and the goal is to raise the qualty of these schools, rather than to expand the number of schools. The economic expansion is provided for additional assistance to the established schools.
Source: Development Plan 1974—78, p. 420.

The purpose of this section on projections, is to discuss what kinds of assumptions can be made, and how closely these are tied up with socio-economic development. Also the purpose is to show how projections of population are used in all planning. Not only is the size of the population relevant, but much more relevant is the availability of funds and resources. For example, how much does it cost in terms of school buildings, teachers and education of teachers to reach the targets of full enrollment in primary school? The kind of projections discussed above will answer this, and the targets can then be modified according to the money actually available.

The dependency of an expanding economy on external factors for reaching the set targets may be illustrated by the effect of the high increase in oil prices. This implied a rise in expenditures of a dimension large enough in Tanzania to delay the whole 5-year plan. Projections under such changing conditions will only reflect how the increasing costs affect the implementation of plans and how the target has to be changed accordingly, thus making the projection assumptions and the projections irrelevant under the new economic situation.

Projection of labour force, manpower and employment

Projection of the labour force is very important for estimating the manpower available and the manpower in the future Development Plan. This is often compared with a projection of the employment, including the problems of generating employment in the different sectors.

For this kind of projection, we first have to make a projection of the population in the different age and sex groups to estimate the population in the working ages for the relevant years. However what is more important is to make an estimation of "manpower" based on the economic activity rates in the different age-sex groups. What we are trying to find out is what proportion of the different groups who is likely to be engaged in work given the size of the population in the working ages. For example, to find the manpower between ages 20 and 25 in Kenya 1980, we project the population to get an estimate of men and women 20—24 years, and multiply by the assumed activity rates for these groups. According to the Kenyan estimates the activity rates are 90.5 % for males and 48 % for females in these age groups.

Once the population has been projected, the number of employment possibilities should also be projected for a comparison, and an estimation of the trend in employment. In the Development Plan of 1974—78, projections was made in order to find the minimal need for employment, given the rate of population growth and stable activity rates. The population is assumed to increase with 2.3 million more people in 1974—78. With an average household size of 5.6 and the need for 1 income earner per household, the creation of 400,000 more jobs is necessary to cater for the increase in the population. But we know that more than one jobs is usually needed and 800,000 more jobs will actually be necessary as a minimum. This is only to cater for the increasing population, whereas already there are not enough jobs for the existing labour force. Therefore if the people now unemployed are also to be catered for, the figure would have to be much higher.[1]

It is unlikely that the modern sector in the cities can absorb more than

---

[1] *Development Plan 1974—78*, Republic of Kenya. Nairobi 1974, pp. 89—90.

approximately 200,000 new job-holders, as there were approximately 545,000 in these jobs in 1970, so most of the jobs must be created within agriculture and in the informal sector.

School-leavers present a special problem; by 1978, 2.5 million will be estimated to have completed standard VII, compared with 800,000 in 1969, and 300,000 will be estimated to have completed form 4—6. However, even the best and most positive estimate of employment indicates the existence of only 995,000 jobs in the modern sector by 1978. Thus, even among the more educated, some of them will have to turn to rural areas and the informal sector for jobs.

Table 65. *Modern sector employment 1972 and projected 1978, with two different alternative assumptions (in thousands).*

Sector	Employment 1972	Projected under Assumptions	
		A	B
Agriculture, Forestry, Fishing	245.9	291.7	281.6
Mining, Quarrying	3.3	8.0	10.0
Construction	35.5	45.0	51.3
Manufacturing	103.9	153.8	158.5
Commerce	63.5	79.4	88.7
Electricity, Gas, Water	5.6	6.4	7.1
Transport	46.2	57.0	69.3
Services	81.5	96.6	104.4
General Govt.	177.0	214.6	224.4
Total	762.4	952.2	995.3

Assumption A = projections equal 1972 employment figures times compound growth in GDP planned for each sector, divided by compound rate of productivity increase for labour that actually occurred during 1967—71 or "What would happen without Government intervention?"

Assumption B = same basic assumption, but modified to include the results of policies to: change relative prices of land, labour, and capital in order to create employment. This is thus a more optimistic assumption.

Source: *Development Plan 1974—78*, Republic of Kenya. Nairobi 1974, p. 94.

This type of projection is one of the most frequently used for planning purposes, i.e. based on assumptions of high vs. low success in the policy implementation, in order to evaluate the necessity of investing more in particular sectors.

In the ILO report on "Employment, Incomes and Equality", which analyses aspects of the employment problem in Kenya, the evaluation of the assumptions may be supplemented by the following evaluation of the annual increase or decrease in employment in the private and the public sector (Table 66). This shows the very high dependency of creating jobs within the public sector and that little employment creation apparently can be expected within the private sector. This also increases the sensitivity toward restrictions in government policy. The problem with this kind of projection and evaluation, however, is that it covers only a small fraction of the population whereas most of the population is outside this sector.

Table 66. *Annual growth in employment in private and public sector, 1966—1970.*

	Private	Public	Total
1966	−2.2	+6.3	+0.6
1967	+0.1	+5.8	+2.1
1968	−0.1	+4.6	+1.5
1969	+1.4	+7.1	+3.4
1970	+1.7	+4.3	+2.7

Source: ILO: *Employment, Incomes and Equality,* Geneva 1972, p. 535.

The proportion of the labour force in the formal/modern sector could be estimated in Nairobi, where the largest proportion of the formally employed are working. Even in Nairobi (table 67) it shows that quite high numbers are still not accounted for by the formal employment or education.

Table 67. *Population over 14 years of age in Nairobi distributed on kind of employment, 1969 (in thousands and percentages).*

	Males		Females		Total	
	Numbers	%	Numbers	%	Numbers	%
Population over 14	179	100	84	100	263	100
accounted for:	137	76.6	26	31.0	163	62.0
Secondary schools	17	9.5	6	7.2	23	8.7
students	2	1.1	—	—	2	0.8
wage employment formal	116	64.6	19	22.6	134	51.0
self employment formal	3	1.7	1	1.2	4	1.5
unaccounted for*	42	23.4	58	69.0	100	38.0

* Unaccounted for = informal sector, housewives, unemployed.

Source: ILO: *Employment, Incomes and Equality,* Geneva, 1972, p. 343.

In relation to projections of the labour force and manpower, one of the most important aspects to be considered is the number and timing of the entrants into the labour force, i.e. what is the size of the population in these age-groups, and when will these generations start working? Will the time for entry be later because of increased school enrollment? An example of the projections of the number of entrants into the labour market is provided in table 68, together with the projection of the pre-school and primary school age population. The projection is given under four alternative assumptions.

These projections show the importance in long term projections of making relevant assumptions about fertility, as the differences are quite large in the long run. Although the differences show up much later for the labour force, they are revealed much earlier among pre-school and school-age population. Most of the entrants into the labour force up to 1990 are already born, and therefore will not be affected by changes in fertility.

Table 68. *Projection of number of pre-school children, children of primary school age, and young entrants into the labour force under different assumptions of growth 1970—2000 (in thousands).*

Year	Assumption alternatives	Preschool pop. 0—5 years	Primary Schoolage 6—12 years	Entrants into labour force 15—19 years
1970	A	2,556	2,235	1,187
	B	2,556	2,235	1,187
	C	2,556	2,235	1,187
	D	2,556	2,235	1,187
1975	A	3,140	2,652	1,401
	B	3,140	2,652	1,401
	C	3,140	2,652	1,401
	D	3,140	2,652	1,401
1980	A	3,780	3,235	1,662
	B	3,605	3,235	1,662
	C	3,517	3,235	1,662
	D	3,480	3,235	1,662
1990	A	5,536	4,795	2,448
	B	4,368	4,312	2,448
	C	3,995	4,140	2,448
	D	3,618	3,997	2,448
2000	A	8,192	7,067	3,627
	B	4,947	5,134	3,154
	C	3,921	4,529	3,001
	D	2,920	3,908	2,847

Assumption alternatives: A = Total fertility rate remaining unchanged at 7.6. B = Total fertility rate beginning to decline in 1975 and falling to 4 by the year of 2000. C = Total fertility rate beginning to decline in 1975 and falling to 3 by the year 2000. D = Total fertility rate beginning to decline in 1975 and falling to 2 by the year 2000.

Source: Kenya Statistical Digest, June 1971, (and ILO p. 123).

Projection of the urban population

In the projection of the urban population, the population existing in urban areas in the census should be projected on the basis of assumptions about fertility and mortality. In addition, the assumptions on migration trends should also be considered, for example:

1. A 7% annual increase in Nairobi's population until 2000.
2. A 7% increase per year between 1970—74, declining to 6% in 1975—80 and 5% from 1980 onwards.
3. A 7% increase between 1970—74, rising to 8% in 1975—80 and 9% from 1980 onwards.

This would give 3 alternative projections, with the high and low limits (3 and 2 respectively).

For the small urban areas, the trend in migration may be extremely varied.

For example, when the Pan African Papermills in Webuye were constructed, a lot of workers came in for a short period just after the opening of the factory, there was also in-migration during the construction period. However once the posts had been filled, the population influx went down to a low level again. Thus the migration rate may be as high as 30% in one year, and as low as 5% in the years after. This means that a very clear indication of the jobs available must be the basis for the projection of the population in such an area.

Supplementary reading

1. *UN. Determinants and Consequences of Population Trends.* N.Y. 1974. Demographic projections, pp. 557—588.

2. *Development Plan 1974—78*, Republic of Kenya. Nairobi 1974, pp. 89—108.

3. ILO; *Employment, Incomes and Equality*, Geneva, 1972. Population Policy, pp. 121—132; Education and Training, pp. 233—235.

4. B. Egero & R. Henin (eds): *The Population of Tanzania.* An Analysis of the 1967 Population Census. Census vol. 6. Dar es Salaam 1973, pp. 212—220.

Chapter XV

Population policies

Population policies contain all deliberate government actions that affect population size, growth and distribution. Often however the difinition of population policies is confined merely to those measures relating to population control. Therefore this wider definition of population policies include most national political and economic measures.

The most salient problem in relation to population policies, is whether the factors of population size, structure and distribution are considered as an essential part of development planning. Secondly, it is related to the whole perception of 1) population *versus* resources, especially land resources, and 2) population growth in relation to economic development potential and employment. Therefore the policies do not only reflect theoretical perceptions about population, but also the specific economic and historical conditions of the different countries.

The official attitudes to population size in relation to resources show great variations in African countries, depending both on the resource base in terms of agricultural land and infrastructure, and on how fast the infrastructure can be developed to cater for the rapidly increasing population. The official statements and arguments of a number of countries are presented to illustrate the different points of view on population:

Somalia's First Five Year Plan (1963—67):

The rate of population growth is not known. The birth rate is probably high, but due to the inadequate health services, it is unlikely that the death rate is very low. Thus, the rate of natural increase cannot be very high. However, the death rate will decline with the improvement in health services as envisaged in the Plan, and this will result in an increase in the rate of population growth. But the Somali Republic is not overpopulated. In view of the relatively small size of the population and the very large area and natural resources which would be progressively exploited through economic development, the country is not likely to have a population problem in the foreseeable future.[1]

Ethiopia's Second Five Year Plan argues along the same lines; that a rapid growth of the population is encouraging, because of the availability of labour and the expansion of the domestic market. Even the Ghanaian 1963—70 plan, which advocates a more restrictive population policy, states the benefits of a large population "as there are more mouths to feed, so also there eventually are more hands to work".[2]

[1] D. K. Ghansah: Population Policies and Programmes in Sub-Saharan Africa. *Rural Africana*, no. 14, 1971, p. 31.
[2] Ibid. p. 31

The views on population in relation to resources are seldom presented as clearly as those mentioned above. Other countries with low population densities either reveal a laissez faire policy concerning the growth rate, i.e. mainly on fertility, or sometimes a restrictive policy. Thus the stand taken by Botswana, where the crude population density is 1 person per square kilometer, may be put forward. In the country's National Development Plan of 1970—75, it is argued that: "Although Botswana is a large country in terms of area it is not markedly underpopulated in terms of resources endowment".[3] Furthermore, it says that the costs of infrastructure and administration are higher per capita than in more densely populated territories, and the quality of water supplies and other services are poorer than they would be if a larger population could share the costs. However, it may be added that even if a higher population would be favourable for sharing expenses in the long run, the burden of expanding the services at the same rate as the population growth might create problems.

These aspects of population policy are also emphasized in Tanzania, where the population density is not yet high, but where the costs of expanding the infrastructure are heavy:

It is very good to increase our population, because our country is large and there is plenty of unused land. But it is necessary to remember that these 350,000 extra people every year will be babies in arms, not workers. They will have to be fed, clothed, given medical attention, schooling, and many other services for very many years before they will be able to contribute to the economy of the country through their work.[4]

The statement continues: "We have done very little more than expand at the same rate as the number of Tanzanian children was increasing because of population growth".[5]

Some of these same arguments are advocated in the Kenyan Development Plan 1974—78. The following quotations illustrate the most essential arguments regarding the perception of population in relation to resources:

Although there is no accurate measure of the number of unemployed people, the grossest measure would derive from a comparison of population growth estimates with recent trends in the creation of job opportunities. Total population is expected to grow by nearly 3.2 million people over the Plan period. If average household size remains at 5.6 persons, the provision of one income earner for each household implies the creation of over 400,000 income earning opportunities during the Plan period, just to provide for the increase in population. In many instances, however, more than one income earner is required in a family. If, therefore one considers instead that 35 percent of population requires employment, the number of new jobs necessary becomes more than 800,000. Still more jobs will be needed for those who are already unemployed.[6]

---

[3] Ibid. p. 31

[4] B. Maxwell Stamper: Population Policy in Development Planning. *Reports on Population/Family Planning*. May 1973, p. 14.

[5] Ibid.

[6] *Development Plan 1974—78*. Republic of Kenya. Nairobi 1974, p. 90.

13 – A demographic...

In addition, the implications of the high growth rates are perceived to be related to other aspects of economic growth:

In a country already suffering from high unemployment, a high population growth rate has only adverse economic effects. First, it will increase the proportion of total income that is consumed, thus diminishing the levels of domestic savings available for investment. Second, the new population requires more capital, schools, houses, hospitals, roads, and machines. Only after the new population is provided for will there be any net increase in these amenities per person. Third, when the dependency ratio is increasing, more people will be employed simply providing for the new people, without increasing the real income per person. Fourth, the pressure of people on land and capital will reduce the productivity of labour.[7]

In Uganda the focus has been on the impact of the age-structure on educational costs:

In Uganda, population pressure as such is not the critical problem it is in many developing countries. However the high growth rate does mean that a large proportion of the population is in the school-age group, which makes the education burden much greater than in more wealthier countries, which experience lower population growth.[8]

The perception of people as producers and consumers therefore shows great variations within the African regions, and the perception of land resources and how these may be utilized also reflects basic differences in resources supply, and in economic-political systems.

First of all, the views expressed by Somalia, Ethiopia and Ghana are very much in line with the theoretical works of Ester Boserup, Samir Amin and of Alfred Sauvy, namely that there is a positive relationship between economic development and high population density, and that a larger population growth would provide the basis for larger markets and more people to share the basic expenses of setting up the necessary infrastructure. The young population structure (creating the high dependency burden) is perceived as an investment into the coming labour force, as the youths who are at present mainly consumers, will eventually become mainly producers after the age of between 15 to 20 years. The problem relating to employment in some of these areas is perceived as a need for more labourers to develop the land.

On the other hand Nigeria and Kenya, and also to some extent Ghana, perceive the young population structure as creating a severe burden as they are mainly consumers; and instead of being perceived as coming producers, they are seen as a further problem since employment will have to be generated for them. The land resources may have the potential to provide for more people, but the pattern of land distribution and adjudication of land leaves very little open land for development. Therefore any increase in employment will be much more related to the urban economy, where there are already serious difficulties in generating jobs for the unemployed from this generation.

The points raised thus reveal where the main problems in the actual econ-

[7] Ibid., p. 102.
[8] B. Maxwell Stamper: op. cit., p. 15.

omic structure exist, and it is not only a reflection of the theories of population, but more a picture of the main economic constraints in the economy. The perspective of a larger population is practically only maintained in countries where the rural areas may absorb a larger population, and maybe even improve the economic potential by expanding the agricultural basis. On the other hand in the countries where the migration to urban areas, and the urban employment problems, create a stress on the housing, water, sanitation, employment of the towns, the planners tend to focus the solution partly in the population control.

Policies to reduce mortality

In all countries of Africa until recently the mortality level has been quite high and all Governments show great concern about the high level of morbidity and mortality in their countries. Development plans emphasize the goal of reducing mortality, especially infant and child mortality, and improving the general health of the population, curtailing malnutrition and epidemic diseases. The desired improvement of the health conditions have social as well as economic reasons. The improved health would secure the survival of infants and children and it would improve the work capacity of the working population.

All countries maintain as basic policy to reduce mortality as a goal in itself, though the means by which they do it and the investments into this sector show great variations. However, extended vaccination campaigns against epidemic diseases like measles and smallpox have been a characteristic feature of many African health programmes.

With respect to improvement of the health conditions, the expansion of the medical service is important, but more important is the distribution of the medical services, mainly in the rural areas, where the majority of the population are living. However, the main causes for poor health are usually found in the general living conditions, i.e. food, housing, sanitation, working conditions, and changes in these will thus have a major impact on health and thus on mortality. These aspects of a health policy are usually found under the concept of preventive medicine, and include all aspects of life improvement, to secure a good general condition, and avoid some of the main sources of infection such as polluted water, mosquitoes and other insects etc.

One aspect of the health policy which should be emphasized is closely related to the process of reproduction. Short intervals between births imply a threat to the health of both the mother and the children, compared to longer intervals above 2 years as prescribed in most tribal norms in East Africa. Thus a spacing of births will imply improved health for mothers and young children, and therefore a greater probability of survival.

The ideology behind the reduction of morbidity and mortality is not seriously questioned, even though the reduction is leading to a higher population growth rate. Nor is it related to any specific theories, but is based on universal goals, and is not seen as a means for other structural changes, but as a goal in itself. Other aspects of the policy, however, may endanger or delay this goal. Wars or other internal conflicts between groups of the population may increase mortality for some periods. The major examples being the liberation wars and the conflicts in Rwanda and Burundi. Some aspects of economic policy may also affect the health conditions for some periods. Monocultural cashcrop cultivation patterns, whether in plantations or on individual plots, may lead to nutritional problems if the salaries are very low or if prices for the cash crops decline to a very low level. Such fluctuations have been frequent for most export crops. In areas where many people are dependent on buying all food, the wage policy and price policy for food has important implications for the nutrition and thus for the health conditions.

Policies affecting fertility

Whereas policy relating to morbidity and mortality are generally agreed upon and the reduction of these is considered a goal in itself, the same is not true for policies concerning fertility. A decline in fertility is not considered a goal in itself, but a means to reduce population growth and to change the age-structure towards a higher proportion in the working ages.

A reduction of fertility may be initiated by a variety of factors, like an increase in the age at marriage, as has been done in China and India, or extended access to family planning services, abortion or sterilization. Historically the governments in Europe and North America were pro-natalist in their population policy. Even during the period of the fertility decline in Europe and USA, most governments had either a policy favouring large families or a laissez-faire policy. The families in Europe had no or very limited support for the reduction of their family size. In France the sale and distribution of contraceptives had been prohibited until 1967, while marriage loans, premiums on births had been measures used to favour and encourage larger families. However, after 1950 most of the industrial countries favoured family planning, even though the economic incentives for having many children were still maintained. Both family planning through a more liberal access to contraceptives and later to abortions have been supported strongly by the womens movements, leading to the legalization of abortion in several European countries, as a means for the woman to have control over her own reproduction, but not as a means for the government to curb the growth rate.

In African countries on the other hand, very few measures to change fertility have been introduced. Only family planning has been advocated, whereas abortions and sterilizations are not legal.

The family planning programmes in Africa are accepted for quite different motivations in the different countries. In some countries they are perceived as a means to improve the relationship between population growth and employment as well as other resources. But family planning may also be introduced for the purpose of improving the health of women and children and as a support for the woman's right to decide on her family size, and the spacing of children.

Table 69 shows the declared policies of African countries concerning birth control and family planning in 1973.

This table reveals that more governments in 1973 were in favour of family planning activities than against them. The main difference between the first two groups of countries are the perception of population growth and the role of government support for family planning programmes. There is a significant difference between the "Anglophone" and the "Francophone" countries, as the Francophone are practically all in the last group, which do not have any family planning activities or are directly in favour of high growth of population.

Table 69. *Government position on population growth and family planning activities in 38 countries in Africa (1973).*

Policy:	*Countries:*
I. Official policy to reduce population growth; also support family planning for reasons of health and human rights.	Botswana, Egypt, Ghana, Kenya, Mauritius, Morocco, Sénégal, Tunisia.
II. Official support to family planning activities for other than demographic reasons; i.e. for reasons of health and as a human right but any anti-natalist effect is a by-product, not an objective.	Algeria, Lesotho, Liberia, Benin (Dahomey), Gambia, Nigeria, Sierra Leone, Sudan, Swaziland, Tanzania, Uganda.
III. Countries which have neither policy to reduce population growth nor do they support family planning programmes for any reason, demographic or otherwise. However, they permit the establishment of family planning services by voluntary agencies.	Ethiopia, Mali, Zambia.
IV. Countries which have neither policy to reduce population nor family planning services, either official or through voluntary agencies; and countries which are pro-natalist.	Burundi, Tchad, Cameroon, Central African Republic, Gabon, Guinea, Ivory Coast, Libya, Madagascar, Malawi, Mauretania, Niger, Rwanda, Somalia, Upper Volta, Zaïre.

Source: ECA: The Data Base for Discussion on the Interrelation between the Integration of Women in Development, Their Situation and Population Factors in Africa. May 1974. Addis Ababa, p. 49.

In 1966 Kenya was one of the first African countries where a family planning programme was accepted. The programme emphasizes the maternal and child health services, education of family planning staff, nurses and the expansion of family planning information. The total cost of the family planning programme in the Plan period of 1974—78 will be K. £10.8 million (most of which will be funded by international agencies like International Development Agency (World Bank) UN and USAID.

Discrepanies between needs at the macro-level (the government) and at the micro-level (the family).

Although in some countries the overall planning perspective has identified population growth as one of the obstacles to development, the introduction of a family planning programme to cope with high fertility may not necessarily imply a change in the behavior of rural families at whom this programme is aimed.

There seems to be a major discrepancy between the macro-level planning and the needs of the rural families. According to the Kenyan Development Plan 1974—78 "it is expected that social and economic development will ultimately change attitudes towards family size, and that the reduced child mortality will induce parents to have fewer children. But that the change of attitude is too slow and positive action to make it change is necessary."[9]

One important aspect has been that the basis or motivation for reducing family size may not exist under conditions of high infant and childhood mortality. However, child mortality has been declining in many areas, and in some areas the decline may be drastic enough to provide the basis for family planning. However, in other areas mortality is still quite high, as has been shown for Tanzania 1967, where one-fourth of all the children born in peasant families died before reaching 5 years of age. With this high level of mortality, the families will have to produce many children in order to ensure that at least some of the children grow up to support them in their old age, and thus will have little motivation to reduce their family size.

From research within the field, it also appears that children still play an important role contributing to the labour force in rural families. The children appear to be essentially needed to assist in agriculture and other activities. But on the other hand, increasing school enrollment and the costs of schooling are also increasing the costs of children rapidly. Thus in areas where the value of the children's labour in agriculture is low due to very small plots of land or dependency on hired labour, and the costs for schooling are high, increasing the relative costs of children, the women tend to want only 5—7 children.[10]

The increased costs of schooling and the changing economic value of children as perceived by the rural families, thus may provide the first basis for limiting family size among rural families in areas where the child mortality has declined. The wanted number of children is still high, on the average higher than 4—5 in most areas, apparently because the above conditions are not yet widespread, and children constitute the only source of old age security.

Family planning programmes, if set up as service programmes, may provide a basic service for women who want larger intervals between births, or fewer children.

In relation to the Kenyan programme a few problems arise. The programme has been so closely tied to the maternal/child care scheme and so much

---

[9] *Development Plan 1974—78.* Republic of Kenya. Nairobi 1974, p. 102
[10] Mette Monsted: Conditions for changing family size in selected rural areas of Kenya. Centre for Development Research, Copenhagen & Dept. of Sociology, Nairobi, March 1977.

emphasis has been put on that aspect, that women tend to consider family planning as a form of alien repression. The large numbers of first time visits, and the heavy drop-out rates in the programme, may be explained by the fact that many women who register as first time clients, do not really want family planning, but rather health services only for their children.[11]

The other point of criticism against family planning, is that one of the problems in many African rural areas has been that of sterility and sub-fertility due to different diseases reducing fertility. In order for the programme to be perceived as a family planning service and not a birth control programme, some provisions also must be made to deal with infertility, so that infertile women also perceive the programme as beneficial to them.

In Kenya only a small fraction of the women in reproductive ages use family planning services. In 1971 only 1.5% of women in reproductive ages had visited a family planning clinic.[12]

This discrepancy between the Government's efforts to curb the birth rate, and the perception by the rural families about the number of children they want has, in some countries, led to a discussion of more efficient measures to persuade the families, and to more efficent measures like abortion and sterilization. Both abortion and sterilization has long been a part of the family planning programme in China, and sterilization has been playing an increasing role in the Indian programme.

However, going "beyond family planning" to a more compulsory programme has long been discussed in certain countries, and Berelson's[13] conclusion on this aspect is that "the worse the problem, the more one is willing to 'give up' an ethical position in order to reach a 'solution'". India has recently embarked on this solution with the introduction of compulsory sterilization in some of the states. The political repercussions of such a drastic measure appear at present to rule this out for a long time in the future.

Policies affecting the population distribution

The "population problem" is most frequently perceived as the problem of insufficient land and employment for the population. The land problem in Kenya was created by the settlement of Europeans in many areas, and restrictions for the African population from gaining access to land under the colonial economic system.

Landlessness was no problem in the traditional societies. All adult males of the clan had rights to use the land, and the more people in a family, the more hands there were to work on the land, and the more land could be cultivated.

[11] J. Mugo Gachuhi: Family Planning in Kenya and the Problem of Drop-outs. in U. U. Uche (ed): Law and Population Change in Africa. Nbi. 1976, pp. 120—131.

[12] Lars Bondestam: Population Growth Control in Kenya. Research Report 12. Scandinavian Institute of African Studies, Uppsala 1972.

[13] B. Berelson: Beyond Family Planning. 1969, p. 8.

However, the alienation of land carried through by the colonial power and the later expansion of the individual land tenure led to increasing individualization of land and the creation of a land market. The increasing population pressure on land has in this new structure resulted in increasing landlessness.

In 1969 the squatter population was estimated to be 200,000 in Kenya,[14] and it is increasing fast each year. After Independence in Kenya, however, a programme was set up to cater for some of the main pressures on land. The settler areas were to a large extent redistributed in a settlement programme for African families, as a means to "satisfy the demand for land so that Kenya could enjoy the economic and social benefits of a prolonged period of political stability".[15] In this programme 1 million acres were allocated to 34,000 African households.

Later settlement schemes and irrigation schemes have had an impact on the population distribution and the expansion of the economic potential in some of the rural areas. Especially the scheduled Tana River scheme, may have a great impact on the reallocation and settlement of the rural population on the marginal agricultural areas. All aspects of land policy could be seen as parts of the population policy, as they have important implications for the distribution of the population and for migrations.

The large scale rural-urban migration is perceived as one of the most severe population problems, especially in relation to the employment possibilities, as urban formal employment only increases as a fraction of the total increase in the urban population. Rural development programmes and rural vocational training aim, among other things, at keeping the potential migrants in productive work in rural areas. But this is a general problem in all of the African countries, and no firm policy to cope with this problem has been initiated. At present no efforts appear to have reverted the migration trends, or to curb the migration rate.

The problems of rural-urban migration are uniform and serious in most countries of the world, although they are most pronounced in the developing countries. However, in practically all countries policies to curtail rural-urban migration are weak or non-existent. Only in China has the policy of population redistribution and movements of large groups of youths to the underpopulated areas of the North-West, and away from the large urban centres, succeeded as an integral part of the rural development strategy.

With respect to the redistribution of population, the Tanzanian villagization policy is important. The dispersed pattern of settlement in rural East Africa makes any Government service difficult and costly. The concentration of the population may create the conditions for an improved provision of services. In the drier, more marginal, farming areas the communal efforts in farming may also lead to a higher productivity within agriculture, and thus to a higher capacity to absorb more people. The long-term implications of the programme

---

[14] P. Mbithi & C. Barnes: *Spontaneous Settlement Problems in Kenya*. Nbi. 1975, p. 1.
[15] An Economic Appraisal of the Settlement Schemes 1964/65—1967/68. Farm Economic Survey Report. No. 27, Nbi. 1971, p. 95.

cannot yet be determined, but it has a definite impact on the settlement of the population, though rural-urban migration is still a serious problem also in Tanzania.

The policies related to population distribution, include all political measures on land tenure and the distribution of land, as well as all rural development and employment policies, thus constituting a complex socio-economic-political pattern. This pattern shows a lot of variation for the African countries, but the problems of creating employment and curbing the rural-urban migration are essentially the same.

Throughout the chapters of this book, the dynamics of population are covered. This shows how different social and economic factors affect the population, and how the demographic factors are interrelated, as well as the implications of different demographic structures for the social and economic development. Economic planning and policies are based on these dynamics, and can thus in many respects be seen as the application of demographic analysis within a specific economic system.

Population policies in the wider application of the concept are thus the result of sociological, economic and demographic considerations, trying to identify the main problems which have to be solved. Population policies are often identifying the social and the economic problems, and the demographic variables appear in many cases either as the basis for the planning, or are perceived as the means to change the economic and social conditions.

Supplementary reading

1. D. K. Ghansah: Population Policies and Programmes in Sub-Saharan Africa. *Rural Africana* no. 14 Spring 1971. "Population and Family Planning in Rural Africa", pp. 28—37.

2. Lars Bondestam: Population Growth Control in Kenya. Research Report no. 12. Scandinavian Institute of African Studies. Uppsala 1972, p. 27—48.

3. *Development Plan 1974—78.* Republic of Kenya. Nairobi 1974. Part I. chapt. 3 "Employment, Population and Manpower", pp. 89—103.

4. Phillip Mbithi & C. Barnes: *Spontaneous Settlement Problem in Kenya.* Nbi. 1975, pp. 81—96 and pp. 108—127.

5. J. C. Caldwell et al. (eds): *Population Growth and Socio-Economic Change in West Africa.* Population Council N. Y. 1975. D. R. Gwatkin: Governmental Population Policies, pp. 169—184.

6. S. H. Ominde & C. N. Ejiogu (eds): *Population Growth and Economic Development in Africa.* London 1972.
    pp. 374—377 J. J. Russel: The Kenya National Family Planning Programme;
    pp. 386—392 C. N. Ejiogu: The Kenya Programme. Policy and Results;
    pp. 393—396 Bonte & Gemert: Evaluation of the Kenya Programme.

7. P. O. Ohadike: Marriage, Family and Family Growth in Lagos. In Caldwell & Okonjo (eds): *The Population of Tropical Africa*, London 1968, pp. 379—392.

Definitions of concepts

Age-specific Death Rate $(_nm_x)$ refers to the number of deaths in 1- or 5-year age groups of the population per mid-year population in the same age-group. For example:

$$_5m_{20} = \frac{_5D_{20}}{_5P_{20}} = \frac{\text{No. of deaths among the pop. 20-24 years}}{\text{mid-year pop. of 20-24 years.}}$$

Age-specific Fertility Rate (ASFR or $_nf_x$) refers to the number of births in 1- or 5-year age groups to women between 15 and 50 years per mid-year population of women in the same age-groups. For example:

$$\text{ASFR}_{30-34} = {_5f_{30}} = \frac{\text{no. of births to women 30-34 years}}{\text{mid-year pop. of women 30-34 years}}$$

Age-structure: The distribution of the population by age. Usually this is illustrated in the age-sex-pyramid, showing the relative distribution of the male population on the left side, and of the female population on the right side.

Childbearing age, see reproductive age.

Child-woman ratio indicates the number of children between 0 and 5 years per woman in the reproductive age in a census or survey.

$$\text{Child-woman ratio} = \frac{\text{no. of children 0-4 years}}{\text{no. of women 15-49 years}}$$

Completed Family Size refers to the total number of live-births for women at the end of the reproductive period. This is equivalent to parity for women above 50 years.

Crude Birth Rate (CBR) refers to the number of births per 1000 of the total population at risk in a given year.

$$\text{CBR} = \frac{\text{No. or births in 1 year}}{\text{mid-year pop. of men and women in all ages}} \cdot 1000$$

Crude Death Rate (CDR) provides the number of deaths in a population per 1000 in the total population at risk in a given year.

$$\text{CDR} = \frac{\text{No. of deaths in 1 year}}{\text{mid-year pop. of men and women in all ages}} \cdot 1000$$

Dependency ratio or *dependency burden* is defined as the number of dependents, i.e. the population below and above the working ages, per 100 persons in the labour force, i.e. population in the working ages.

$$\text{Dependency Ratio} = \frac{\text{pop. 0-14 years + 65 years and above}}{\text{pop. 15-64 years}} \cdot 100$$

e_0 see life expectancy at birth.

206

Economically active population shows the number of persons in some form of employment plus those seeking employment.

Fecundity is the biological capacity of women to reproduce themselves. Fertility is always lower than fecundity, as all societies have some social norms to restrict the fertility performance.

Fertility is the actual performance of women in terms of reproduction. This is measured by the number of live births.

General Fertility Rate (GFR) is number of births per 1000 women in the reproductive ages of risk given in a year.

$$GFR = \frac{\text{no. of births in 1 year}}{\text{mid-year pop. of women 15—49 years}} \cdot 1000$$

Gross Reproduction Rate (GRR) is the average number of female births a woman would have if she experienced the current age-specific fertility and sex-ratio of children at each age-group as she passed through her reproductive period. It is assumed that all women survive to 50 years of age, which is the end of the reproductive period.

$$GRR = TFR \cdot \frac{\text{female births}}{\text{male + female births}}$$

Infant mortality $(_1q_0)$ refers to the number of deaths among infants under 1 year of age in a given year, divided by the number of births in the same year.

$_nL_x$ shows the total number of man-years lived by the generation in the life-table between the age x and x + n. This is used to calculate the life-expectancy.

Labour force is defined as the population in the working ages, i.e. the population between 15 and 65 years (sometimes defined up to 60 years). This indicates the potentially economically active population.

Life-expectancy (e_x) shows the average number of years left to live for a person who has reached age x, if the level and structure of mortality remains the same as at the time the life-table was constructed.

Life-expectancy at birth (e_o) shows the average number of years to live for a newborn baby, if the level and structure of mortality remains the same as at the time the life-table was constructed.

Life-Table (l_x) shows for a standard generation, how it is reduced by mortality through the ages, until all the persons have died at the maximum age, which is usually defined as 100 years.

Mid-year population indicates an estimation of the population at risk in a given year, by calculating the population in the middle of the year, or the average number in the population in that year. (population at the end plus the population in the beginning, and divided by 2).

Migration is defined as a movement from one permanent residence to another. In relation to migration the borders crossed are essential as rural-urban migration and rural-rural migration in the statistics have to be related to a certain area, district, province, or Nation.

Mortality indicates the level and pattern of deaths occurring in the population. Usually we measure the mortality for certain age-groups of the population.

Natural Growth Rate (r) indicates the population increase due to only the difference between births and deaths per 1000 in the population. Any increase caused by migration is not included. r = CBR−CDR.

Net Reproduction Rate (NRR) measures the average number of female births a woman would have if she experienced the current age-specific fertility and sex-ratio of children at each age-group as she passed through her reproductive period. It is assumed that the generation of women will experience the current age-specific mortality. This last assumption makes the measure lower than the Gross Reproduction Rate, but also more realistic in terms of predicting reproduction.

Nuptuality indicates the measurement of marriage and changes in the married population.

Parity shows the total number of live-births per woman in the different age-groups of the reproductive period. Parity for women of 50 years and over is equal to the Completed Family Size.

Population at risk indicates the number of people in a certain period who are under the risk of certain demographic events, i.e. the population in an area who may die during the year, or the population of women who may give birth or migrate. This indicates the number of persons multiplied by the time period lived by the generation. Usually for a one year period, the approximation of the mid-year population is used.

Probability of dying between age x *and* x + n ($_nq_x$) This is a measure derived from the life-table, indicating the number of deaths in relation to the population at the beginning of the age interval.

$$_nq_n = (l_x - l_{x+n})/l_x$$

Probability of surviving between age x *and* x + n ($_np_x$) This is a measure in the life-table, indicating the number of survivors in the life-table relative to the population at the beginning of the age interval. It is complementary to the probability of dying.

$$_np_x = l_{x+n}/l_x = 1 - {}_nq_x$$

Radix in the life-table (l_o) indicates the standardized generation at birth in the life-table. Usually we define this as 1,000, 10,000 or 100,000.

Reproductive age or period, or the childbearing age for women, is defined from the age of 15 up to the age of 50 years.

Sex-ratio is defined as the number of males per 100 females in the same age-groups.

T_x. This is a measure from the life-table, indicating the number of man-years lived by the generation between age x and the maximum age (100). It is the sum of $_nL_x$ from age x to 100, and is used to calculate the life-expectancy.

Total Fertility Rate (TFR) shows the average number of children a woman would have, if she experienced the set of current age-specific fertility rates of each age-group as she passed through her childbearing ages, and it is assumed that she survives the whole of her reproductive period.

208

List of Tables

Lists of Graphs